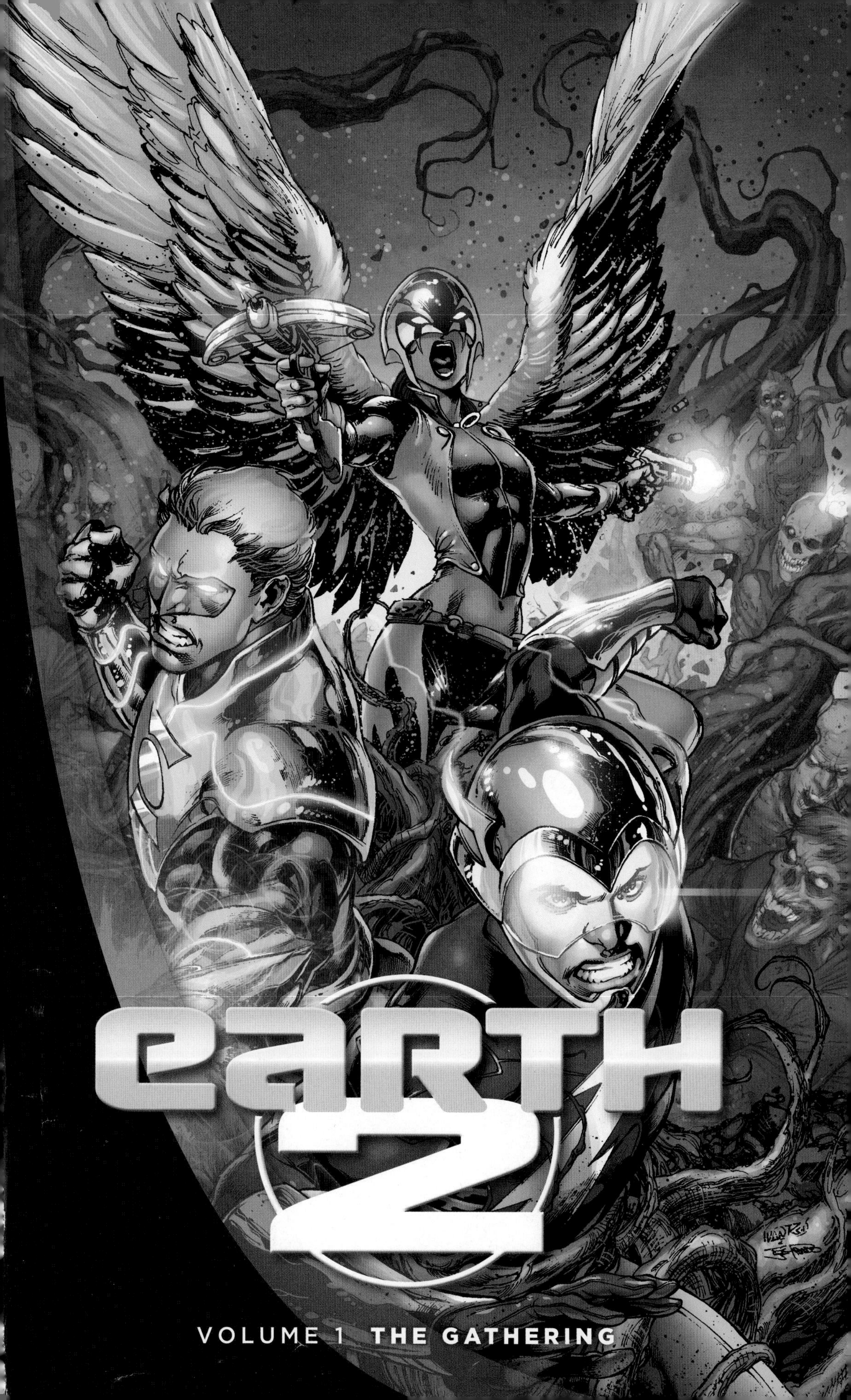
EARTH 2
VOLUME 1 THE GATHERING

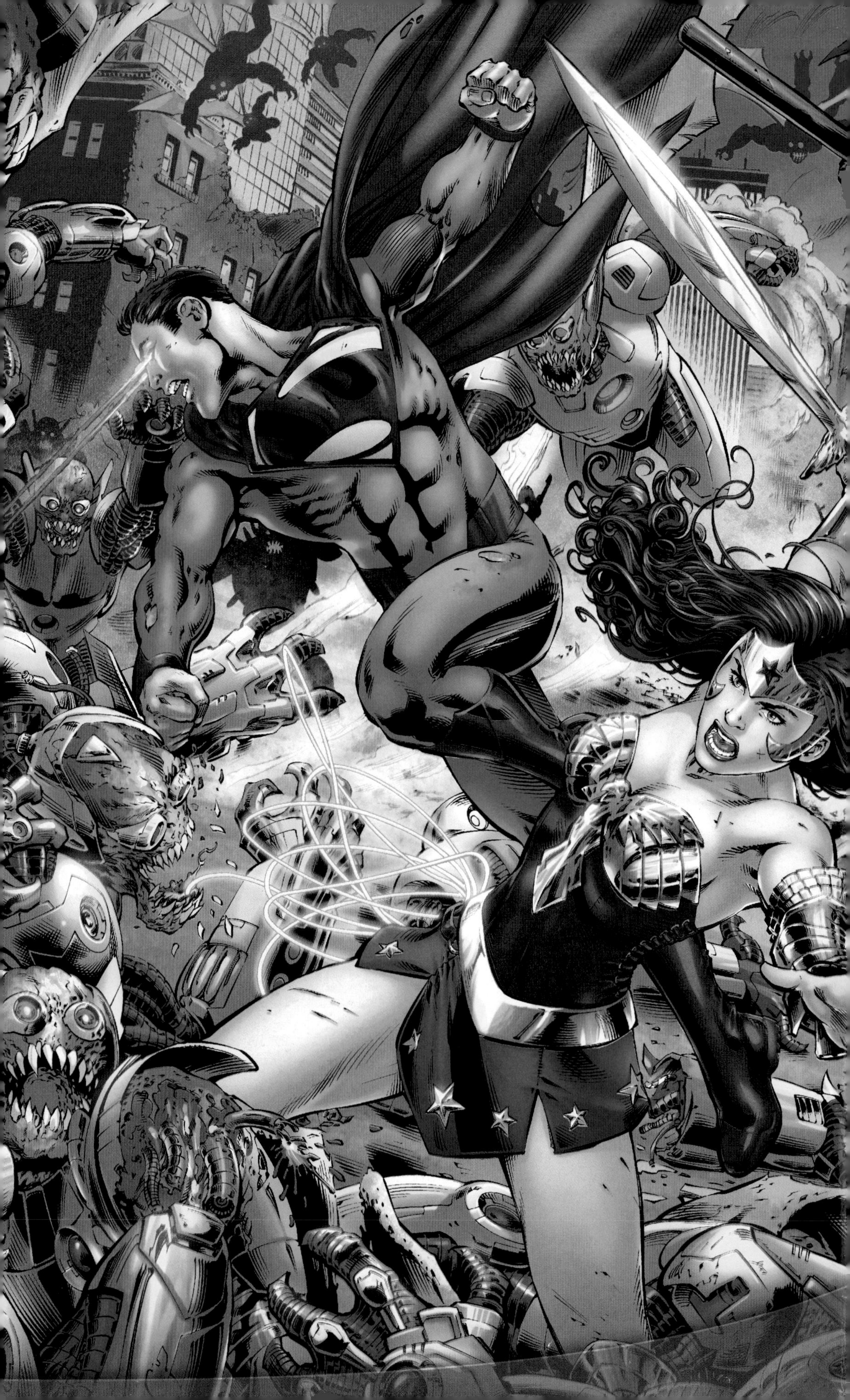

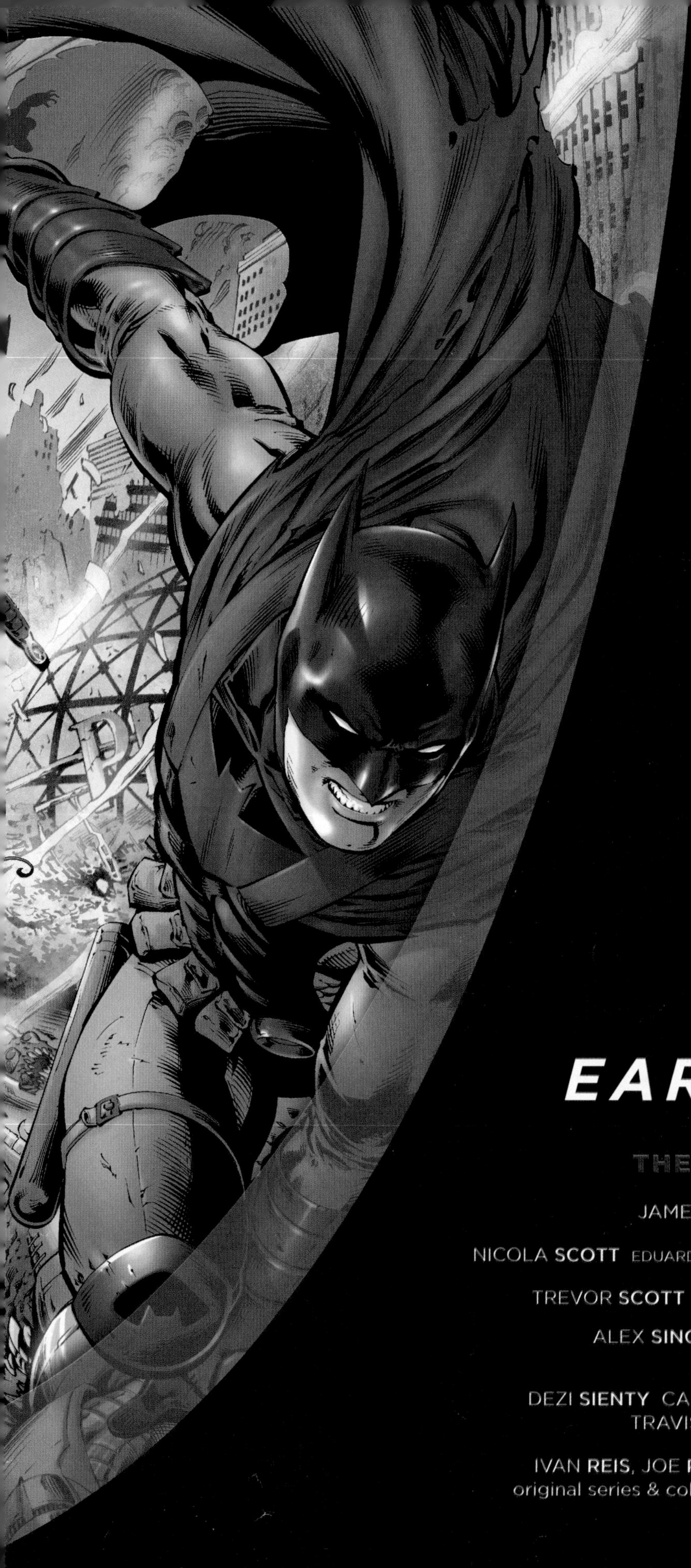

EARTH 2

VOLUME 1

THE GATHERING

JAMES **ROBINSON** writer

NICOLA **SCOTT** EDUARDO **PANSICA** pencillers

TREVOR **SCOTT** SEAN **PARSONS** inkers

ALEX **SINCLAIR** PETE **PANTAZIS**
TONY **AVINA** colorists

DEZI **SIENTY** CARLOS M. **MANGUAL**
TRAVIS **LANHAM** letterers

IVAN **REIS**, JOE **PRADO** & ROD **REIS**
original series & collection cover artists

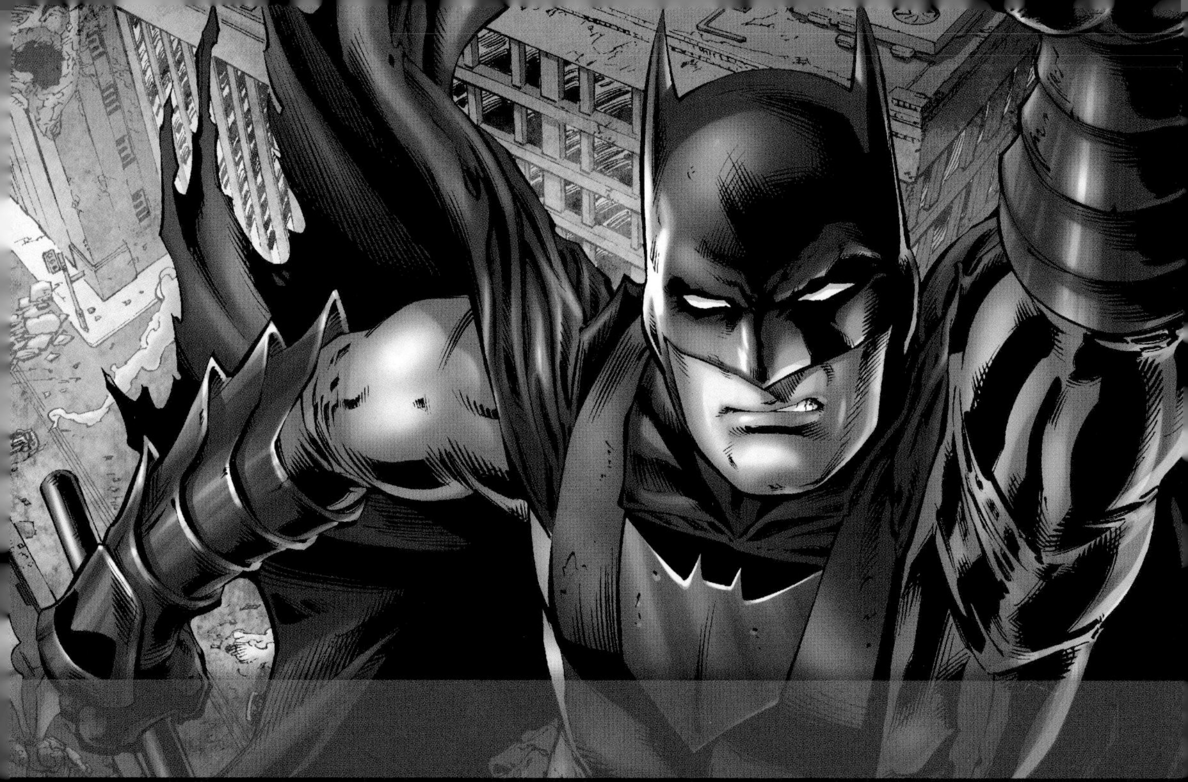

PAT MCCALLUM Editor – Original Series SEAN MACKIEWICZ KATE STEWART Assistant Editors – Original Series
PETER HAMBOUSSI Editor ROBBIN BROSTERMAN Design Director – Books
ROBBIE BIEDERMAN Publication Design

BOB HARRAS VP – Editor-in-Chief

DIANE NELSON President DAN DIDIO and JIM LEE Co-Publishers
GEOFF JOHNS Chief Creative Officer
JOHN ROOD Executive VP – Sales, Marketing and Business Development
AMY GENKINS Senior VP – Business and Legal Affairs NAIRI GARDINER Senior VP – Finance
JEFF BOISON VP – Publishing Operations MARK CHIARELLO VP – Art Direction and Design
JOHN CUNNINGHAM VP – Marketing TERRI CUNNINGHAM VP – Talent Relations and Services
ALISON GILL Senior VP – Manufacturing and Operations HANK KANALZ Senior VP – Digital
JAY KOGAN VP – Business and Legal Affairs, Publishing JACK MAHAN VP – Business Affairs, Talent
NICK NAPOLITANO VP – Manufacturing Administration SUE POHJA VP – Book Sales
COURTNEY SIMMONS Senior VP – Publicity BOB WAYNE Senior VP – Sales

EARTH 2 VOLUME 1: THE GATHERING

DC Comics, 1700 Broadway, New York, NY 10019
A Warner Bros. Entertainment Company.
Printed by RR Donnelley, Salem, VA, USA. 2/8/13. First Printing.

ISBN HC: 978-1-4012-3774-5
ISBN SC: 978-1-4012-4281-7

Library of Congress Cataloging-in-Publication Data

Robinson, James Dale, author.
Earth 2. Volume 1, The gathering / James Robinson, Nicola Scott, Trevor Scott.
pages cm
"Originally published in single magazine form in Earth 2 1-6."
ISBN 978-1-4012-3774-5
1. Graphic novels. I. Scott, Nicola, illustrator. II. Scott, Trevor, illustrator. III. Title. IV. Title: Gathering.
PN6727.R58E23 2013
741.5'973—dc23
2012046491

SUSTAINABLE FORESTRY INITIATIVE
Certified Chain of Custody
At Least 20% Certified Forest Content
www.sfiprogram.org
SFI-01042
APPLIES TO TEXT STOCK ONLY

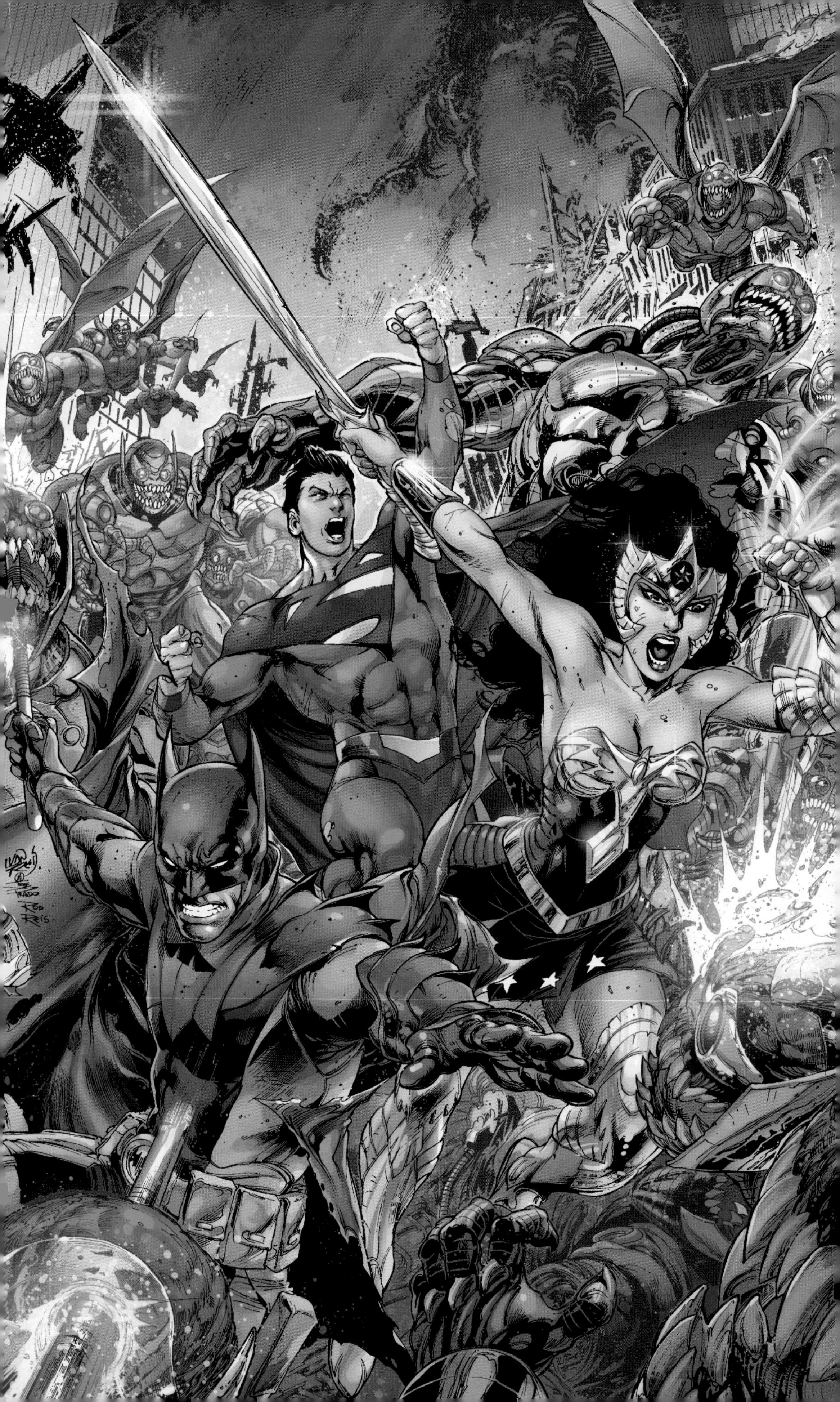

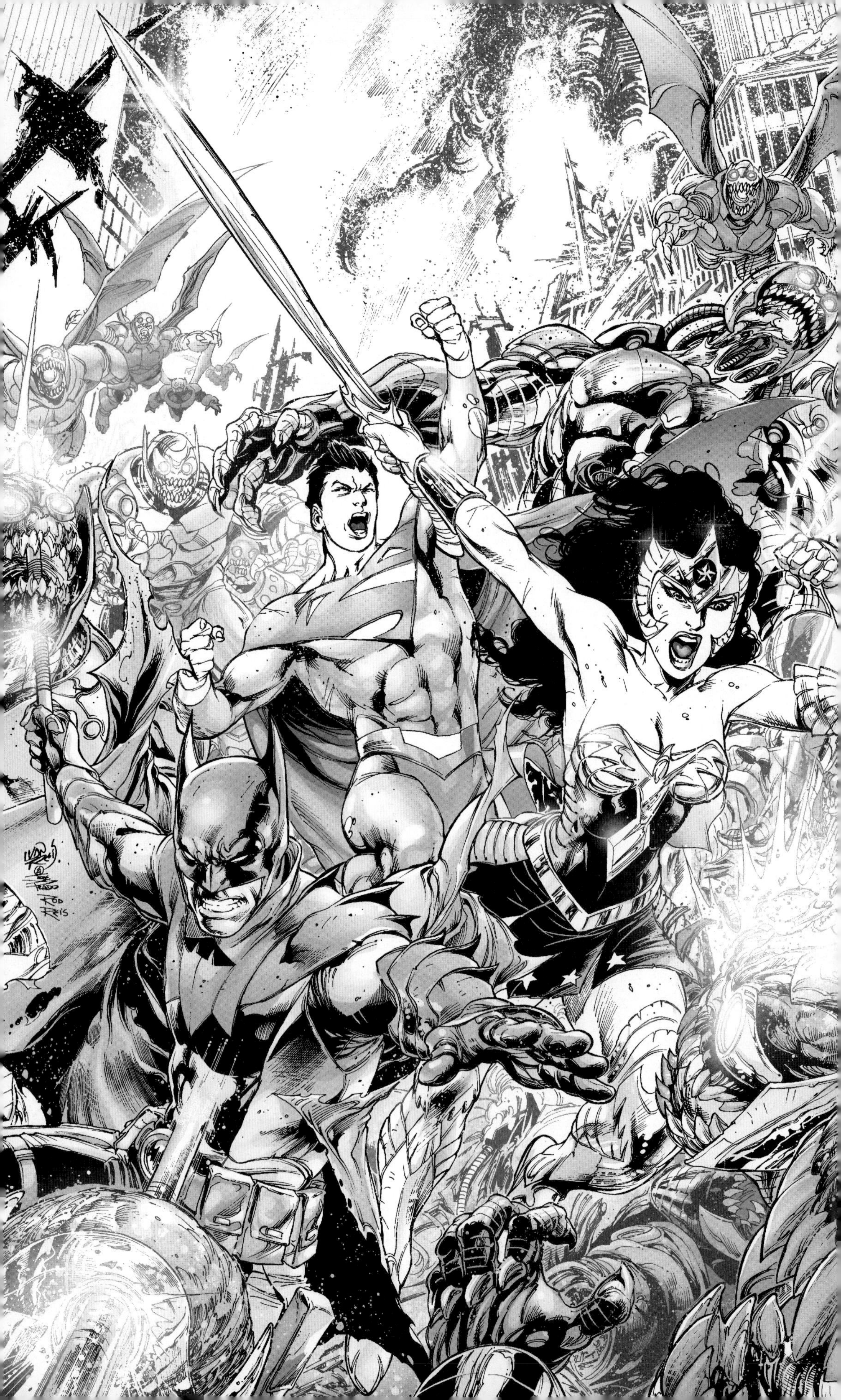

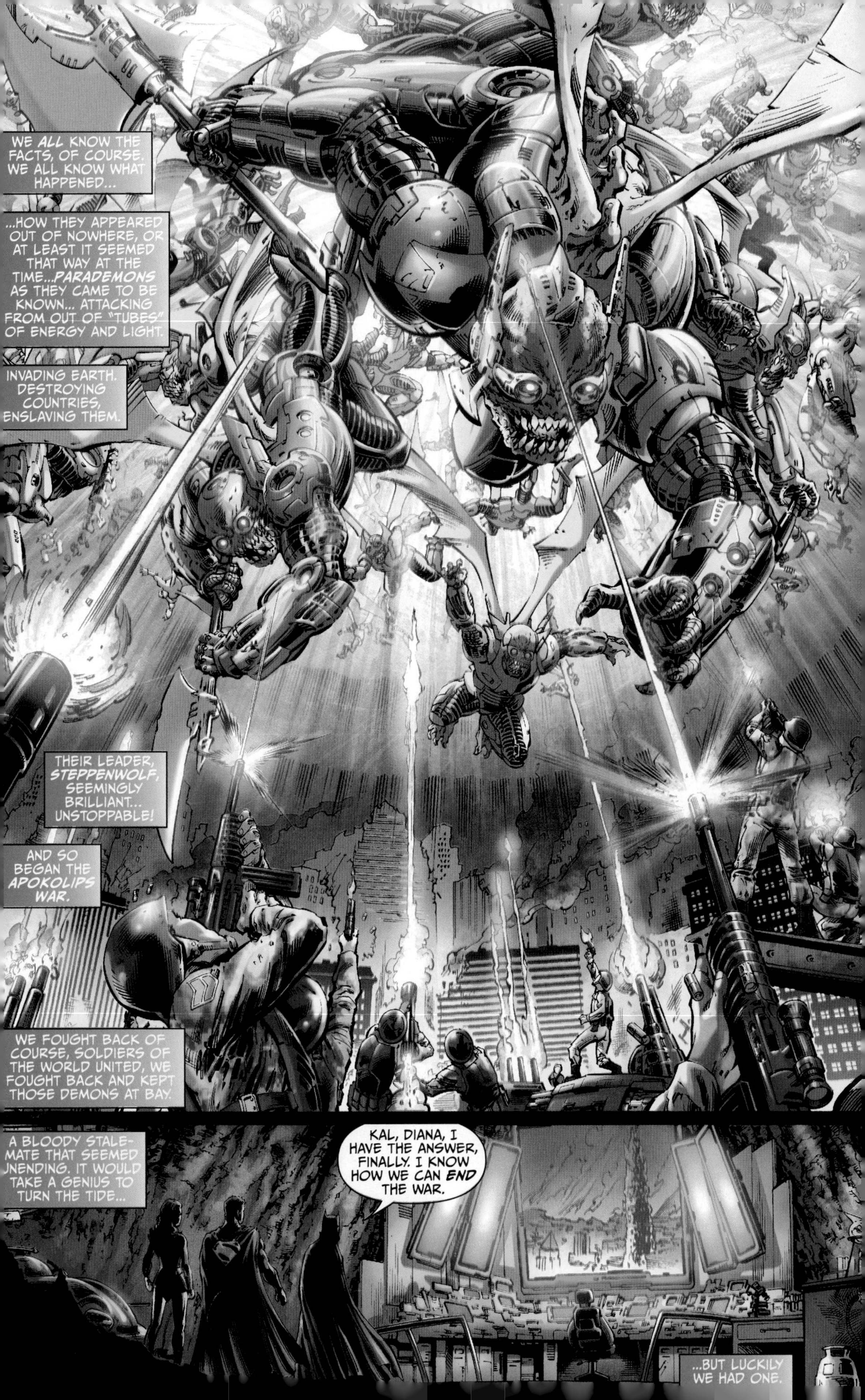
WE ALL KNOW THE FACTS, OF COURSE. WE ALL KNOW WHAT HAPPENED...
...HOW THEY APPEARED OUT OF NOWHERE, OR AT LEAST IT SEEMED THAT WAY AT THE TIME...PARADEMONS AS THEY CAME TO BE KNOWN... ATTACKING FROM OUT OF "TUBES" OF ENERGY AND LIGHT.
INVADING EARTH. DESTROYING COUNTRIES, ENSLAVING THEM.
THEIR LEADER, STEPPENWOLF, SEEMINGLY BRILLIANT... UNSTOPPABLE!
AND SO BEGAN THE APOKOLIPS WAR.
WE FOUGHT BACK OF COURSE, SOLDIERS OF THE WORLD UNITED, WE FOUGHT BACK AND KEPT THOSE DEMONS AT BAY.
A BLOODY STALEMATE THAT SEEMED UNENDING. IT WOULD TAKE A GENIUS TO TURN THE TIDE...
KAL, DIANA, I HAVE THE ANSWER, FINALLY. I KNOW HOW WE CAN END THE WAR.
...BUT LUCKILY WE HAD ONE.

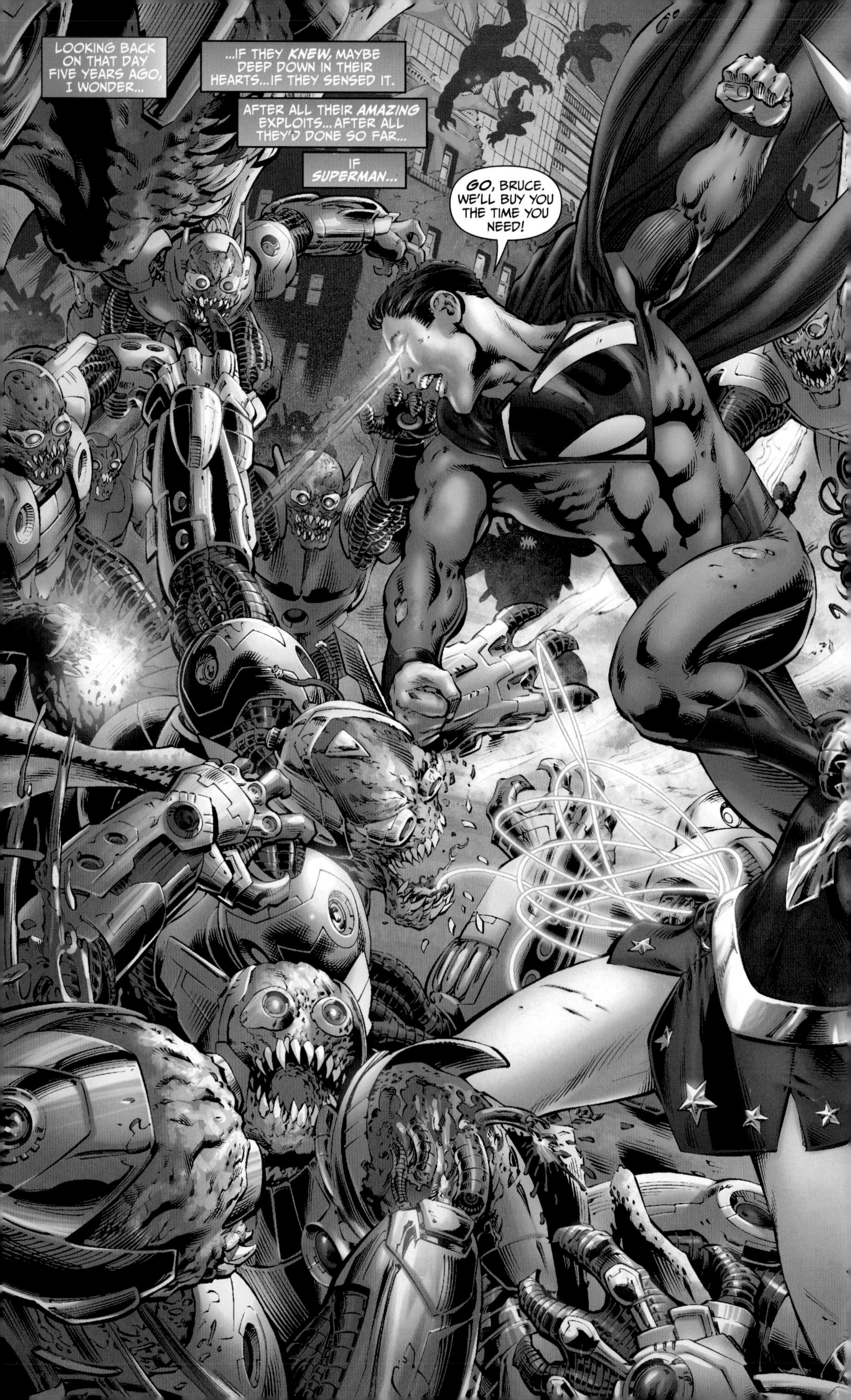
LOOKING BACK ON THAT DAY FIVE YEARS AGO, I WONDER...
...IF THEY KNEW, MAYBE DEEP DOWN IN THEIR HEARTS...IF THEY SENSED IT.
AFTER ALL THEIR AMAZING EXPLOITS...AFTER ALL THEY'D DONE SO FAR...
IF SUPERMAN...
GO, BRUCE. WE'LL BUY YOU THE TIME YOU NEED!

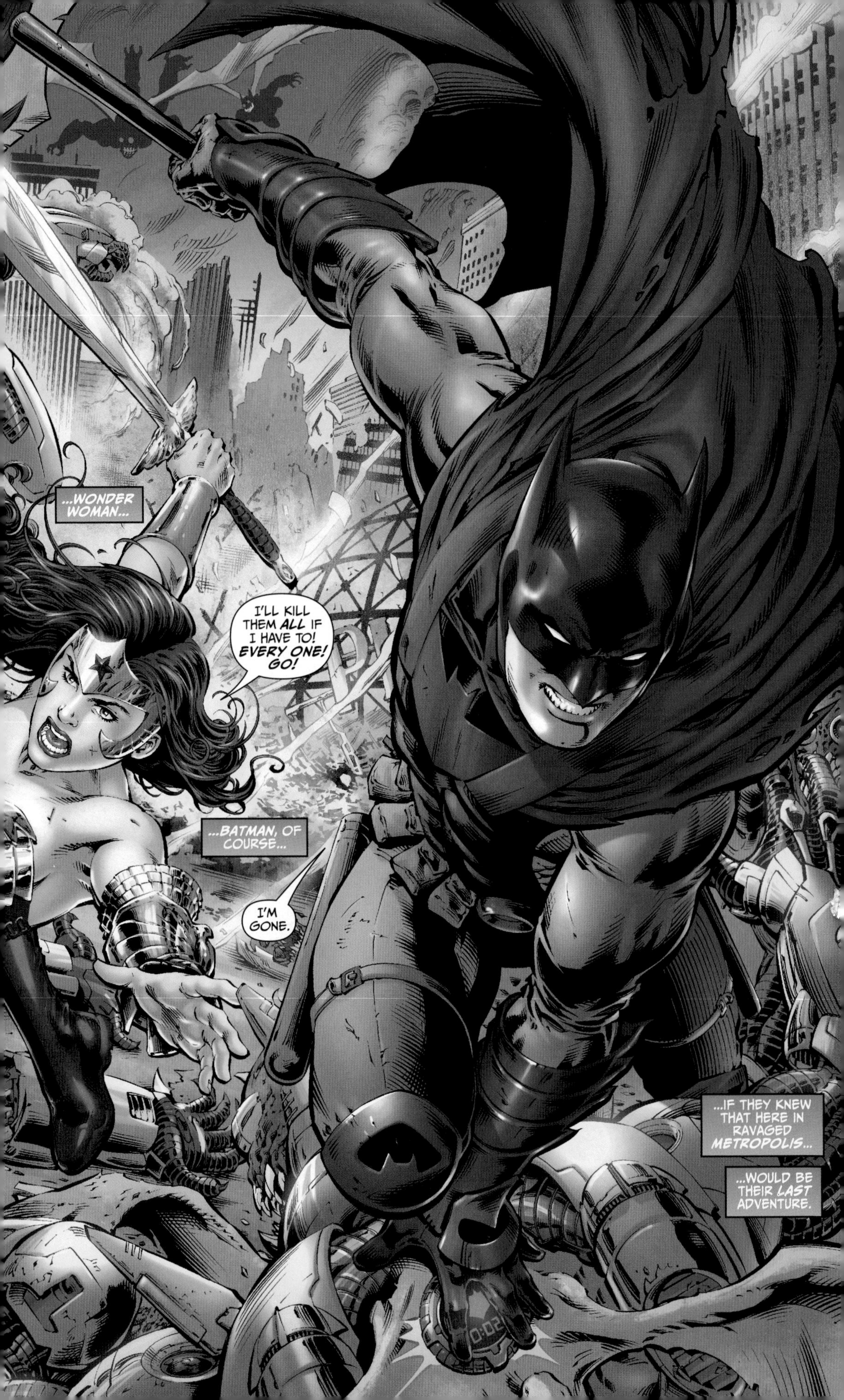
...WONDER WOMAN...
I'LL KILL THEM ALL IF I HAVE TO! EVERY ONE! GO!
...BATMAN, OF COURSE...
I'M GONE.
...IF THEY KNEW THAT HERE IN RAVAGED METROPOLIS...
...WOULD BE THEIR LAST ADVENTURE.

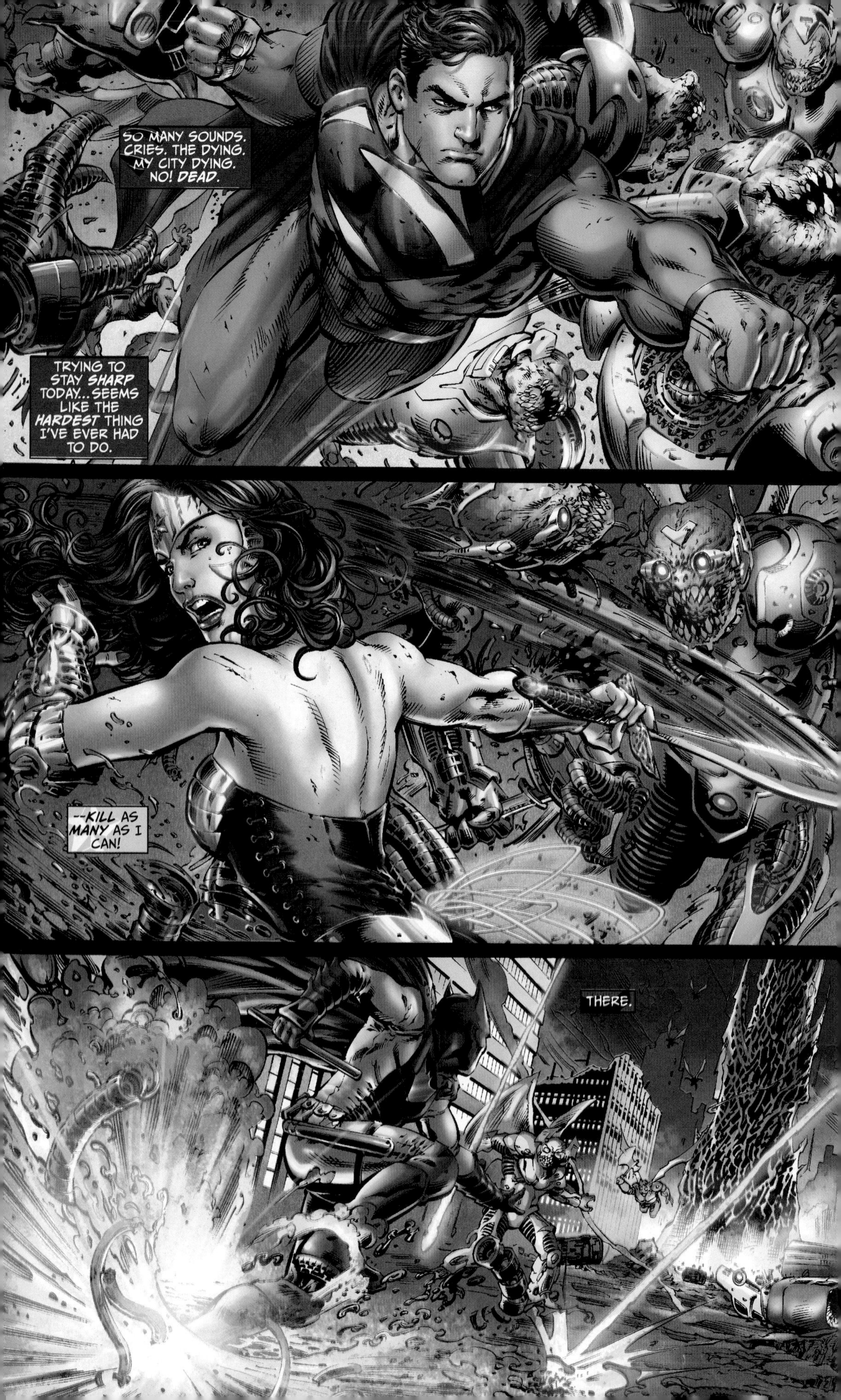
SO MANY SOUNDS. CRIES. THE DYING. MY CITY DYING. NO! DEAD.
TRYING TO STAY SHARP TODAY... SEEMS LIKE THE HARDEST THING I'VE EVER HAD TO DO.
--KILL AS MANY AS I CAN!
THERE.

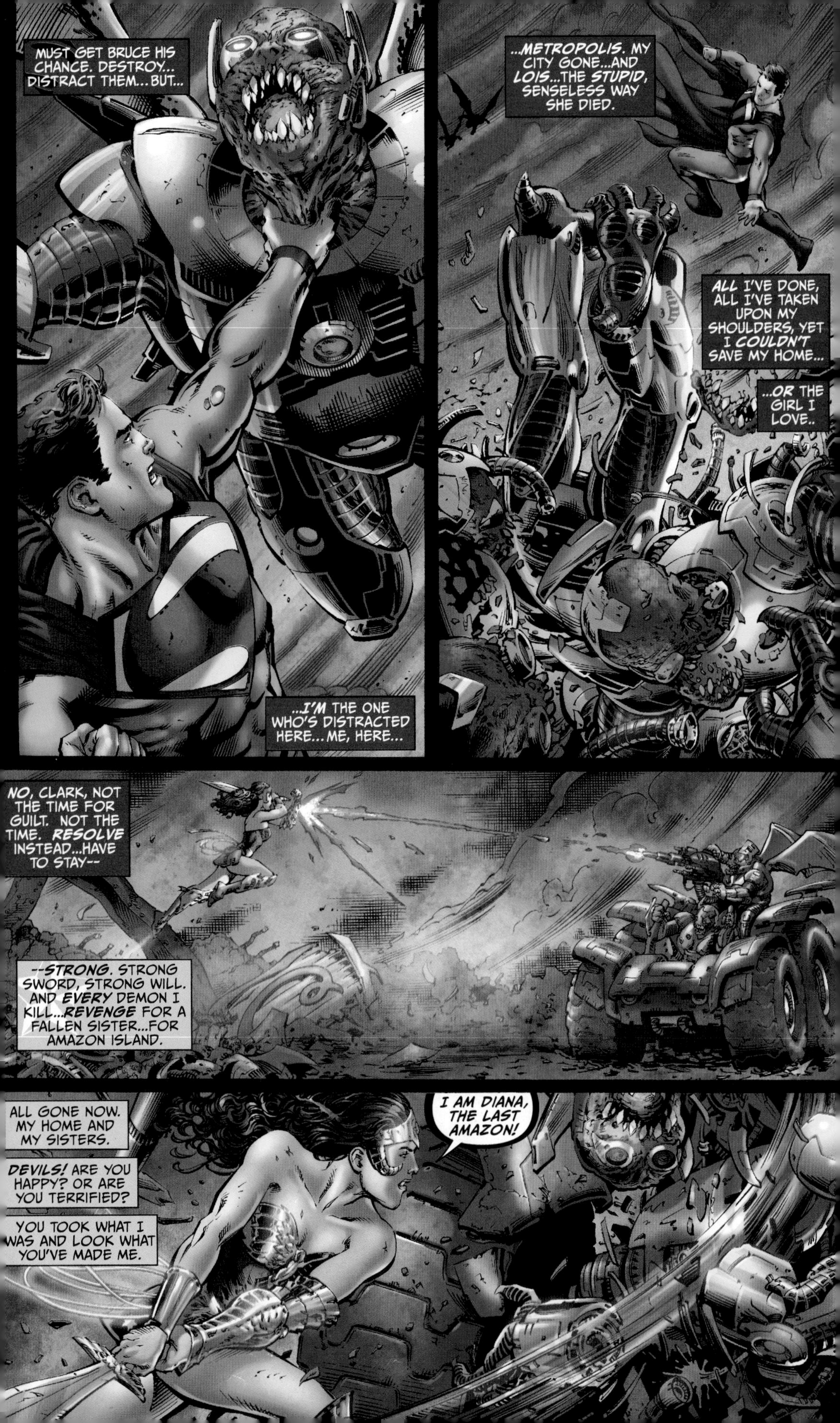
MUST GET BRUCE HIS CHANCE. DESTROY... DISTRACT THEM... BUT...
...I'M THE ONE WHO'S DISTRACTED HERE... ME, HERE...
...METROPOLIS. MY CITY GONE...AND LOIS...THE STUPID, SENSELESS WAY SHE DIED.
ALL I'VE DONE, ALL I'VE TAKEN UPON MY SHOULDERS, YET I COULDN'T SAVE MY HOME...
...OR THE GIRL I LOVE..
NO, CLARK, NOT THE TIME FOR GUILT. NOT THE TIME. RESOLVE INSTEAD...HAVE TO STAY--
--STRONG. STRONG SWORD, STRONG WILL. AND EVERY DEMON I KILL...REVENGE FOR A FALLEN SISTER...FOR AMAZON ISLAND.
ALL GONE NOW. MY HOME AND MY SISTERS.
DEVILS! ARE YOU HAPPY? OR ARE YOU TERRIFIED?
YOU TOOK WHAT I WAS AND LOOK WHAT YOU'VE MADE ME.
I AM DIANA, THE LAST AMAZON!

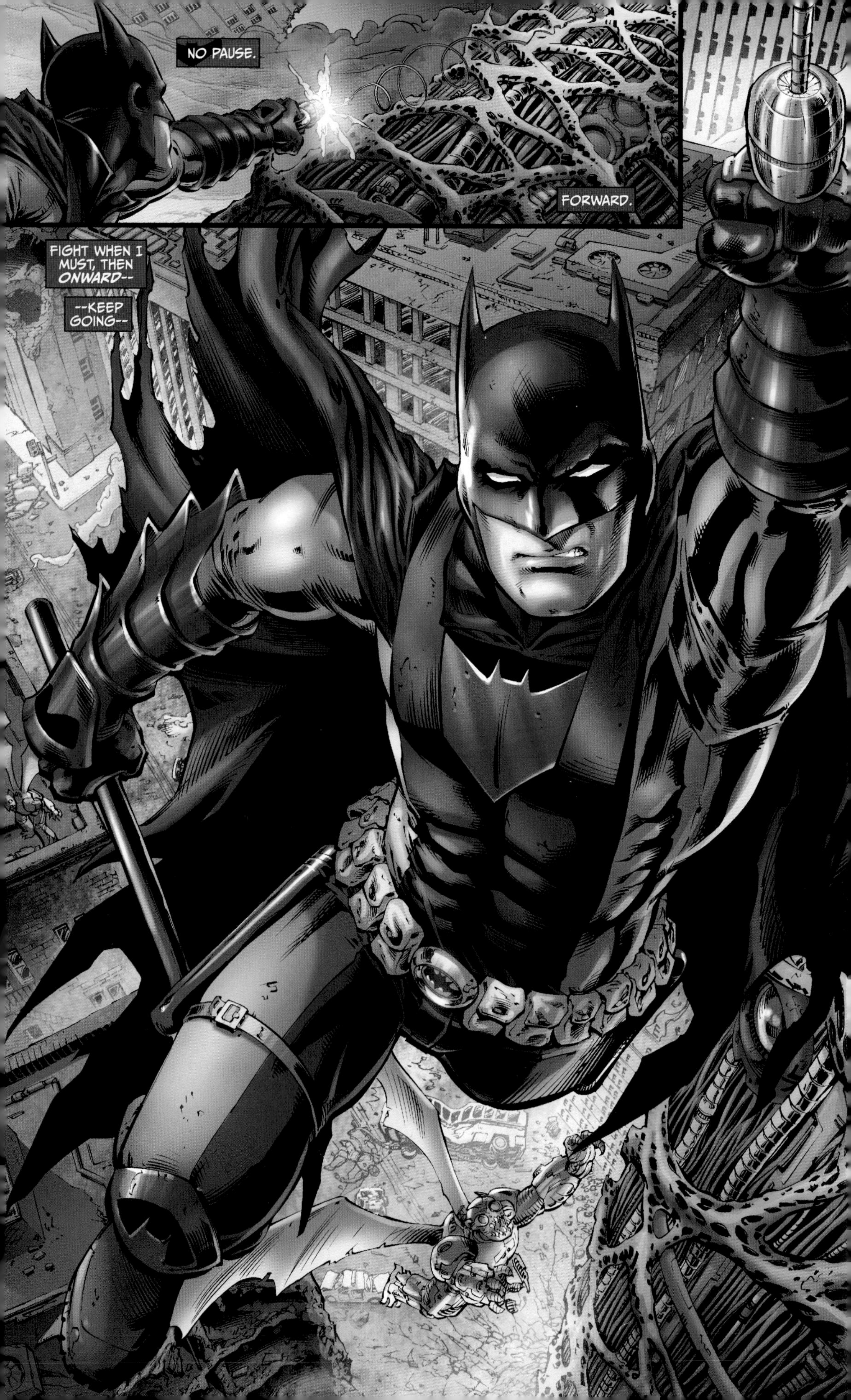
NO PAUSE.
FORWARD.
FIGHT WHEN I MUST, THEN *ONWARD*--
--KEEP GOING--

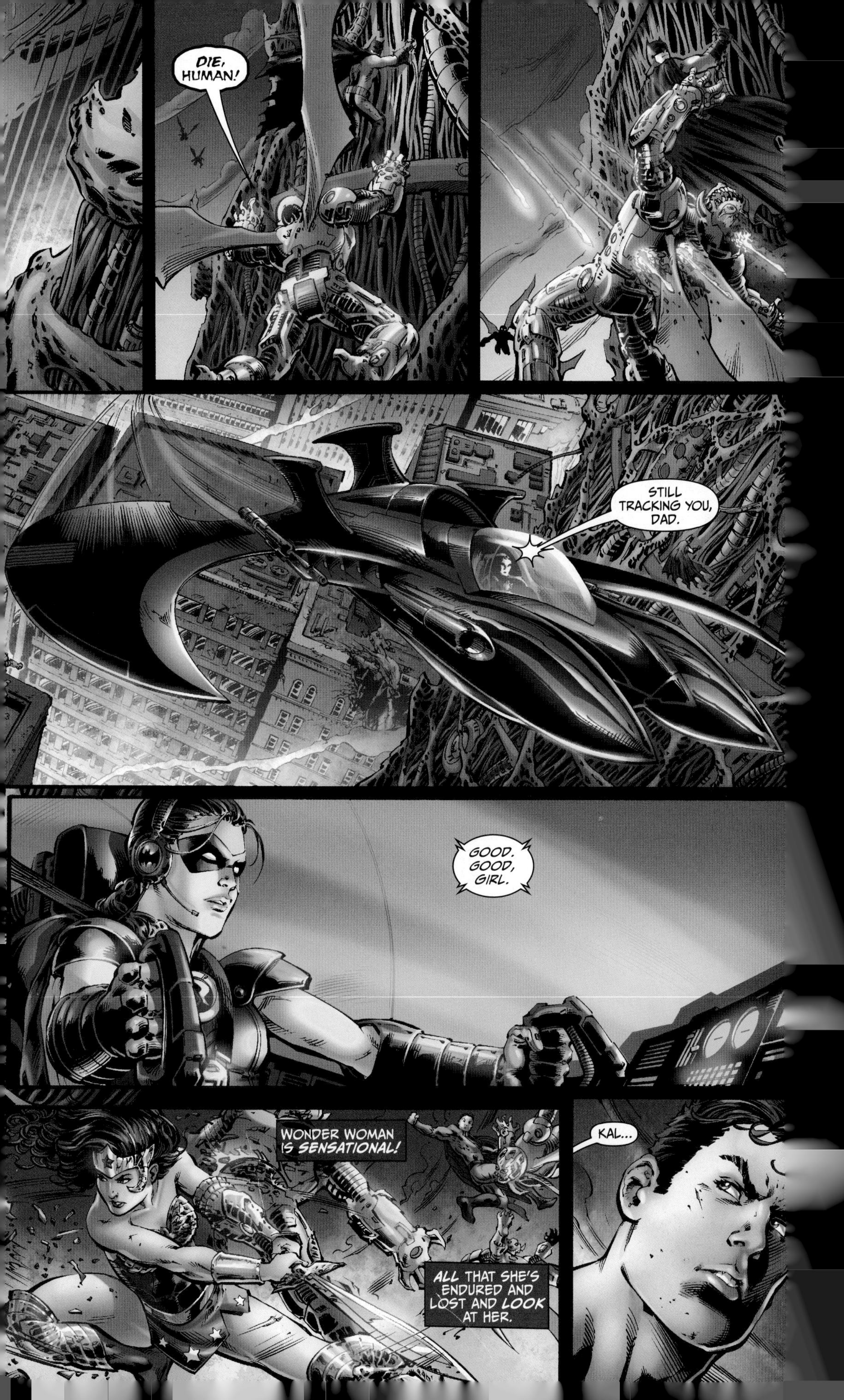
DIE, HUMAN!
STILL TRACKING YOU, DAD.
GOOD. GOOD, GIRL.
WONDER WOMAN IS SENSATIONAL!
ALL THAT SHE'S ENDURED AND LOST AND LOOK AT HER.
KAL...

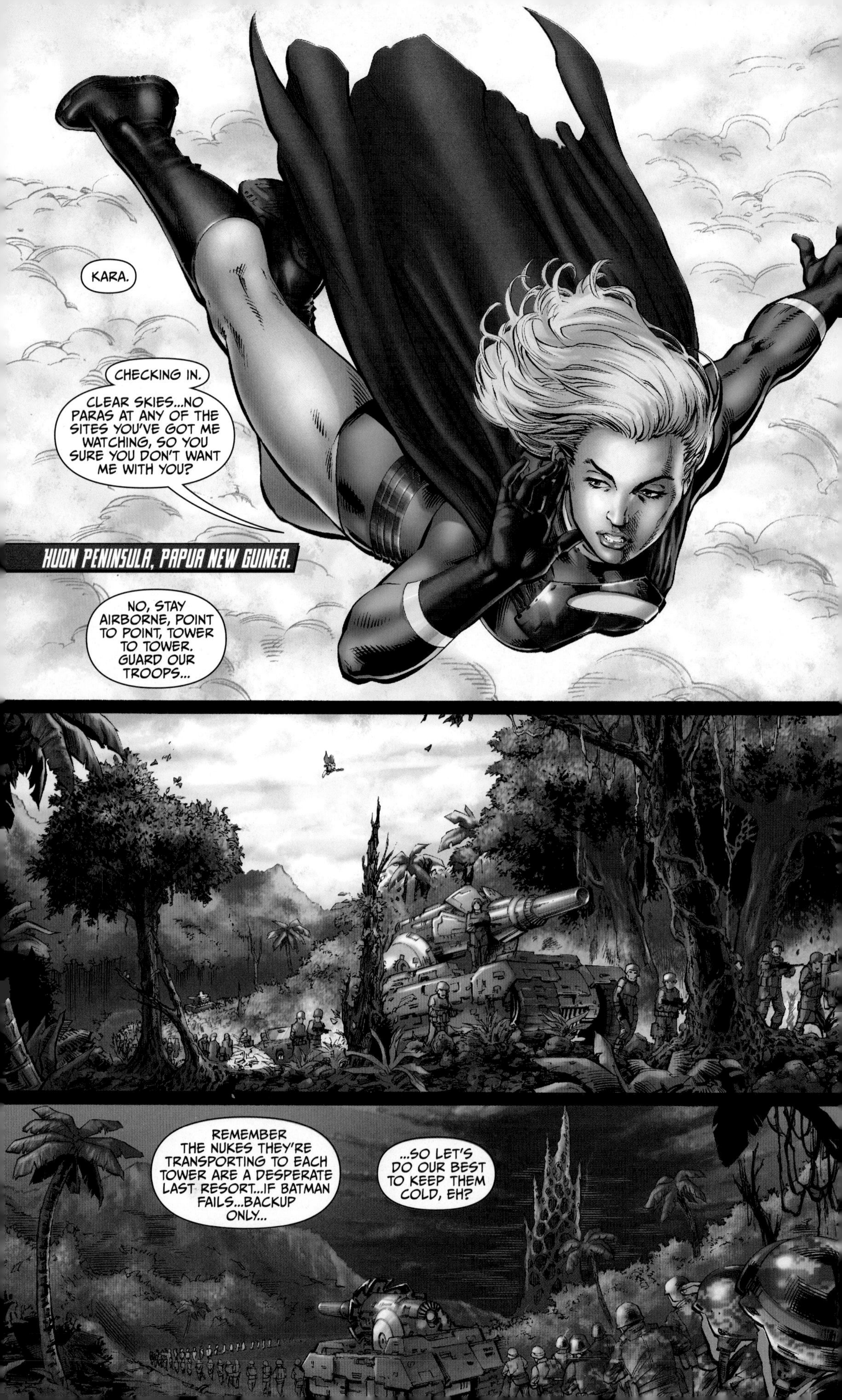

KARA.
CHECKING IN.
CLEAR SKIES...NO PARAS AT ANY OF THE SITES YOU'VE GOT ME WATCHING, SO YOU SURE YOU DON'T WANT ME WITH YOU?
HUON PENINSULA, PAPUA NEW GUINEA.
NO, STAY AIRBORNE, POINT TO POINT, TOWER TO TOWER. GUARD OUR TROOPS...
REMEMBER THE NUKES THEY'RE TRANSPORTING TO EACH TOWER ARE A DESPERATE LAST RESORT...IF BATMAN FAILS...BACKUP ONLY...
...SO LET'S DO OUR BEST TO KEEP THEM COLD, EH?

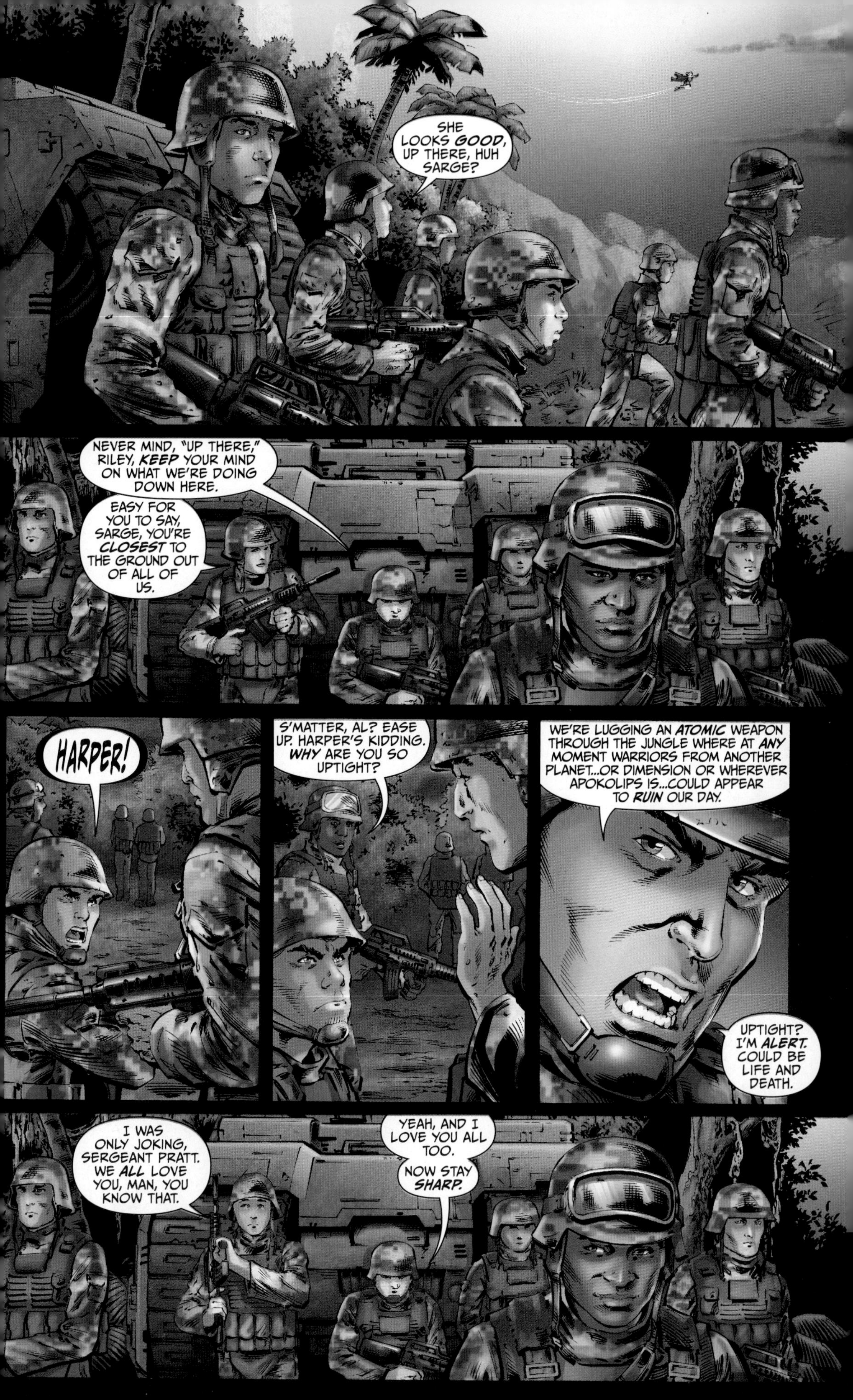
SHE LOOKS GOOD, UP THERE, HUH SARGE?
NEVER MIND, "UP THERE," RILEY, KEEP YOUR MIND ON WHAT WE'RE DOING DOWN HERE.
EASY FOR YOU TO SAY, SARGE, YOU'RE CLOSEST TO THE GROUND OUT OF ALL OF US.
HARPER!
S'MATTER, AL? EASE UP. HARPER'S KIDDING. WHY ARE YOU SO UPTIGHT?
WE'RE LUGGING AN ATOMIC WEAPON THROUGH THE JUNGLE WHERE AT ANY MOMENT WARRIORS FROM ANOTHER PLANET...OR DIMENSION OR WHEREVER APOKOLIPS IS...COULD APPEAR TO RUIN OUR DAY.
UPTIGHT? I'M ALERT. COULD BE LIFE AND DEATH.
I WAS ONLY JOKING, SERGEANT PRATT. WE ALL LOVE YOU, MAN, YOU KNOW THAT.
YEAH, AND I LOVE YOU ALL TOO.
NOW STAY SHARP.

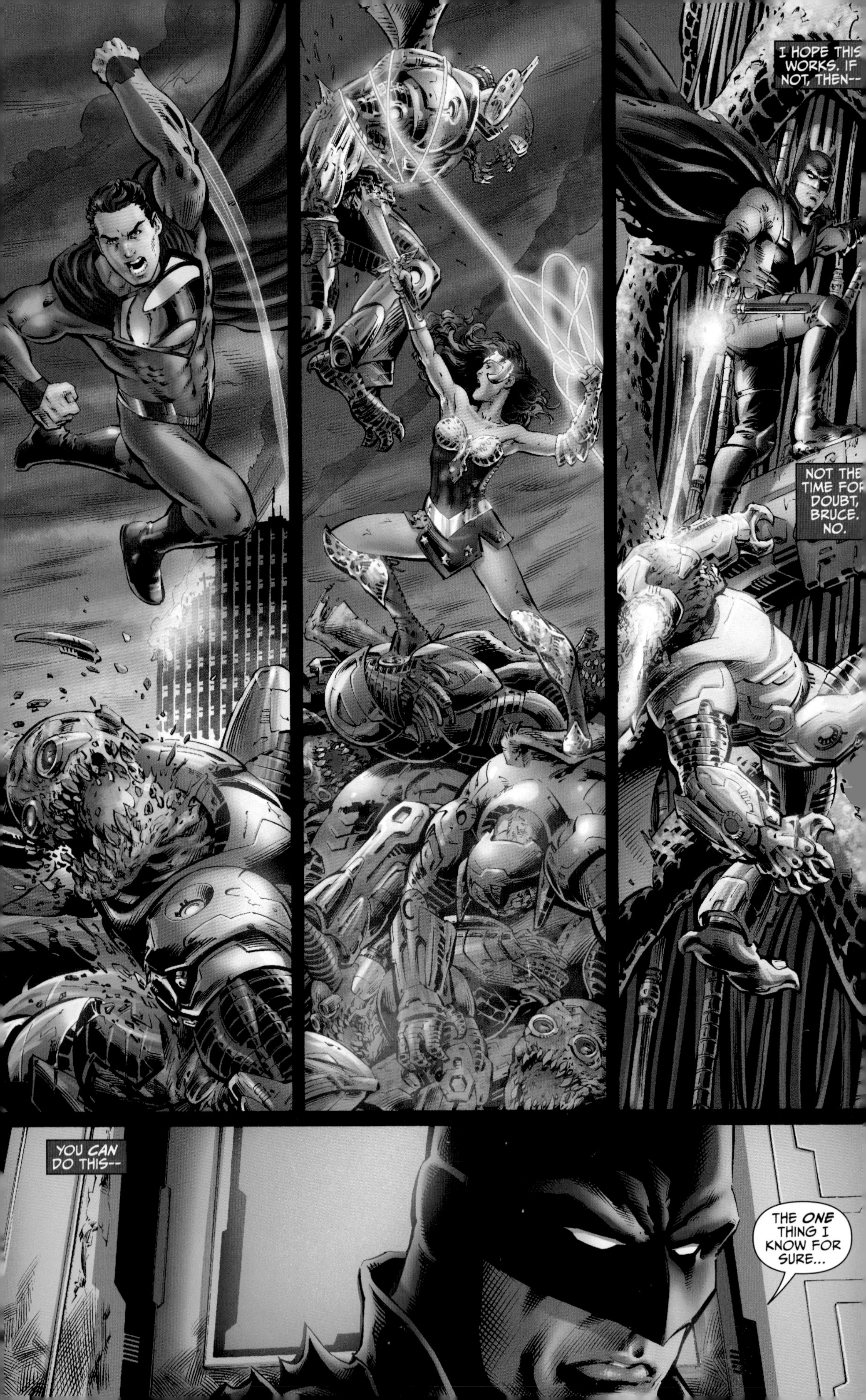
I HOPE THIS WORKS. IF NOT, THEN--
NOT THE TIME FOR DOUBT, BRUCE. NO.
YOU CAN DO THIS--
THE ONE THING I KNOW FOR SURE...

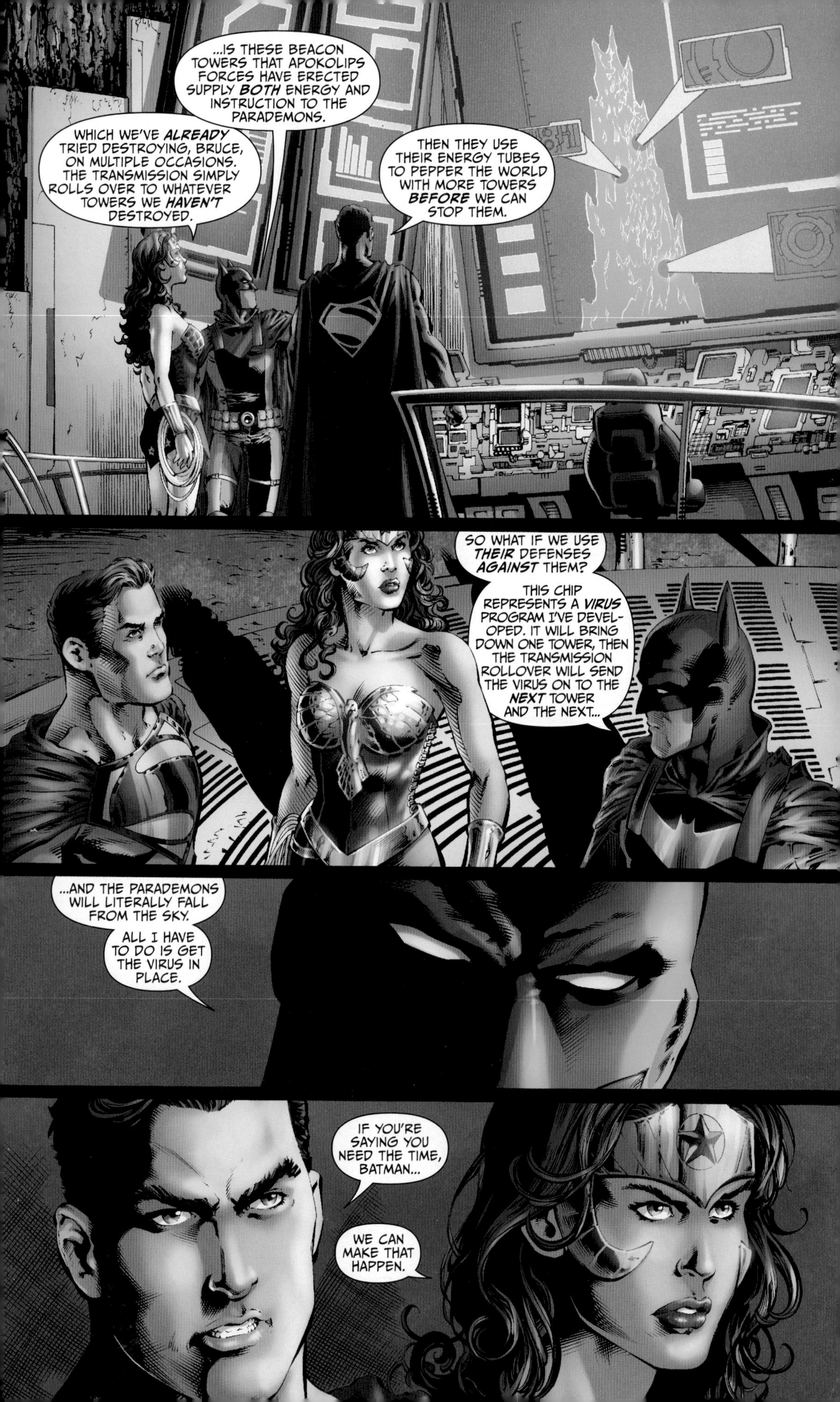
...IS THESE BEACON TOWERS THAT APOKOLIPS FORCES HAVE ERECTED SUPPLY BOTH ENERGY AND INSTRUCTION TO THE PARADEMONS.
WHICH WE'VE ALREADY TRIED DESTROYING, BRUCE, ON MULTIPLE OCCASIONS. THE TRANSMISSION SIMPLY ROLLS OVER TO WHATEVER TOWERS WE HAVEN'T DESTROYED.
THEN THEY USE THEIR ENERGY TUBES TO PEPPER THE WORLD WITH MORE TOWERS BEFORE WE CAN STOP THEM.
SO WHAT IF WE USE THEIR DEFENSES AGAINST THEM?
THIS CHIP REPRESENTS A VIRUS PROGRAM I'VE DEVELOPED. IT WILL BRING DOWN ONE TOWER, THEN THE TRANSMISSION ROLLOVER WILL SEND THE VIRUS ON TO THE NEXT TOWER AND THE NEXT...
...AND THE PARADEMONS WILL LITERALLY FALL FROM THE SKY.
ALL I HAVE TO DO IS GET THE VIRUS IN PLACE.
IF YOU'RE SAYING YOU NEED THE TIME, BATMAN...
WE CAN MAKE THAT HAPPEN.

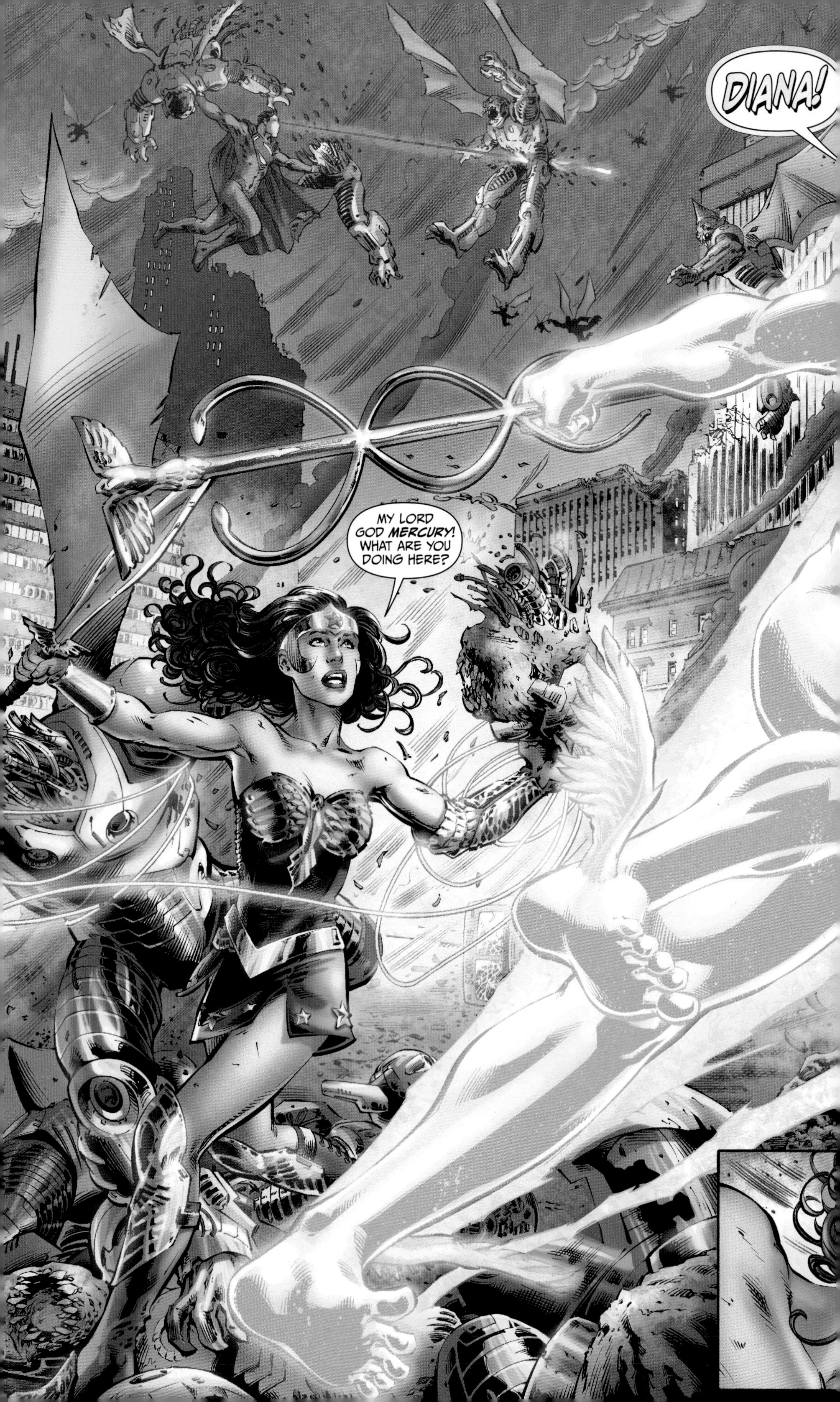
DIANA!
MY LORD GOD MERCURY! WHAT ARE YOU DOING HERE?

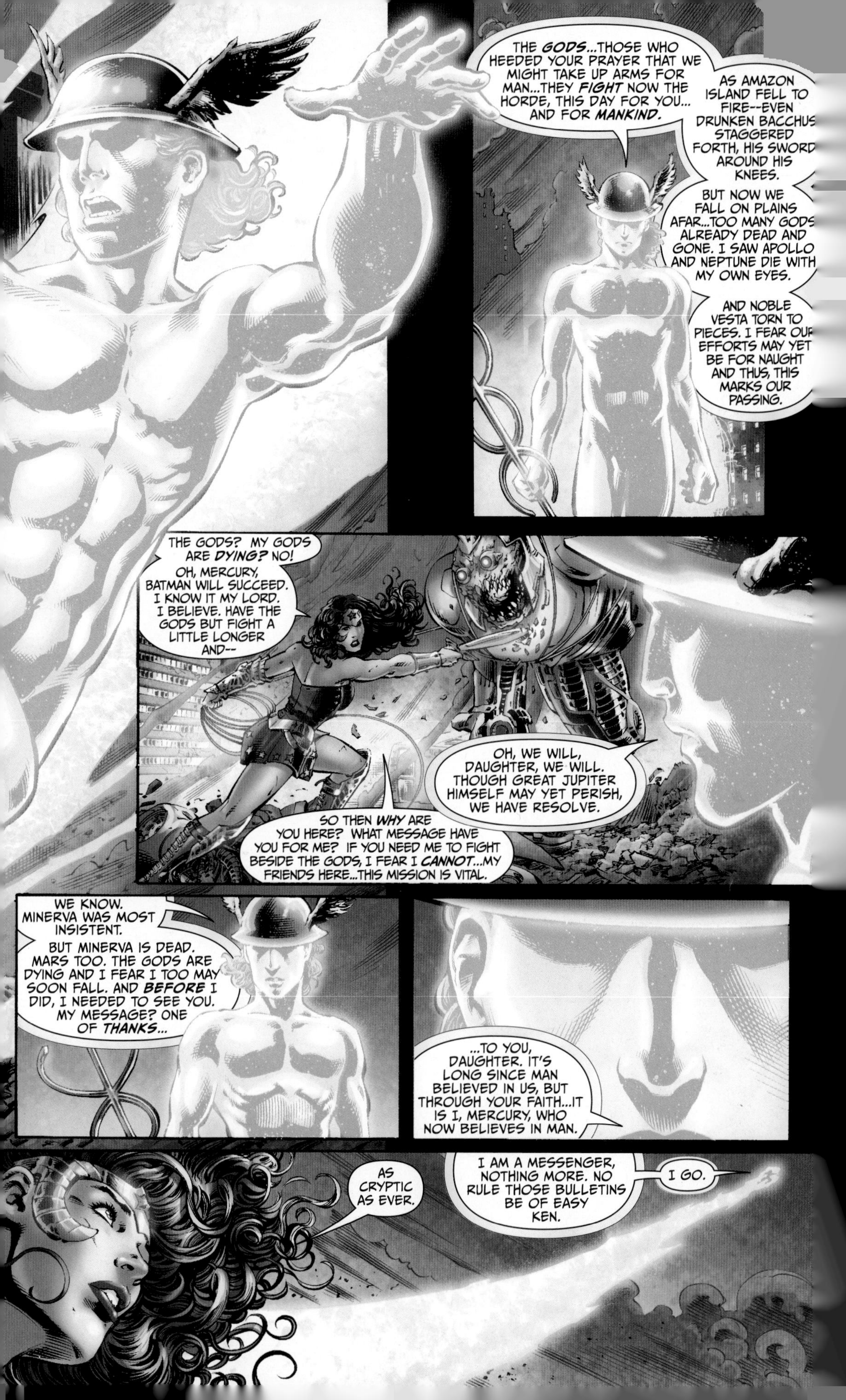
THE GODS...THOSE WHO HEEDED YOUR PRAYER THAT WE MIGHT TAKE UP ARMS FOR MAN...THEY FIGHT NOW THE HORDE, THIS DAY FOR YOU... AND FOR MANKIND.
AS AMAZON ISLAND FELL TO FIRE--EVEN DRUNKEN BACCHUS STAGGERED FORTH, HIS SWORD AROUND HIS KNEES.
BUT NOW WE FALL ON PLAINS AFAR...TOO MANY GODS ALREADY DEAD AND GONE. I SAW APOLLO AND NEPTUNE DIE WITH MY OWN EYES.
AND NOBLE VESTA TORN TO PIECES. I FEAR OUR EFFORTS MAY YET BE FOR NAUGHT AND THUS, THIS MARKS OUR PASSING.
THE GODS? MY GODS ARE DYING? NO!
OH, MERCURY, BATMAN WILL SUCCEED. I KNOW IT MY LORD. I BELIEVE. HAVE THE GODS BUT FIGHT A LITTLE LONGER AND--
OH, WE WILL, DAUGHTER, WE WILL. THOUGH GREAT JUPITER HIMSELF MAY YET PERISH, WE HAVE RESOLVE.
SO THEN WHY ARE YOU HERE? WHAT MESSAGE HAVE YOU FOR ME? IF YOU NEED ME TO FIGHT BESIDE THE GODS, I FEAR I CANNOT...MY FRIENDS HERE...THIS MISSION IS VITAL.
WE KNOW. MINERVA WAS MOST INSISTENT.
BUT MINERVA IS DEAD. MARS TOO. THE GODS ARE DYING AND I FEAR I TOO MAY SOON FALL. AND BEFORE I DID, I NEEDED TO SEE YOU. MY MESSAGE? ONE OF THANKS...
...TO YOU, DAUGHTER. IT'S LONG SINCE MAN BELIEVED IN US, BUT THROUGH YOUR FAITH...IT IS I, MERCURY, WHO NOW BELIEVES IN MAN.
AS CRYPTIC AS EVER.
I AM A MESSENGER, NOTHING MORE. NO RULE THOSE BULLETINS BE OF EASY KEN.
I GO.

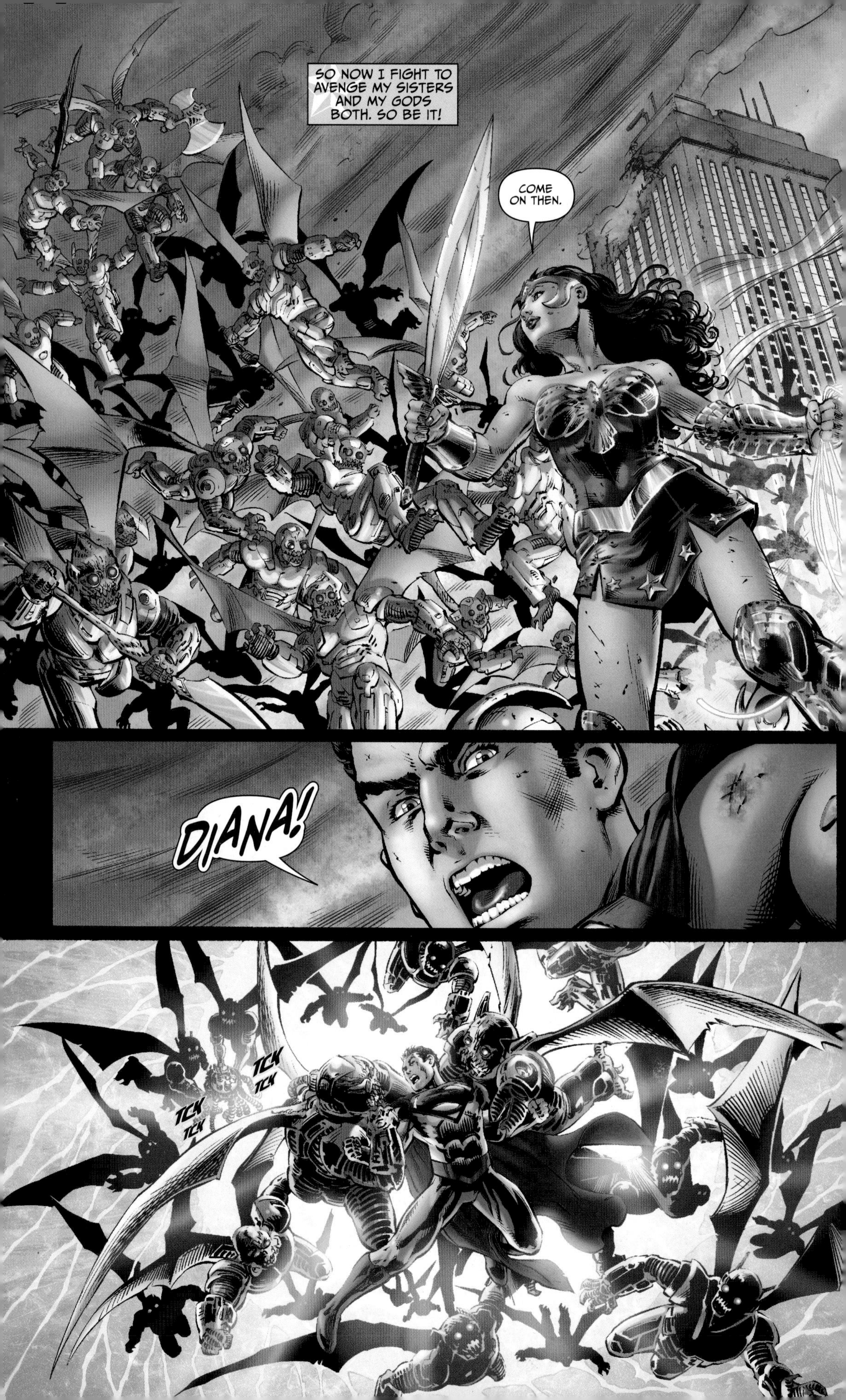
SO NOW I FIGHT TO AVENGE MY SISTERS AND MY GODS BOTH. SO BE IT!
COME ON THEN.
DIANA!
TCK TCK
TCK TCK

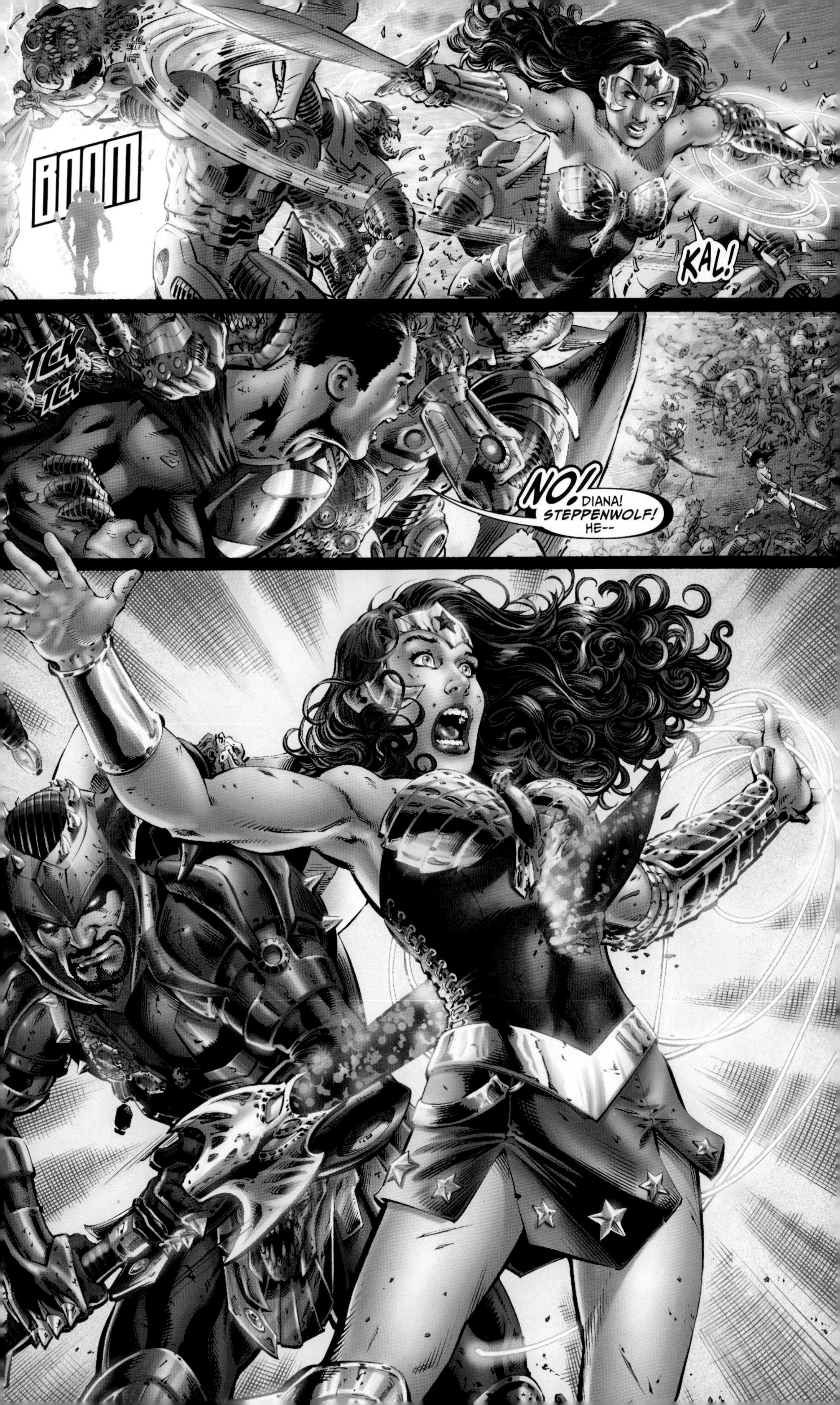
BOOM
KAL!
TCK TCK
NO! DIANA! STEPPENWOLF! HE--

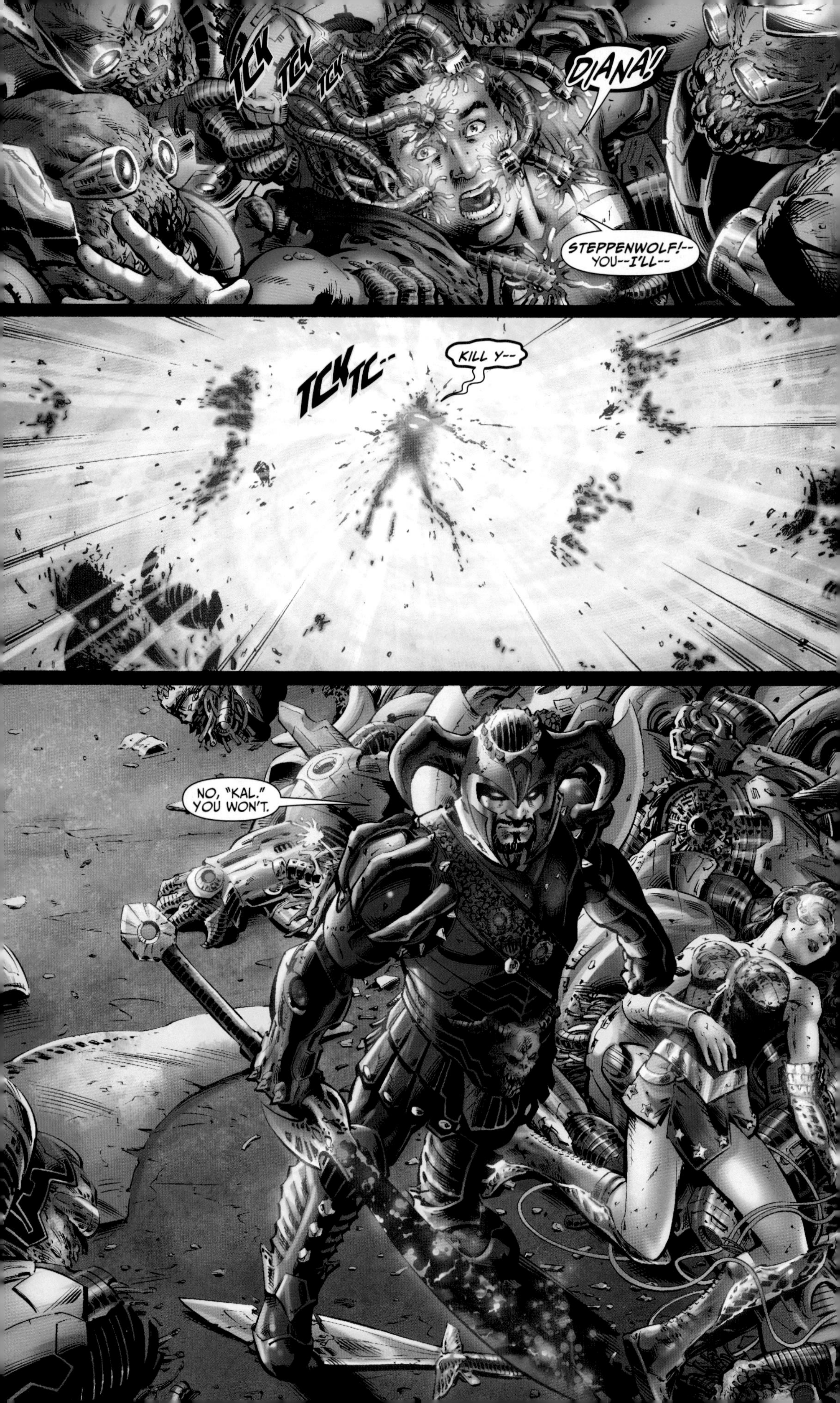
TCK
TCK
TCK
DIANA!
STEPPENWOLF!--
YOU--I'LL--
TCK TC--
KILL Y--
NO, "KAL."
YOU WON'T.

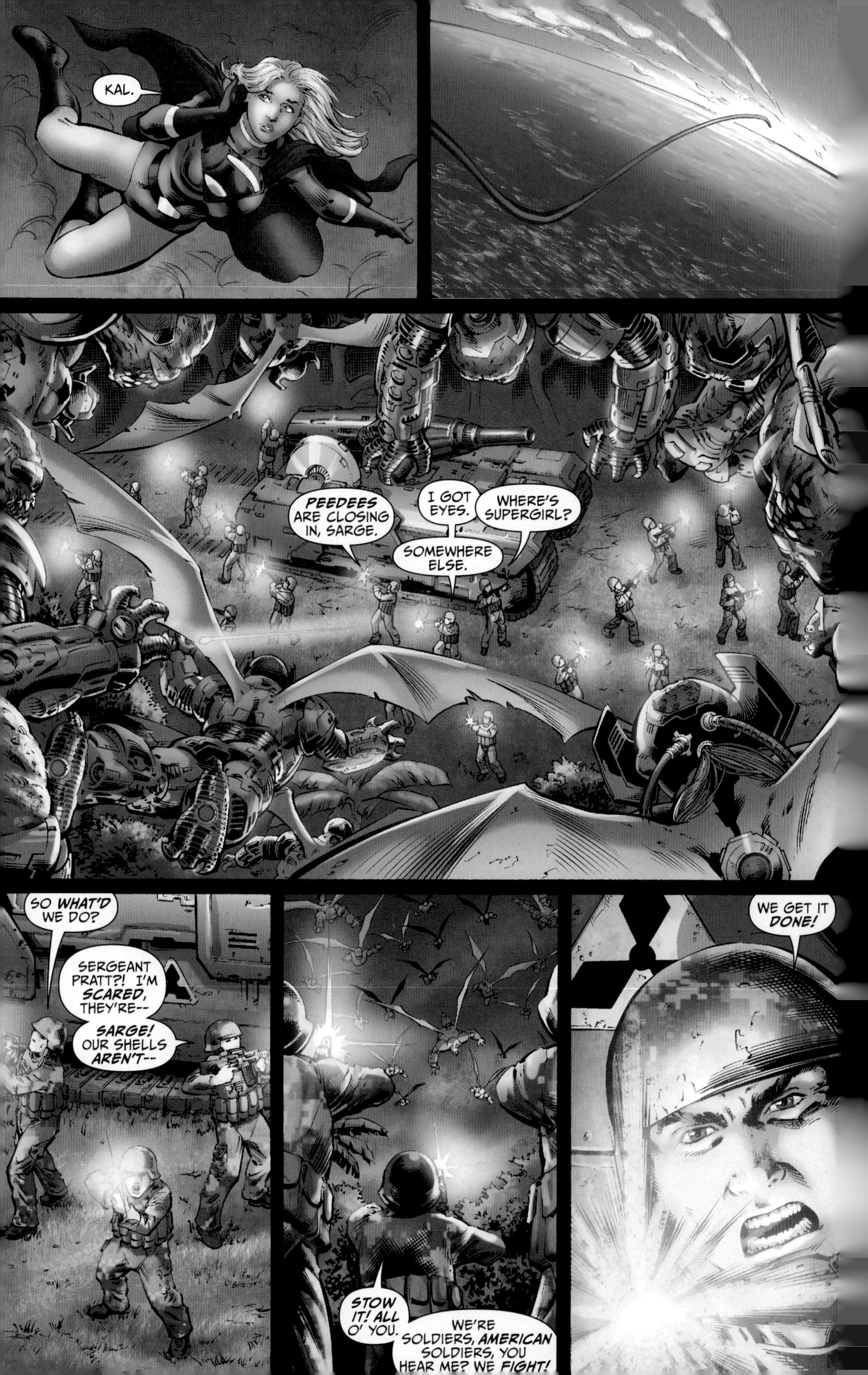
KAL.
PEEDEES ARE CLOSING IN, SARGE.
I GOT EYES.
WHERE'S SUPERGIRL?
SOMEWHERE ELSE.
SO WHAT'D WE DO?
SERGEANT PRATT?! I'M SCARED, THEY'RE--
SARGE! OUR SHELLS AREN'T--
STOW IT! ALL O' YOU.
WE'RE SOLDIERS, AMERICAN SOLDIERS, YOU HEAR ME? WE FIGHT!
WE GET IT DONE!

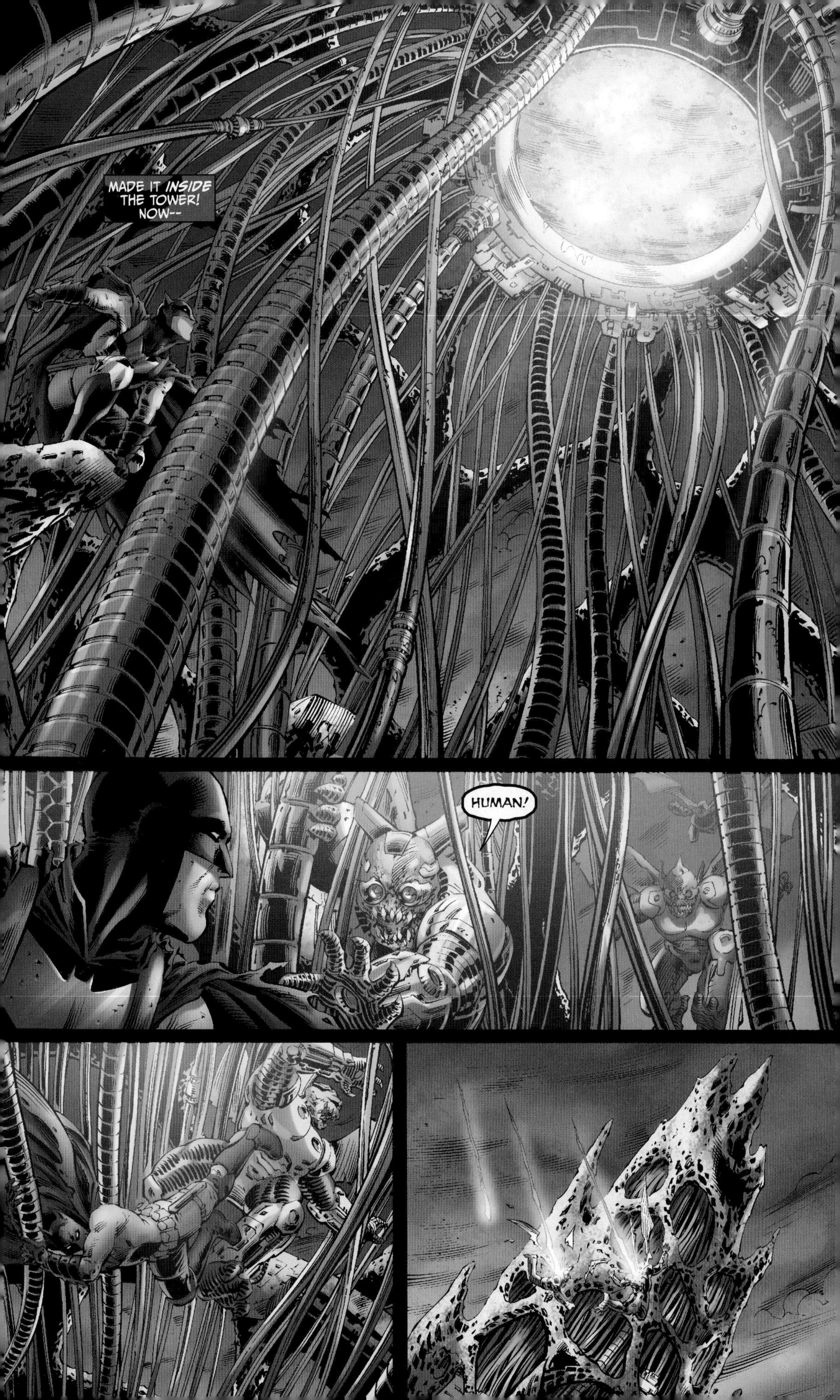
MADE IT *INSIDE* THE TOWER! NOW--
HUMAN!

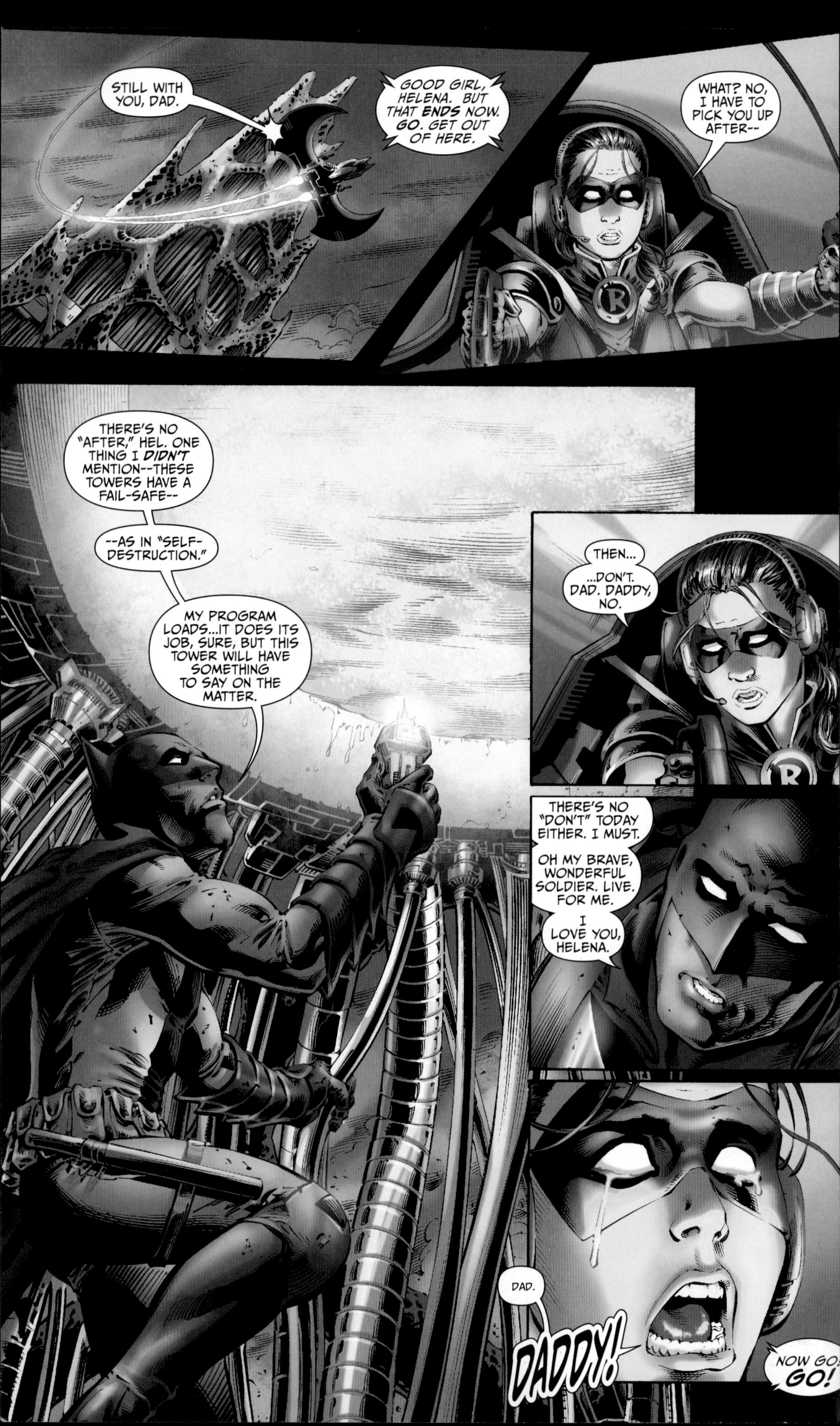

STILL WITH YOU, DAD.
GOOD GIRL, HELENA. BUT THAT ENDS NOW. GO. GET OUT OF HERE.
WHAT? NO, I HAVE TO PICK YOU UP AFTER--
THERE'S NO "AFTER," HEL. ONE THING I DIDN'T MENTION--THESE TOWERS HAVE A FAIL-SAFE--
--AS IN "SELF-DESTRUCTION."
MY PROGRAM LOADS...IT DOES ITS JOB, SURE, BUT THIS TOWER WILL HAVE SOMETHING TO SAY ON THE MATTER.
THEN...
...DON'T. DAD. DADDY, NO.
THERE'S NO "DON'T" TODAY EITHER. I MUST.
OH MY BRAVE, WONDERFUL SOLDIER. LIVE. FOR ME.
I LOVE YOU, HELENA.
DAD.
DADDY!
NOW GO. GO!

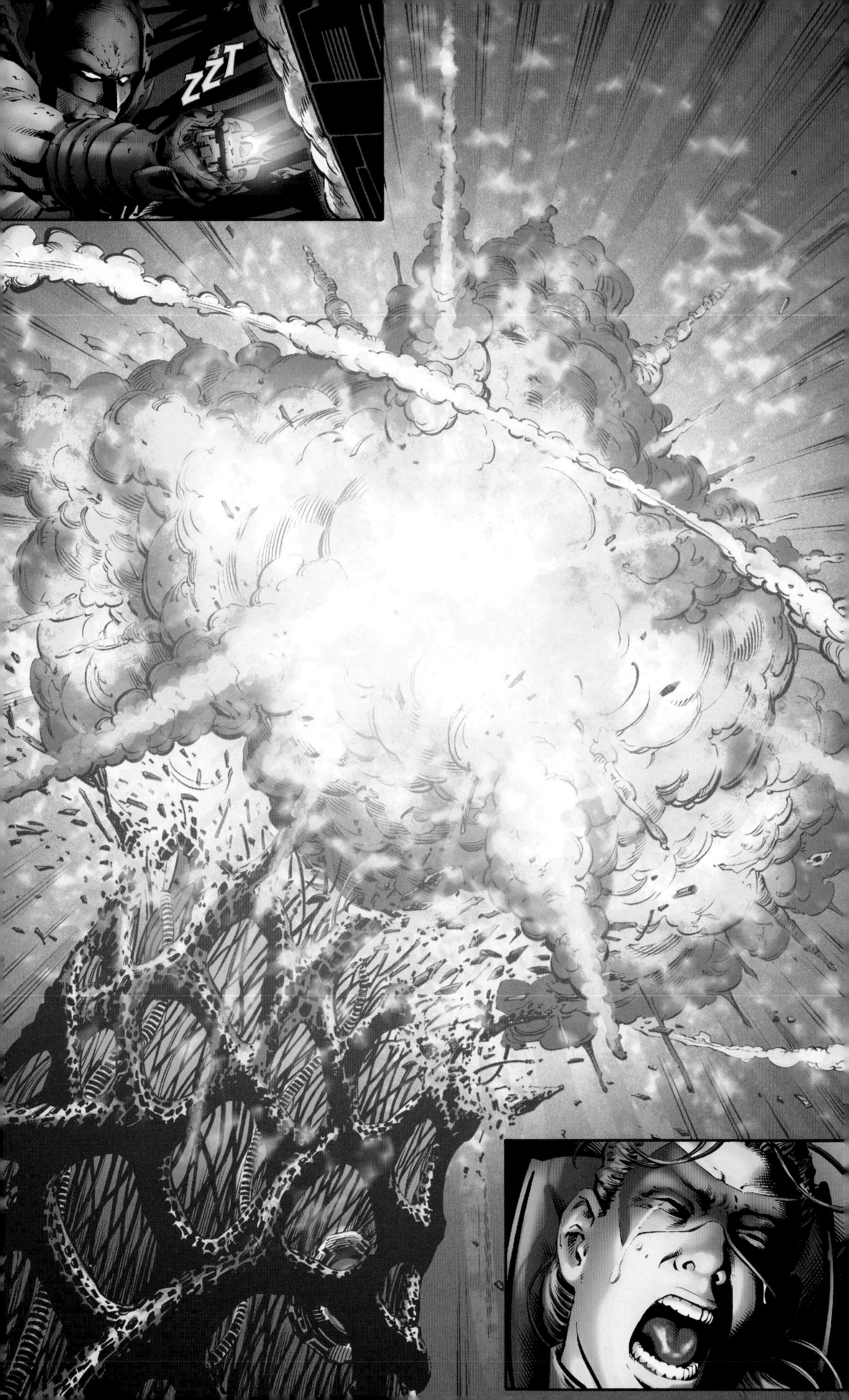
ZZT

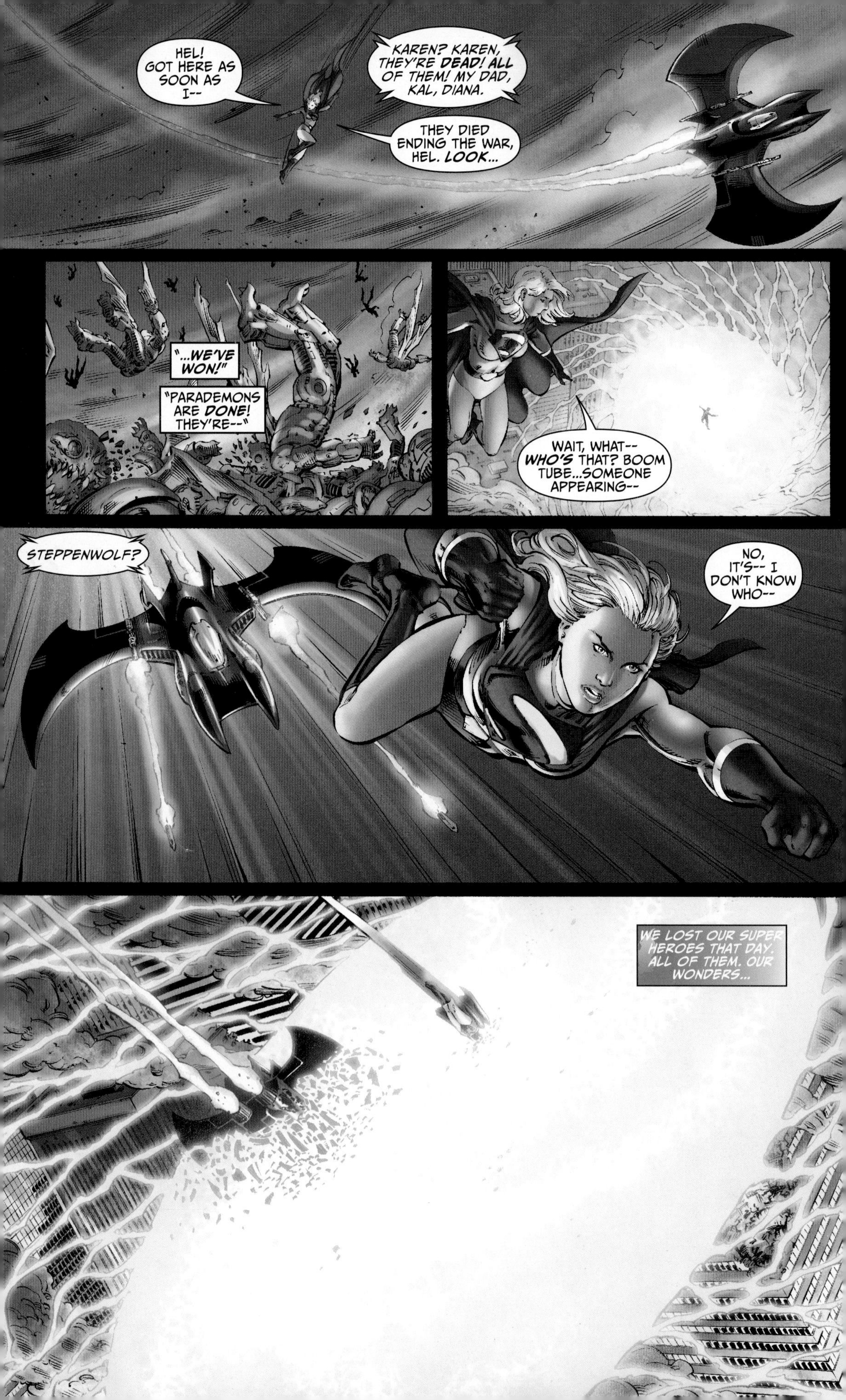
HEL! GOT HERE AS SOON AS I--
KAREN? KAREN, THEY'RE DEAD! ALL OF THEM! MY DAD, KAL, DIANA.
THEY DIED ENDING THE WAR, HEL. LOOK...
"...WE'VE WON!"
"PARADEMONS ARE DONE! THEY'RE--"
WAIT, WHAT-- WHO'S THAT? BOOM TUBE...SOMEONE APPEARING--
STEPPENWOLF?
NO, IT'S-- I DON'T KNOW WHO--
WE LOST OUR SUPER HEROES THAT DAY. ALL OF THEM. OUR WONDERS...

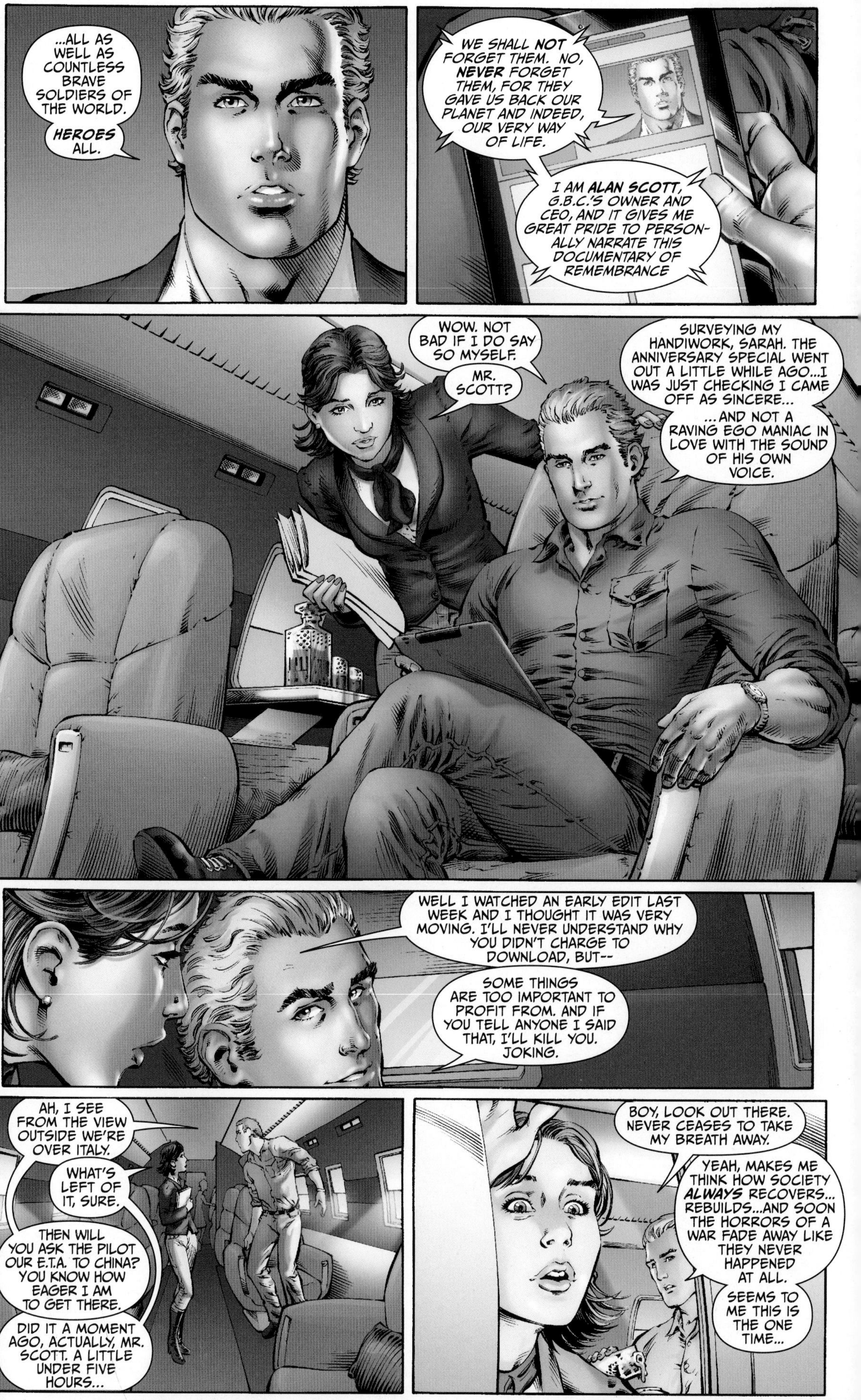
...ALL AS WELL AS COUNTLESS BRAVE SOLDIERS OF THE WORLD.
HEROES ALL.
WE SHALL NOT FORGET THEM. NO, NEVER FORGET THEM, FOR THEY GAVE US BACK OUR PLANET AND INDEED, OUR VERY WAY OF LIFE.
I AM ALAN SCOTT, G.B.C.'S OWNER AND CEO, AND IT GIVES ME GREAT PRIDE TO PERSONALLY NARRATE THIS DOCUMENTARY OF REMEMBRANCE
WOW. NOT BAD IF I DO SAY SO MYSELF.
MR. SCOTT?
SURVEYING MY HANDIWORK, SARAH. THE ANNIVERSARY SPECIAL WENT OUT A LITTLE WHILE AGO...I WAS JUST CHECKING I CAME OFF AS SINCERE...
...AND NOT A RAVING EGO MANIAC IN LOVE WITH THE SOUND OF HIS OWN VOICE.
WELL I WATCHED AN EARLY EDIT LAST WEEK AND I THOUGHT IT WAS VERY MOVING. I'LL NEVER UNDERSTAND WHY YOU DIDN'T CHARGE TO DOWNLOAD, BUT--
SOME THINGS ARE TOO IMPORTANT TO PROFIT FROM. AND IF YOU TELL ANYONE I SAID THAT, I'LL KILL YOU. JOKING.
AH, I SEE FROM THE VIEW OUTSIDE WE'RE OVER ITALY.
WHAT'S LEFT OF IT, SURE.
THEN WILL YOU ASK THE PILOT OUR E.T.A. TO CHINA? YOU KNOW HOW EAGER I AM TO GET THERE.
DID IT A MOMENT AGO, ACTUALLY, MR. SCOTT. A LITTLE UNDER FIVE HOURS...
BOY, LOOK OUT THERE. NEVER CEASES TO TAKE MY BREATH AWAY.
YEAH, MAKES ME THINK HOW SOCIETY ALWAYS RECOVERS... REBUILDS...AND SOON THE HORRORS OF A WAR FADE AWAY LIKE THEY NEVER HAPPENED AT ALL.
SEEMS TO ME THIS IS THE ONE TIME...

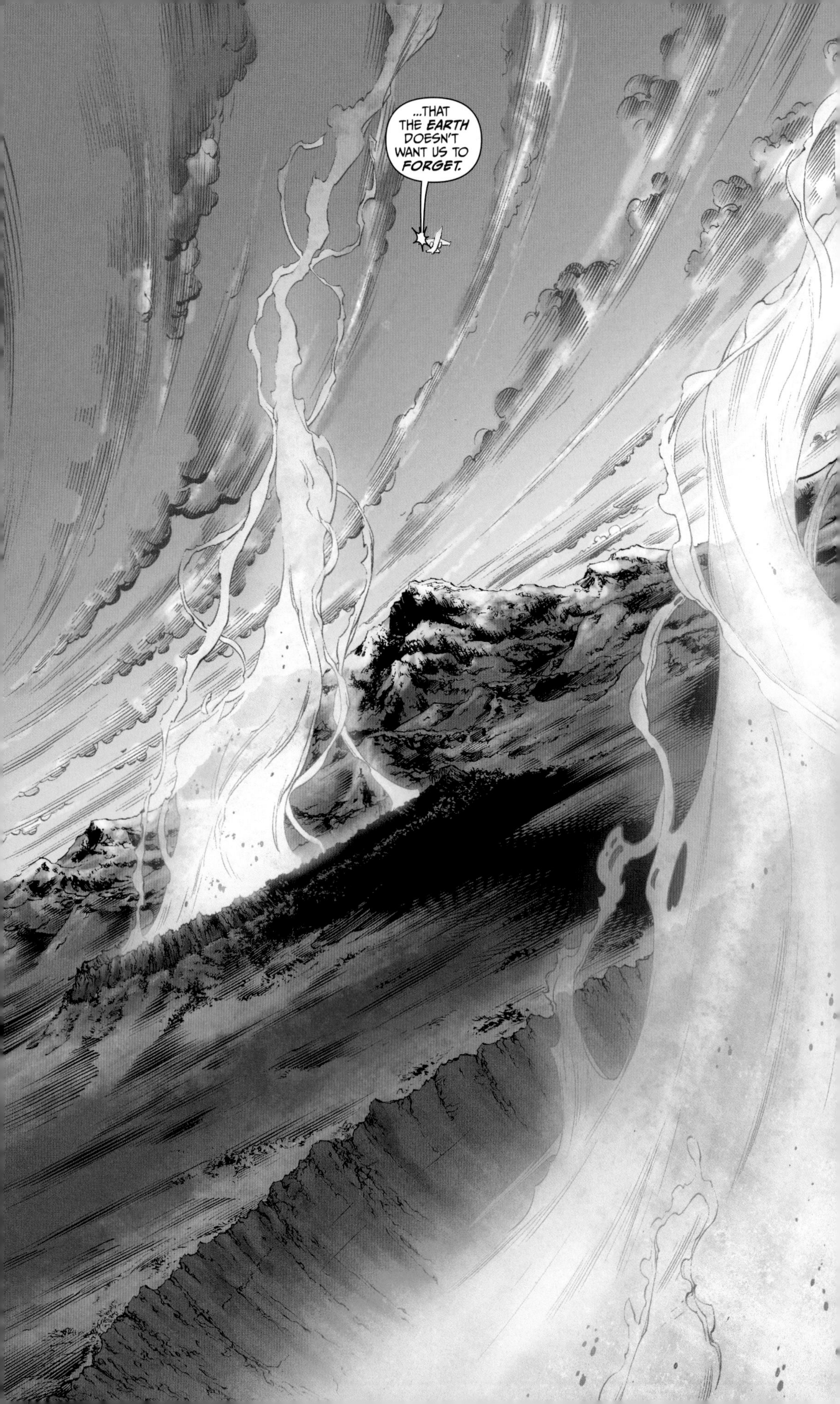
...THAT THE EARTH DOESN'T WANT US TO FORGET.

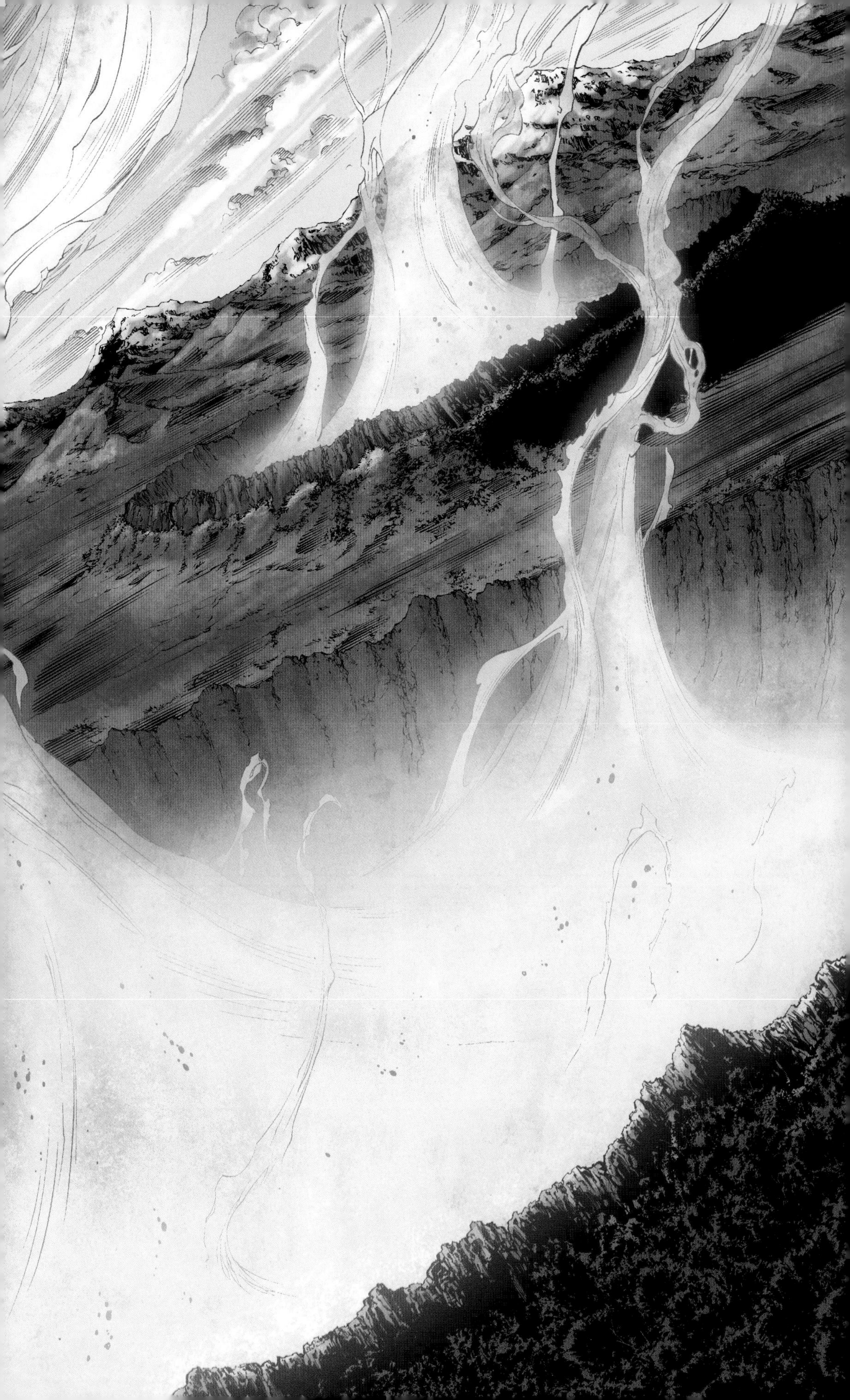

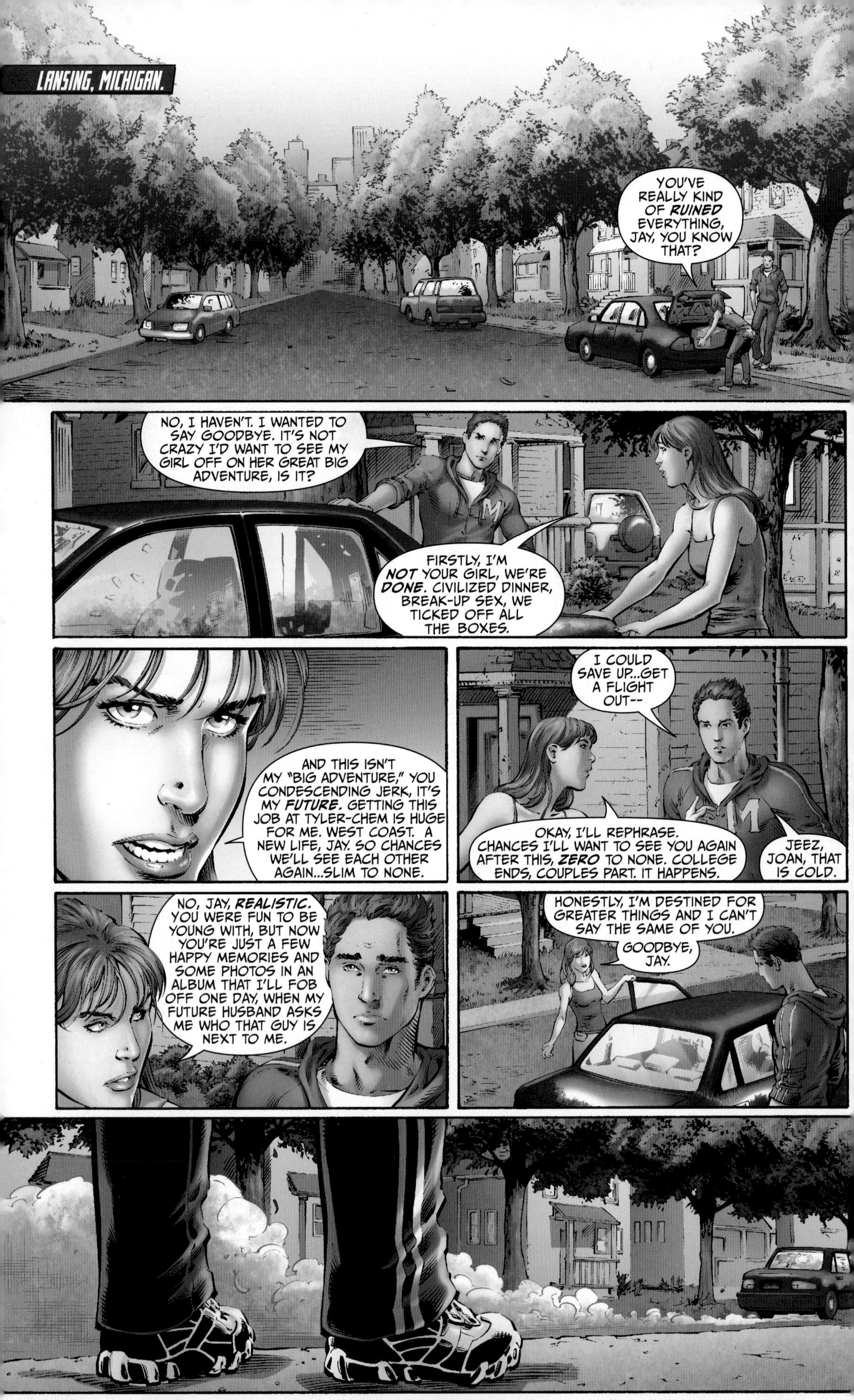

LANSING, MICHIGAN.
YOU'VE REALLY KIND OF RUINED EVERYTHING, JAY, YOU KNOW THAT?
NO, I HAVEN'T. I WANTED TO SAY GOODBYE. IT'S NOT CRAZY I'D WANT TO SEE MY GIRL OFF ON HER GREAT BIG ADVENTURE, IS IT?
FIRSTLY, I'M NOT YOUR GIRL, WE'RE DONE. CIVILIZED DINNER, BREAK-UP SEX, WE TICKED OFF ALL THE BOXES.
AND THIS ISN'T MY "BIG ADVENTURE," YOU CONDESCENDING JERK, IT'S MY FUTURE. GETTING THIS JOB AT TYLER-CHEM IS HUGE FOR ME. WEST COAST. A NEW LIFE, JAY. SO CHANCES WE'LL SEE EACH OTHER AGAIN...SLIM TO NONE.
I COULD SAVE UP...GET A FLIGHT OUT--
OKAY, I'LL REPHRASE. CHANCES I'LL WANT TO SEE YOU AGAIN AFTER THIS, ZERO TO NONE. COLLEGE ENDS, COUPLES PART. IT HAPPENS.
JEEZ, JOAN, THAT IS COLD.
NO, JAY, REALISTIC. YOU WERE FUN TO BE YOUNG WITH, BUT NOW YOU'RE JUST A FEW HAPPY MEMORIES AND SOME PHOTOS IN AN ALBUM THAT I'LL FOB OFF ONE DAY, WHEN MY FUTURE HUSBAND ASKS ME WHO THAT GUY IS NEXT TO ME.
HONESTLY, I'M DESTINED FOR GREATER THINGS AND I CAN'T SAY THE SAME OF YOU.
GOODBYE, JAY.

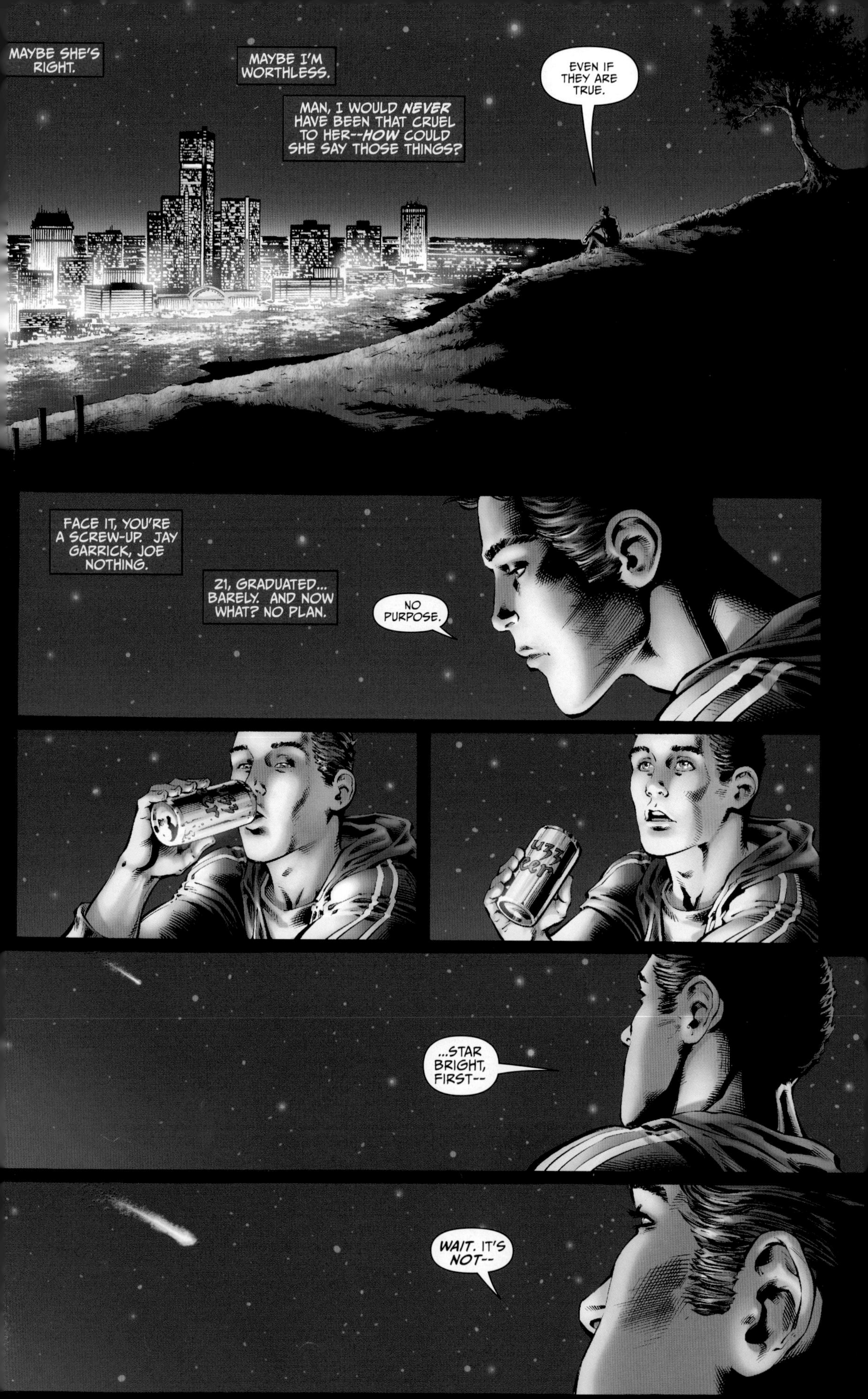
MAYBE SHE'S RIGHT.
MAYBE I'M WORTHLESS.
MAN, I WOULD NEVER HAVE BEEN THAT CRUEL TO HER--HOW COULD SHE SAY THOSE THINGS?
EVEN IF THEY ARE TRUE.
FACE IT, YOU'RE A SCREW-UP. JAY GARRICK, JOE NOTHING.
21, GRADUATED... BARELY. AND NOW WHAT? NO PLAN.
NO PURPOSE.
...STAR BRIGHT, FIRST--
WAIT. IT'S NOT--

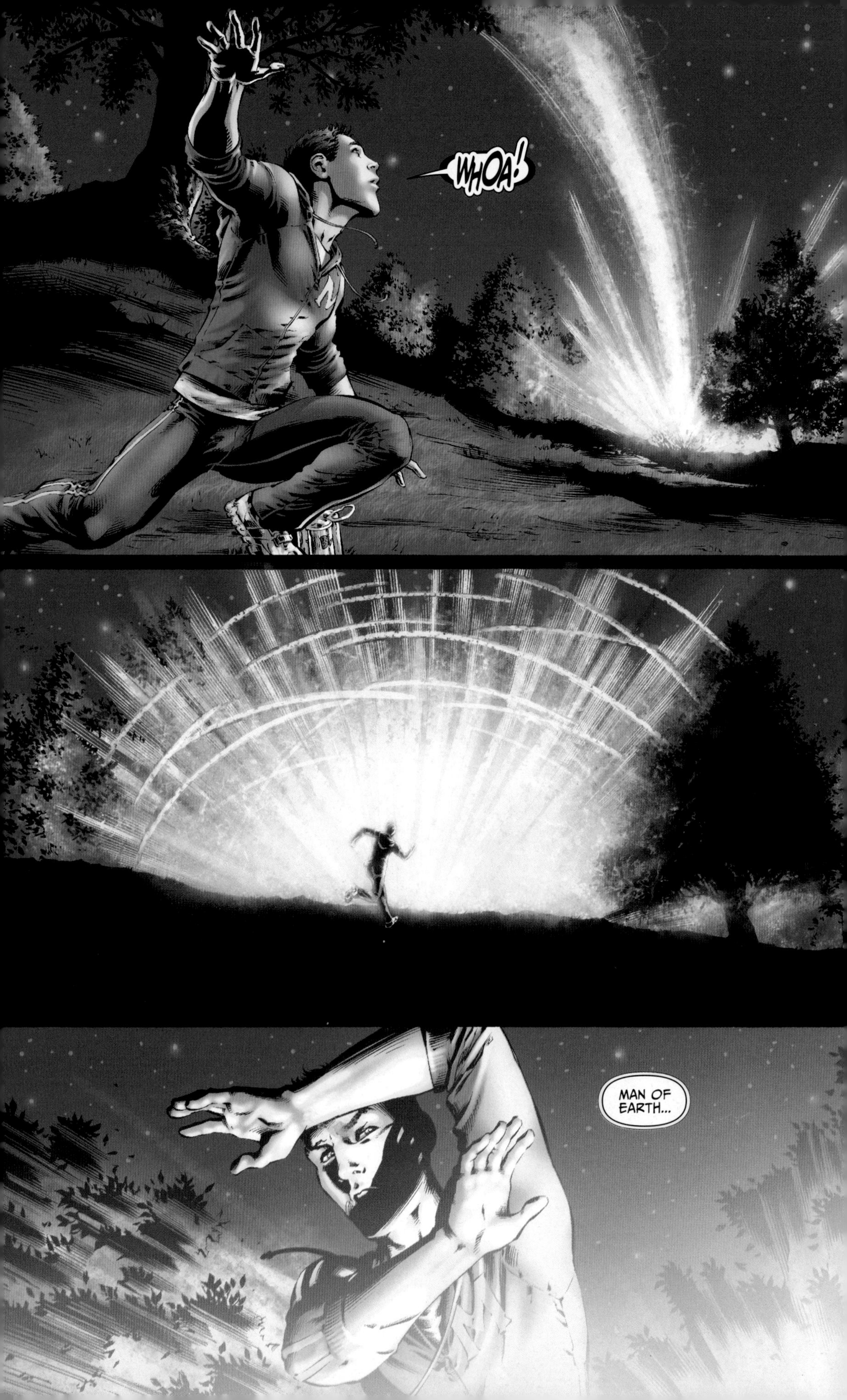
WHOA!
MAN OF EARTH...

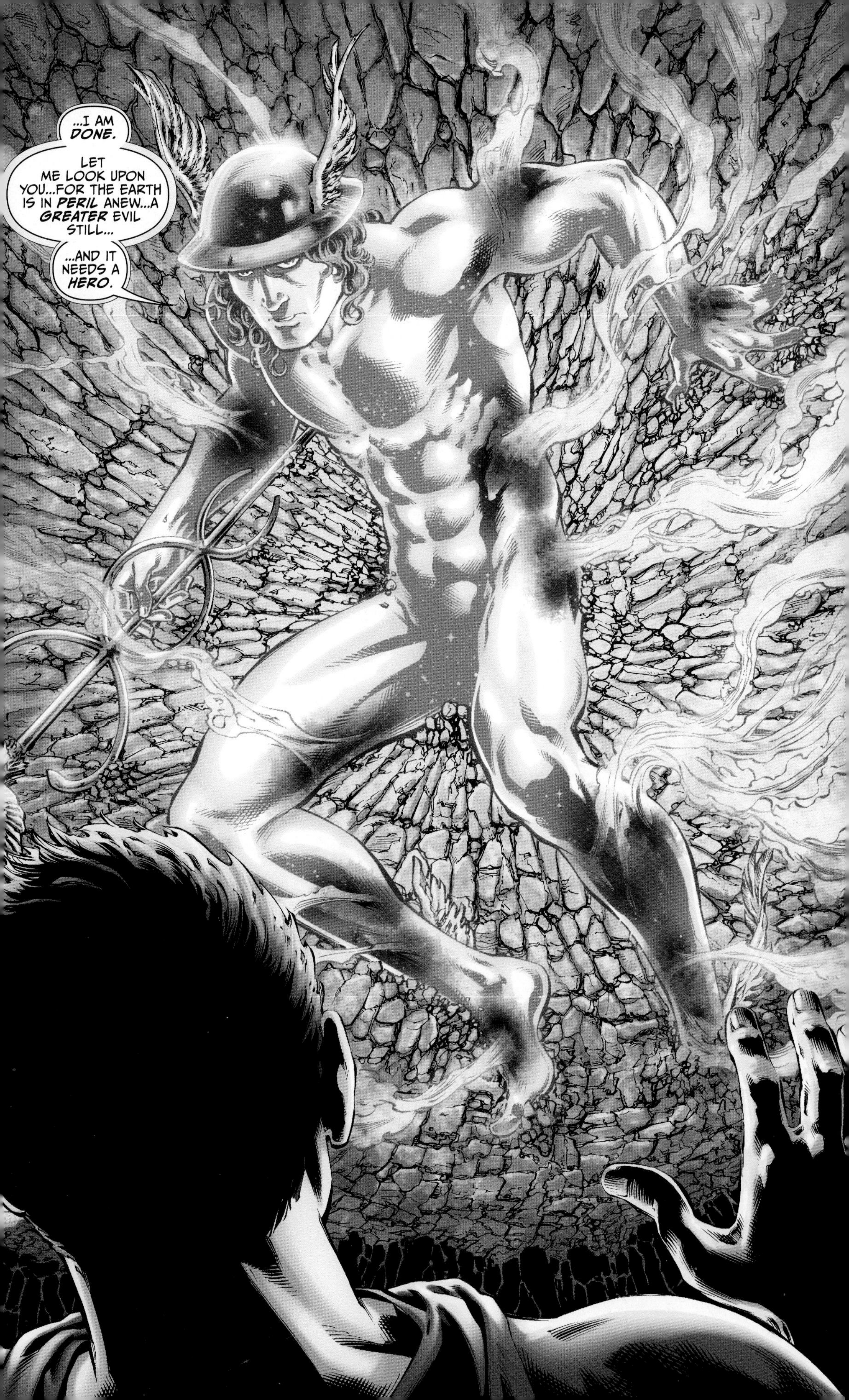
...I AM DONE.
LET ME LOOK UPON YOU...FOR THE EARTH IS IN PERIL ANEW...A GREATER EVIL STILL...
...AND IT NEEDS A HERO.

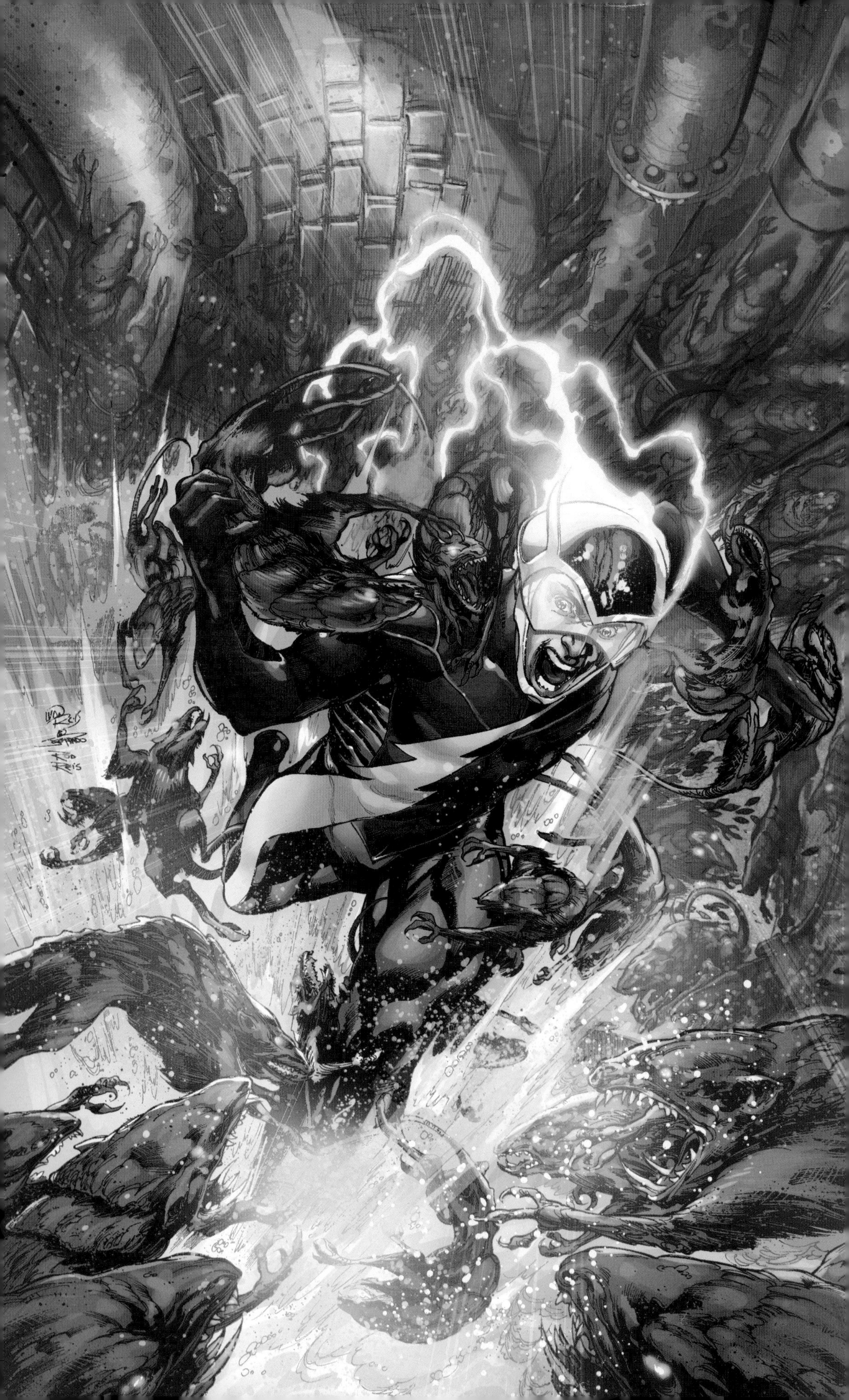

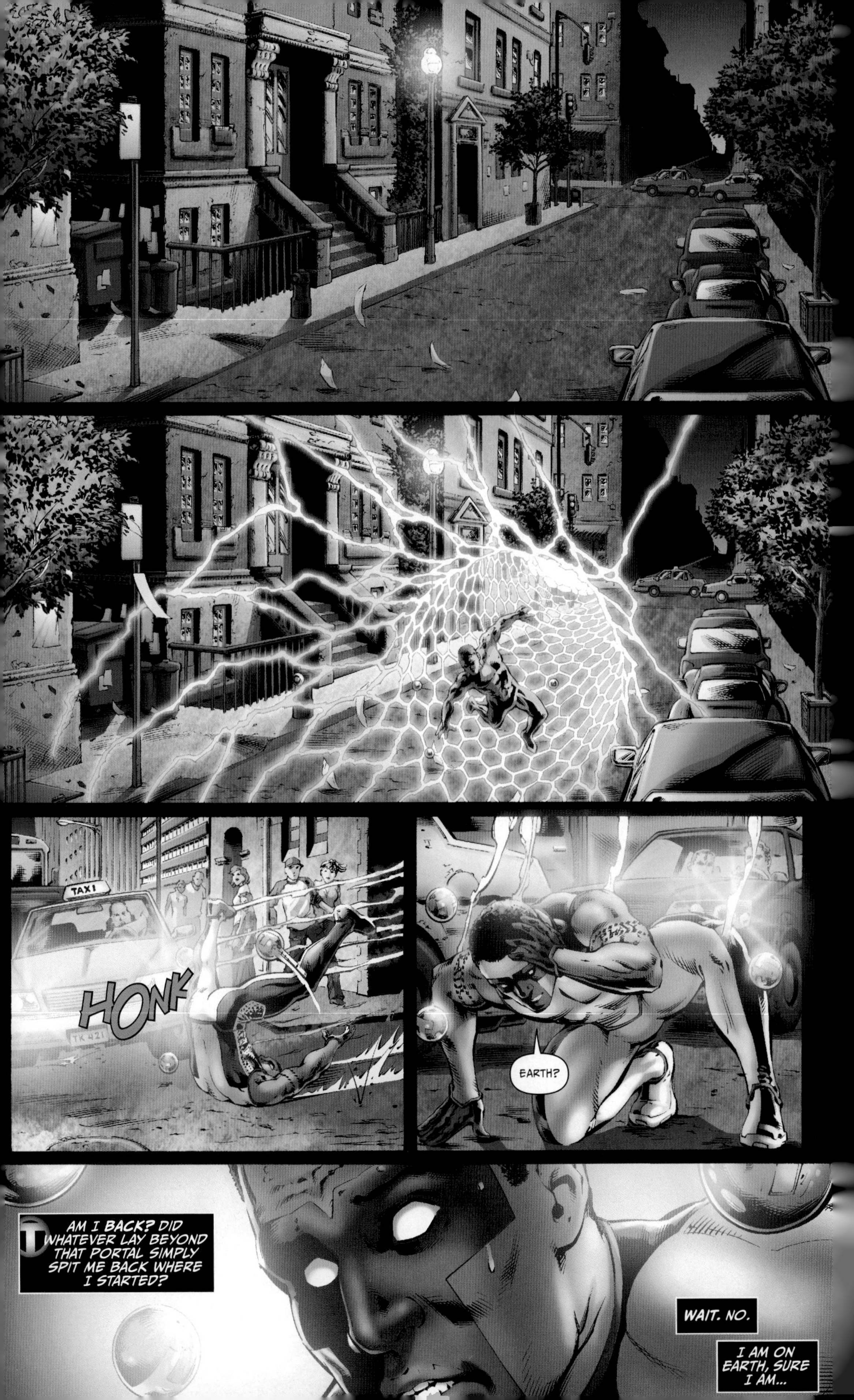
TAXI
HONK
TK 421
EARTH?
AM I BACK? DID WHATEVER LAY BEYOND THAT PORTAL SIMPLY SPIT ME BACK WHERE I STARTED?
WAIT. NO.
I AM ON EARTH, SURE I AM...

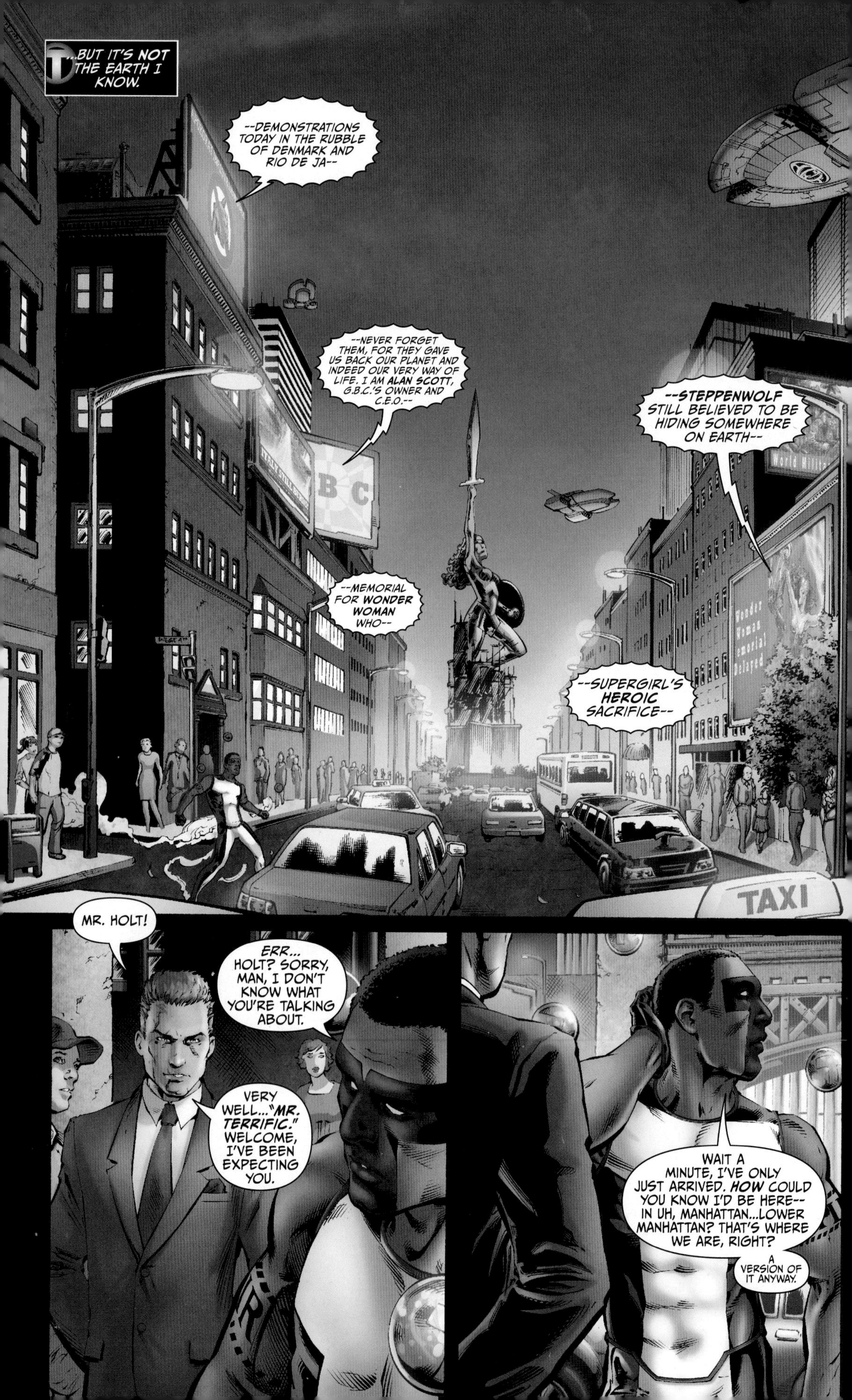
...BUT IT'S NOT THE EARTH I KNOW.
--DEMONSTRATIONS TODAY IN THE RUBBLE OF DENMARK AND RIO DE JA--
--NEVER FORGET THEM, FOR THEY GAVE US BACK OUR PLANET AND INDEED OUR VERY WAY OF LIFE. I AM ALAN SCOTT, G.B.C.'S OWNER AND C.E.O.--
--STEPPENWOLF STILL BELIEVED TO BE HIDING SOMEWHERE ON EARTH--
--MEMORIAL FOR WONDER WOMAN WHO--
--SUPERGIRL'S HEROIC SACRIFICE--
Wonder Woman Memorial Delayed
TAXI
MR. HOLT!
ERR... HOLT? SORRY, MAN, I DON'T KNOW WHAT YOU'RE TALKING ABOUT.
VERY WELL..."MR. TERRIFIC." WELCOME, I'VE BEEN EXPECTING YOU.
WAIT A MINUTE, I'VE ONLY JUST ARRIVED. HOW COULD YOU KNOW I'D BE HERE--IN UH, MANHATTAN...LOWER MANHATTAN? THAT'S WHERE WE ARE, RIGHT?
A VERSION OF IT ANYWAY.

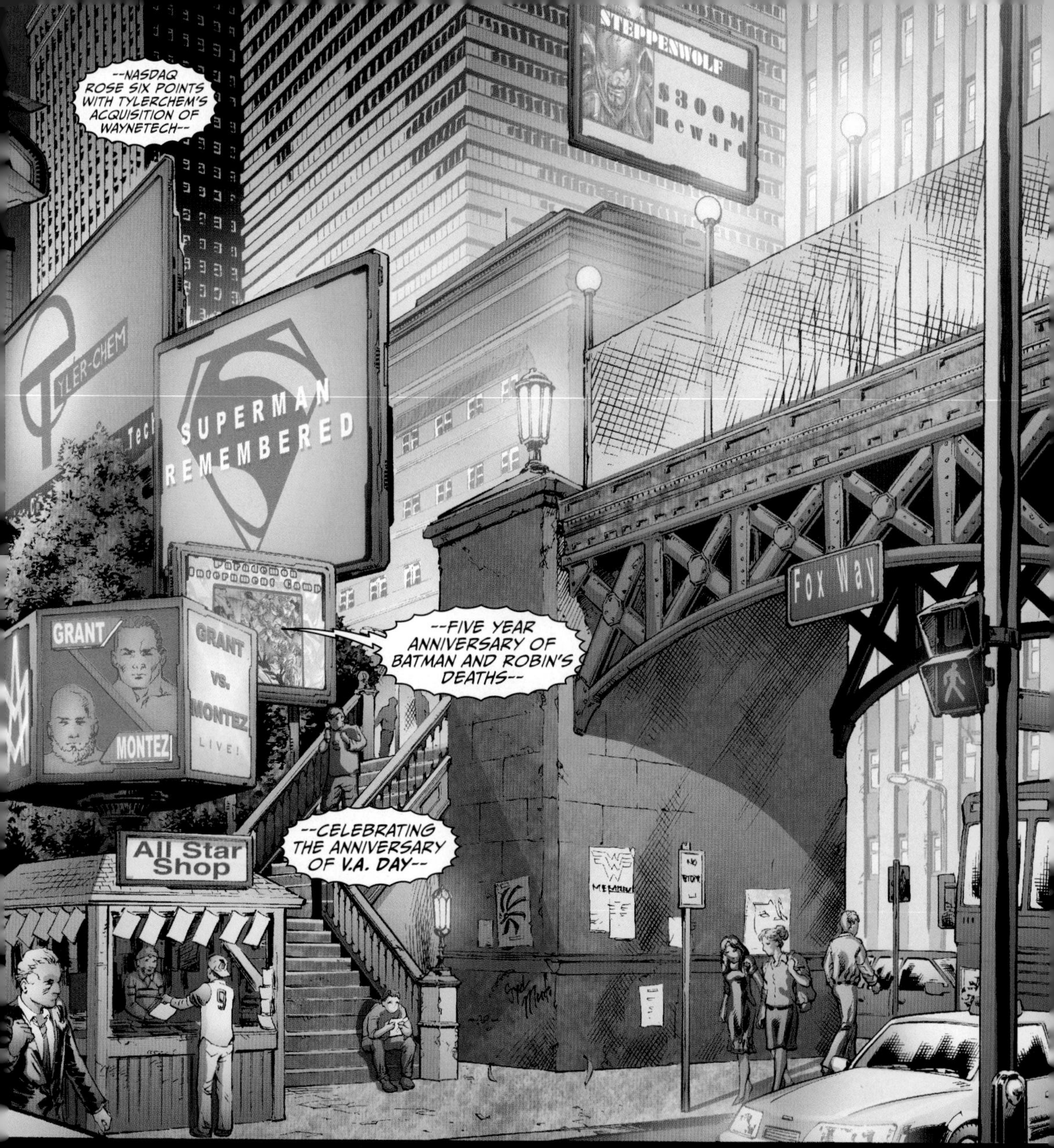

--NASDAQ ROSE SIX POINTS WITH TYLERCHEM'S ACQUISITION OF WAYNETECH--
STEPPENWOLF
$300M Reward
TYLER-CHEM
Tech
SUPERMAN REMEMBERED
Parademon Internment Camp
GRANT
MONTEZ
GRANT vs. MONTEZ LIVE!
--FIVE YEAR ANNIVERSARY OF BATMAN AND ROBIN'S DEATHS--
Fox Way
--CELEBRATING THE ANNIVERSARY OF V.A. DAY--
All Star Shop

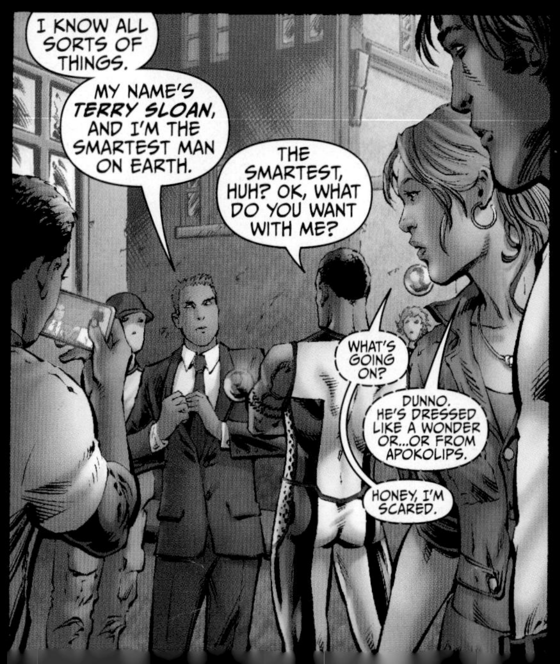

I KNOW ALL SORTS OF THINGS.
MY NAME'S TERRY SLOAN, AND I'M THE SMARTEST MAN ON EARTH.
THE SMARTEST, HUH? OK, WHAT DO YOU WANT WITH ME?
WHAT'S GOING ON?
DUNNO. HE'S DRESSED LIKE A WONDER OR...OR FROM APOKOLIPS.
HONEY, I'M SCARED.

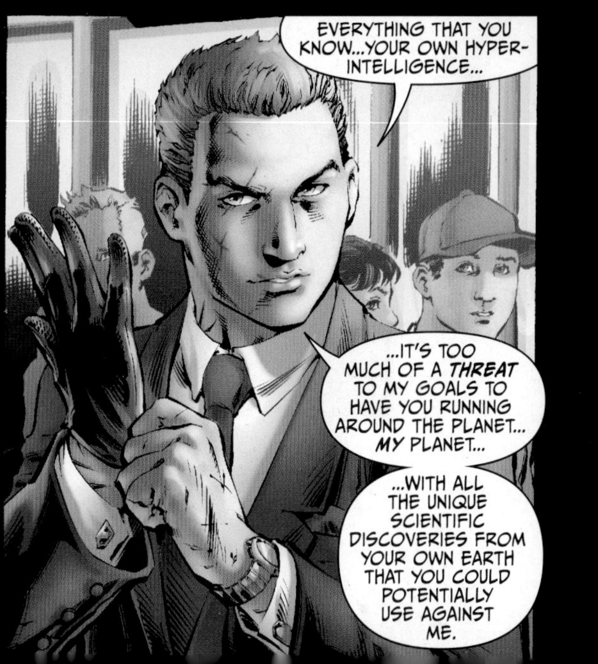

EVERYTHING THAT YOU KNOW...YOUR OWN HYPER-INTELLIGENCE...
...IT'S TOO MUCH OF A THREAT TO MY GOALS TO HAVE YOU RUNNING AROUND THE PLANET... MY PLANET...
...WITH ALL THE UNIQUE SCIENTIFIC DISCOVERIES FROM YOUR OWN EARTH THAT YOU COULD POTENTIALLY USE AGAINST ME.

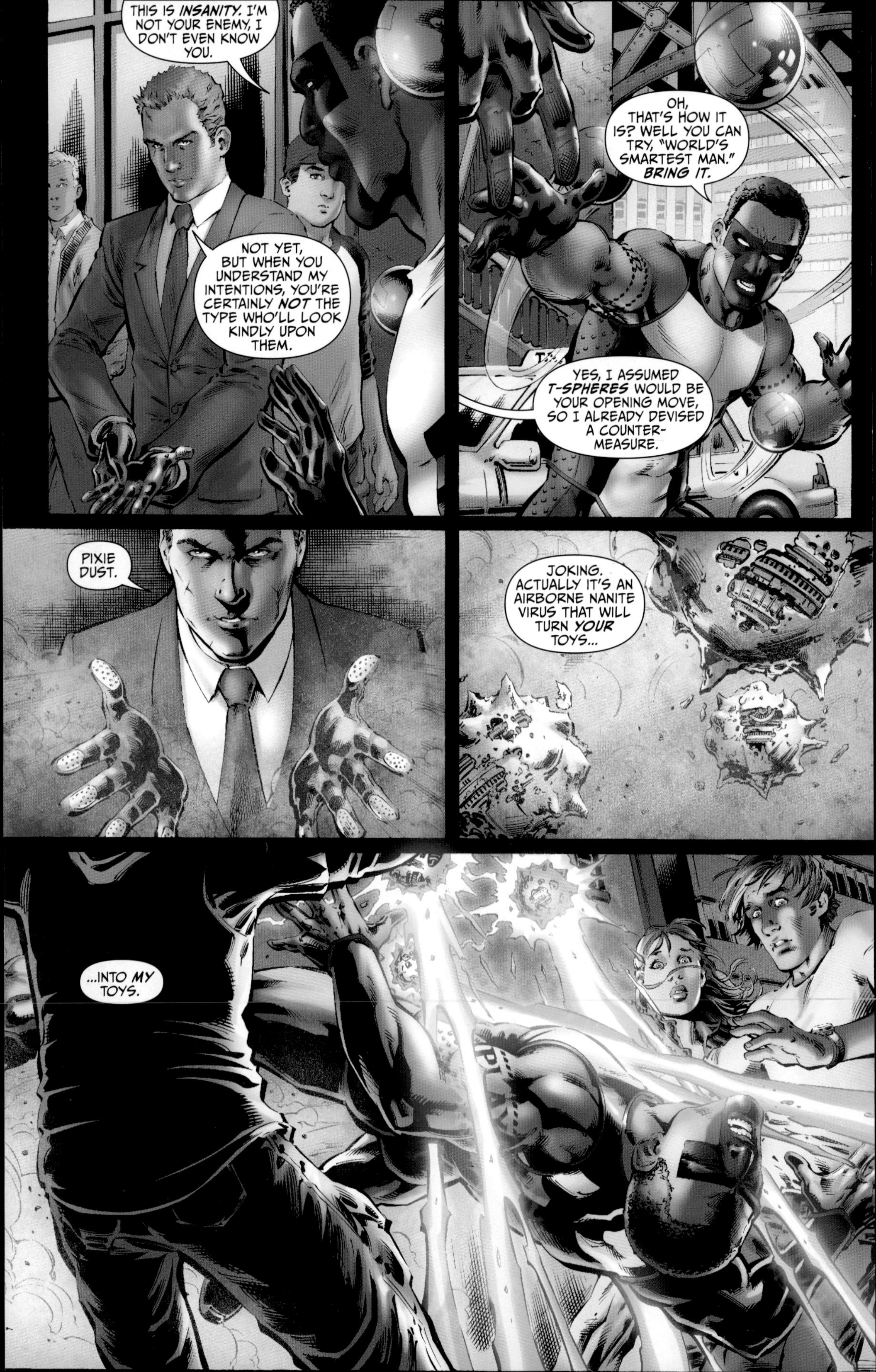
THIS IS *INSANITY.* I'M NOT YOUR ENEMY, I DON'T EVEN KNOW YOU.
NOT YET, BUT WHEN YOU UNDERSTAND MY INTENTIONS, YOU'RE CERTAINLY *NOT* THE TYPE WHO'LL LOOK KINDLY UPON THEM.
OH, THAT'S HOW IT IS? WELL YOU CAN TRY, "WORLD'S SMARTEST MAN." *BRING IT.*
YES, I ASSUMED *T-SPHERES* WOULD BE YOUR OPENING MOVE, SO I ALREADY DEVISED A COUNTER-MEASURE.
PIXIE DUST.
JOKING. ACTUALLY IT'S AN AIRBORNE NANITE VIRUS THAT WILL TURN *YOUR* TOYS...
...INTO *MY* TOYS.

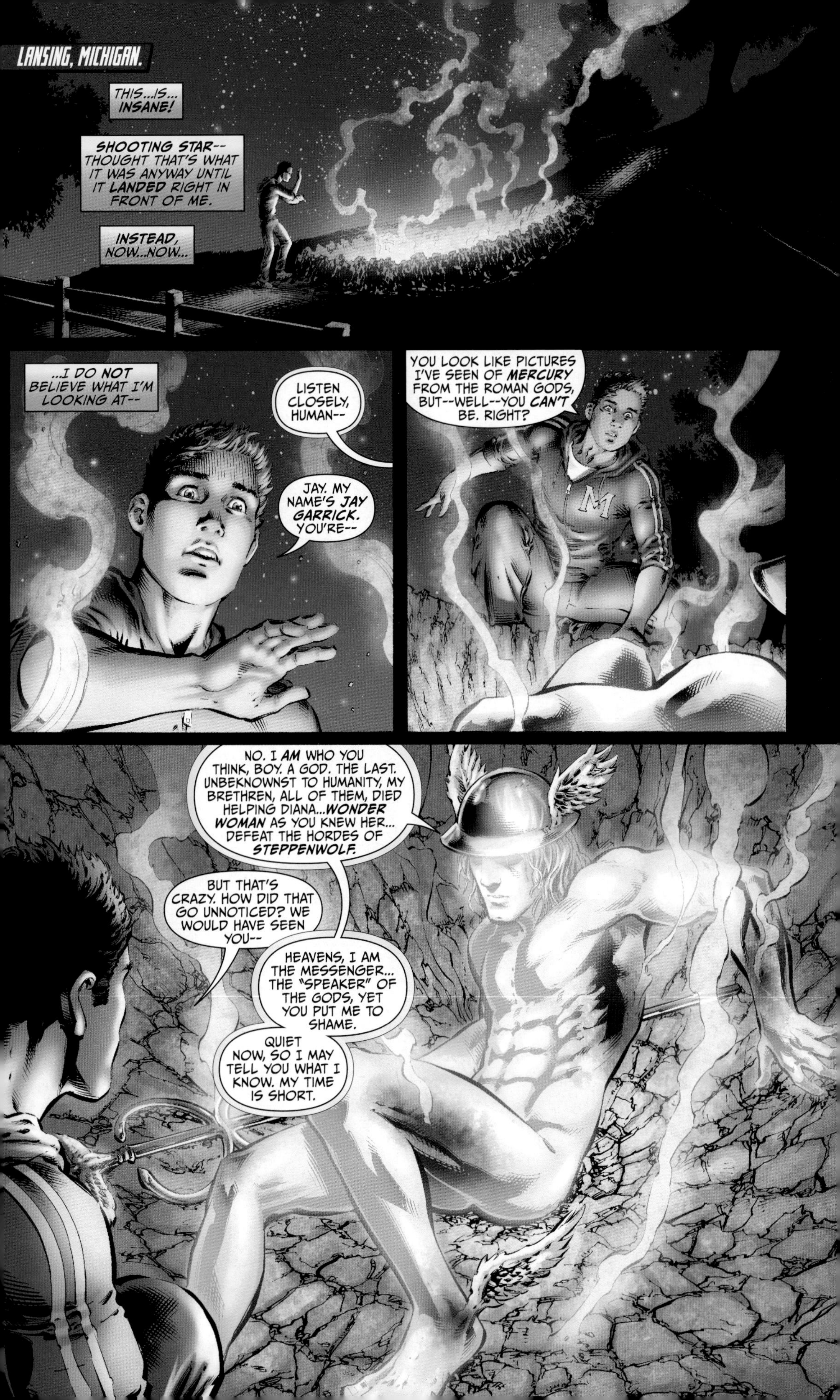
LANSING, MICHIGAN.
THIS...IS... INSANE!
SHOOTING STAR--THOUGHT THAT'S WHAT IT WAS ANYWAY UNTIL IT LANDED RIGHT IN FRONT OF ME.
INSTEAD, NOW...NOW...
...I DO NOT BELIEVE WHAT I'M LOOKING AT--
LISTEN CLOSELY, HUMAN--
JAY. MY NAME'S JAY GARRICK. YOU'RE--
YOU LOOK LIKE PICTURES I'VE SEEN OF MERCURY FROM THE ROMAN GODS, BUT--WELL--YOU CAN'T BE. RIGHT?
NO. I AM WHO YOU THINK, BOY. A GOD. THE LAST. UNBEKNOWNST TO HUMANITY, MY BRETHREN, ALL OF THEM, DIED HELPING DIANA...WONDER WOMAN AS YOU KNEW HER... DEFEAT THE HORDES OF STEPPENWOLF.
BUT THAT'S CRAZY. HOW DID THAT GO UNNOTICED? WE WOULD HAVE SEEN YOU--
HEAVENS, I AM THE MESSENGER... THE "SPEAKER" OF THE GODS, YET YOU PUT ME TO SHAME.
QUIET NOW, SO I MAY TELL YOU WHAT I KNOW. MY TIME IS SHORT.

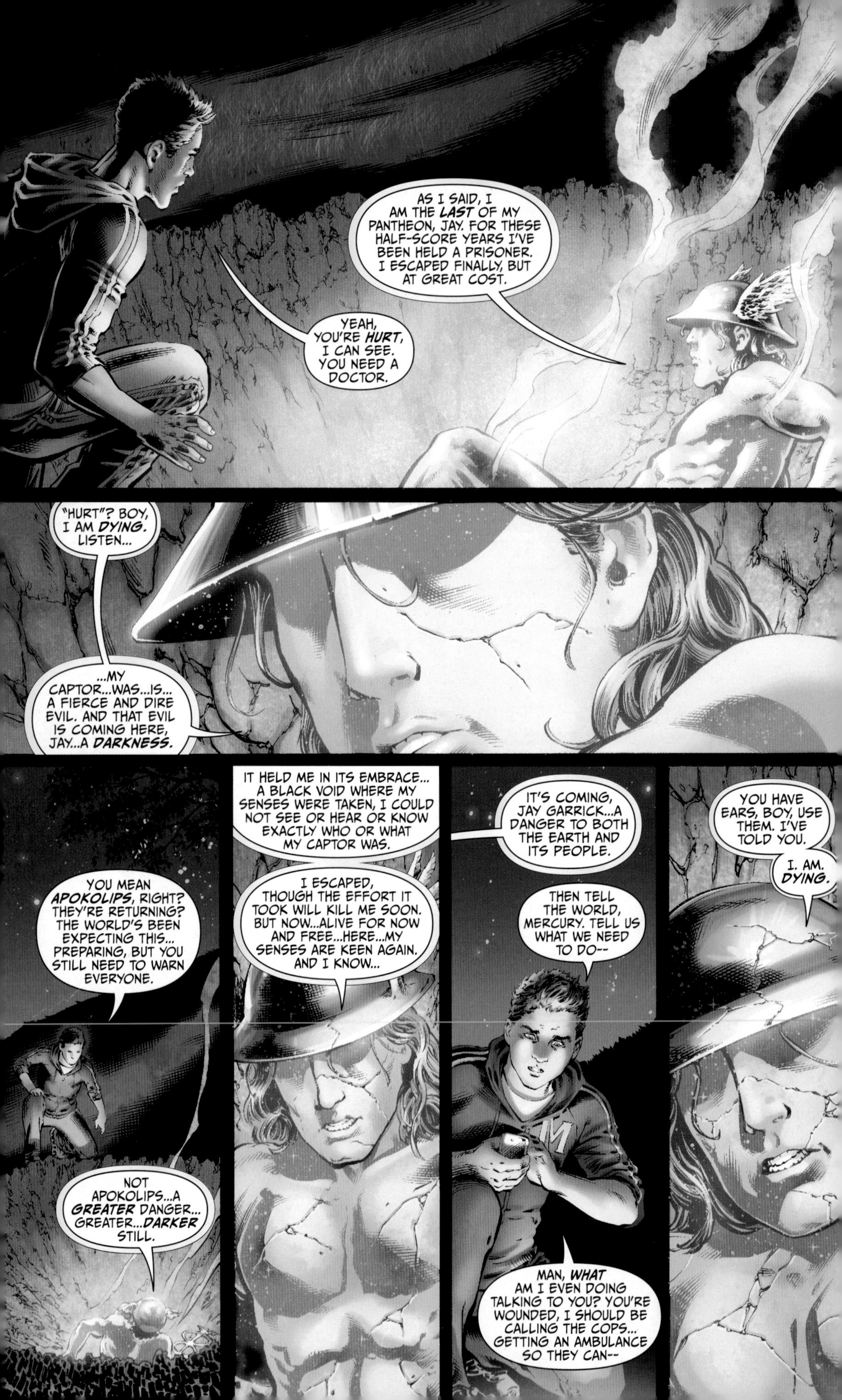

AS I SAID, I AM THE LAST OF MY PANTHEON, JAY. FOR THESE HALF-SCORE YEARS I'VE BEEN HELD A PRISONER. I ESCAPED FINALLY, BUT AT GREAT COST.
YEAH, YOU'RE HURT, I CAN SEE. YOU NEED A DOCTOR.
"HURT"? BOY, I AM DYING. LISTEN...
...MY CAPTOR...WAS...IS... A FIERCE AND DIRE EVIL. AND THAT EVIL IS COMING HERE, JAY...A DARKNESS.
YOU MEAN APOKOLIPS, RIGHT? THEY'RE RETURNING? THE WORLD'S BEEN EXPECTING THIS... PREPARING, BUT YOU STILL NEED TO WARN EVERYONE.
NOT APOKOLIPS...A GREATER DANGER... GREATER...DARKER STILL.
IT HELD ME IN ITS EMBRACE... A BLACK VOID WHERE MY SENSES WERE TAKEN, I COULD NOT SEE OR HEAR OR KNOW EXACTLY WHO OR WHAT MY CAPTOR WAS.
I ESCAPED, THOUGH THE EFFORT IT TOOK WILL KILL ME SOON. BUT NOW...ALIVE FOR NOW AND FREE...HERE...MY SENSES ARE KEEN AGAIN. AND I KNOW...
IT'S COMING, JAY GARRICK...A DANGER TO BOTH THE EARTH AND ITS PEOPLE.
THEN TELL THE WORLD, MERCURY. TELL US WHAT WE NEED TO DO--
MAN, WHAT AM I EVEN DOING TALKING TO YOU? YOU'RE WOUNDED, I SHOULD BE CALLING THE COPS... GETTING AN AMBULANCE SO THEY CAN--
YOU HAVE EARS, BOY, USE THEM. I'VE TOLD YOU.
I. AM. DYING.

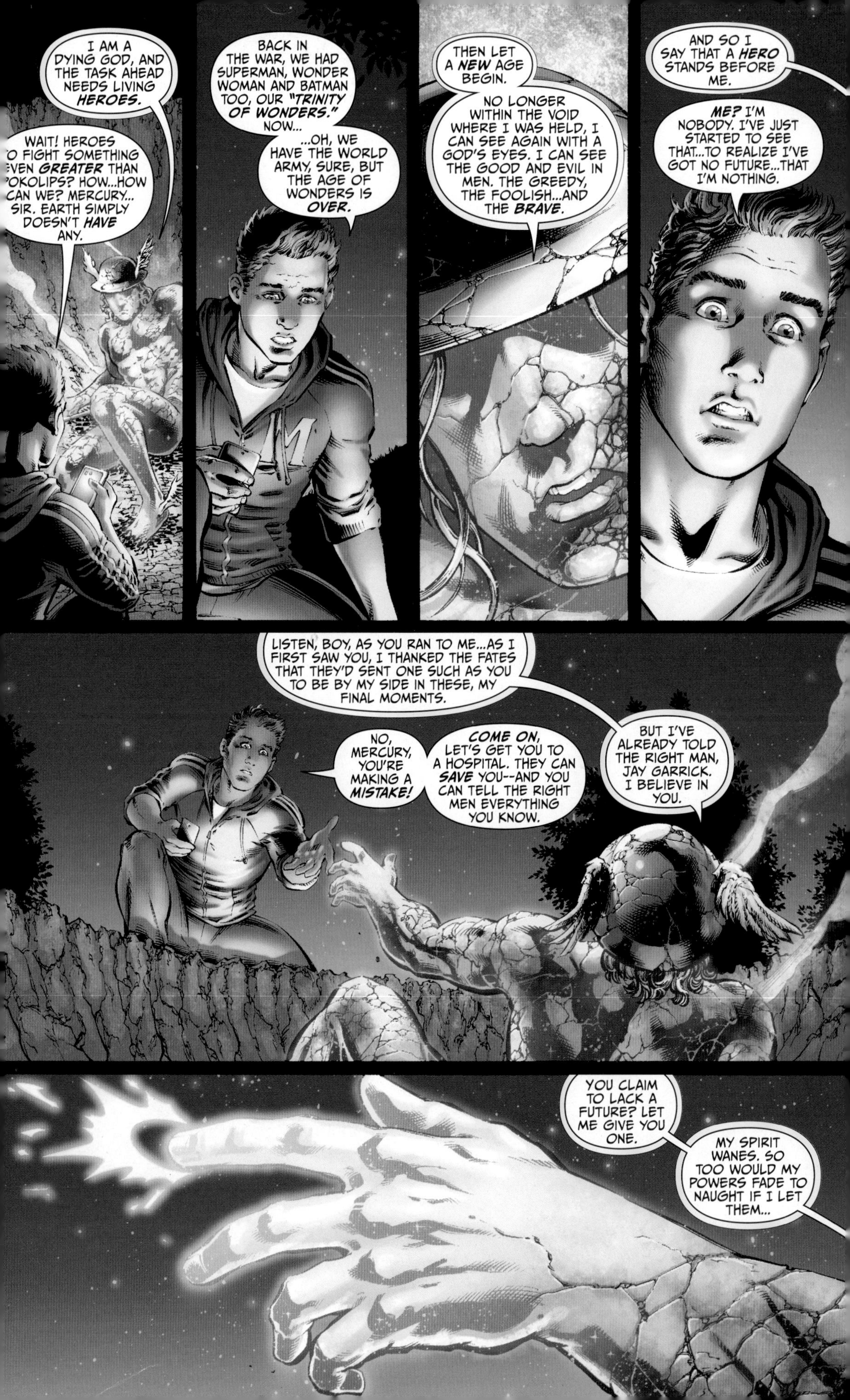

I AM A DYING GOD, AND THE TASK AHEAD NEEDS LIVING HEROES.
WAIT! HEROES O FIGHT SOMETHING EVEN GREATER THAN OKOLIPS? HOW...HOW CAN WE? MERCURY... SIR. EARTH SIMPLY DOESN'T HAVE ANY.
BACK IN THE WAR, WE HAD SUPERMAN, WONDER WOMAN AND BATMAN TOO, OUR "TRINITY OF WONDERS." NOW...
...OH, WE HAVE THE WORLD ARMY, SURE, BUT THE AGE OF WONDERS IS OVER.
THEN LET A NEW AGE BEGIN.
NO LONGER WITHIN THE VOID WHERE I WAS HELD, I CAN SEE AGAIN WITH A GOD'S EYES. I CAN SEE THE GOOD AND EVIL IN MEN. THE GREEDY, THE FOOLISH...AND THE BRAVE.
AND SO I SAY THAT A HERO STANDS BEFORE ME.
ME? I'M NOBODY. I'VE JUST STARTED TO SEE THAT...TO REALIZE I'VE GOT NO FUTURE...THAT I'M NOTHING.
LISTEN, BOY, AS YOU RAN TO ME...AS I FIRST SAW YOU, I THANKED THE FATES THAT THEY'D SENT ONE SUCH AS YOU TO BE BY MY SIDE IN THESE, MY FINAL MOMENTS.
NO, MERCURY, YOU'RE MAKING A MISTAKE!
COME ON, LET'S GET YOU TO A HOSPITAL. THEY CAN SAVE YOU--AND YOU CAN TELL THE RIGHT MEN EVERYTHING YOU KNOW.
BUT I'VE ALREADY TOLD THE RIGHT MAN, JAY GARRICK. I BELIEVE IN YOU.
YOU CLAIM TO LACK A FUTURE? LET ME GIVE YOU ONE.
MY SPIRIT WANES. SO TOO WOULD MY POWERS FADE TO NAUGHT IF I LET THEM...

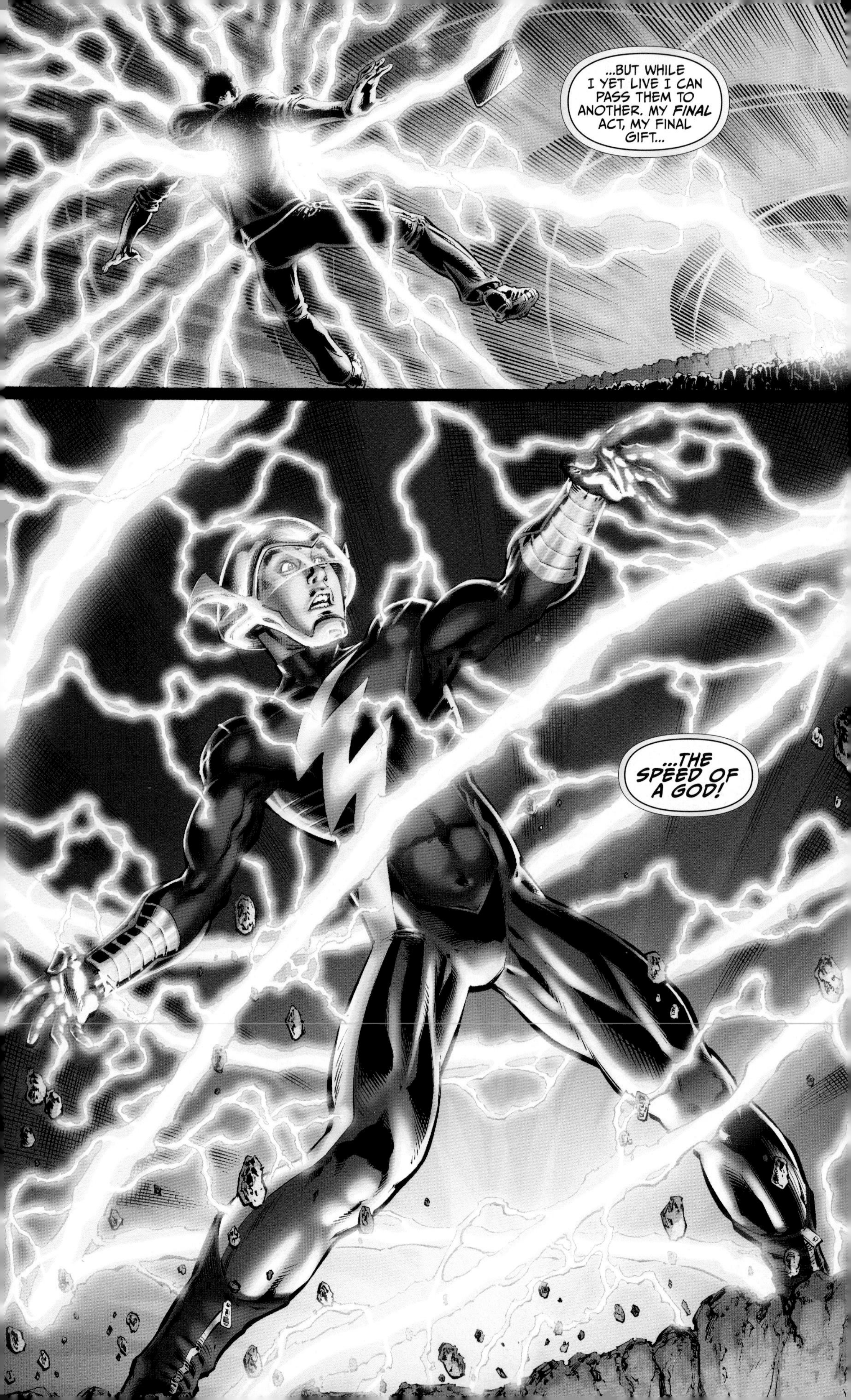
...BUT WHILE I YET LIVE I CAN PASS THEM TO ANOTHER. MY FINAL ACT, MY FINAL GIFT...
...THE SPEED OF A GOD!

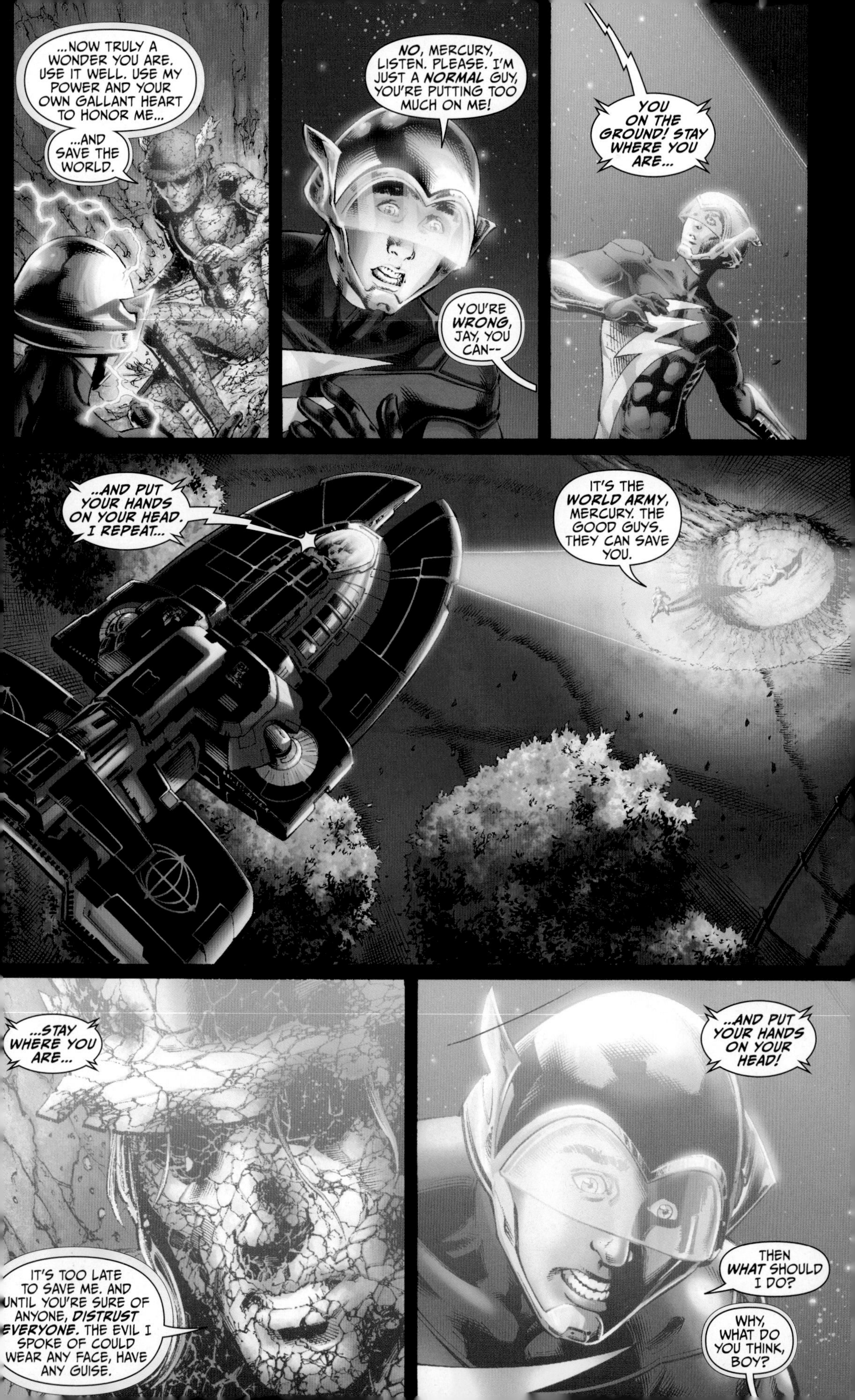
...NOW TRULY A WONDER YOU ARE. USE IT WELL. USE MY POWER AND YOUR OWN GALLANT HEART TO HONOR ME...
...AND SAVE THE WORLD.
NO, MERCURY, LISTEN. PLEASE. I'M JUST A NORMAL GUY, YOU'RE PUTTING TOO MUCH ON ME!
YOU'RE WRONG, JAY, YOU CAN--
YOU ON THE GROUND! STAY WHERE YOU ARE...
...AND PUT YOUR HANDS ON YOUR HEAD. I REPEAT...
IT'S THE WORLD ARMY, MERCURY. THE GOOD GUYS. THEY CAN SAVE YOU.
...STAY WHERE YOU ARE...
IT'S TOO LATE TO SAVE ME. AND UNTIL YOU'RE SURE OF ANYONE, DISTRUST EVERYONE. THE EVIL I SPOKE OF COULD WEAR ANY FACE, HAVE ANY GUISE.
...AND PUT YOUR HANDS ON YOUR HEAD!
THEN WHAT SHOULD I DO?
WHY, WHAT DO YOU THINK, BOY?

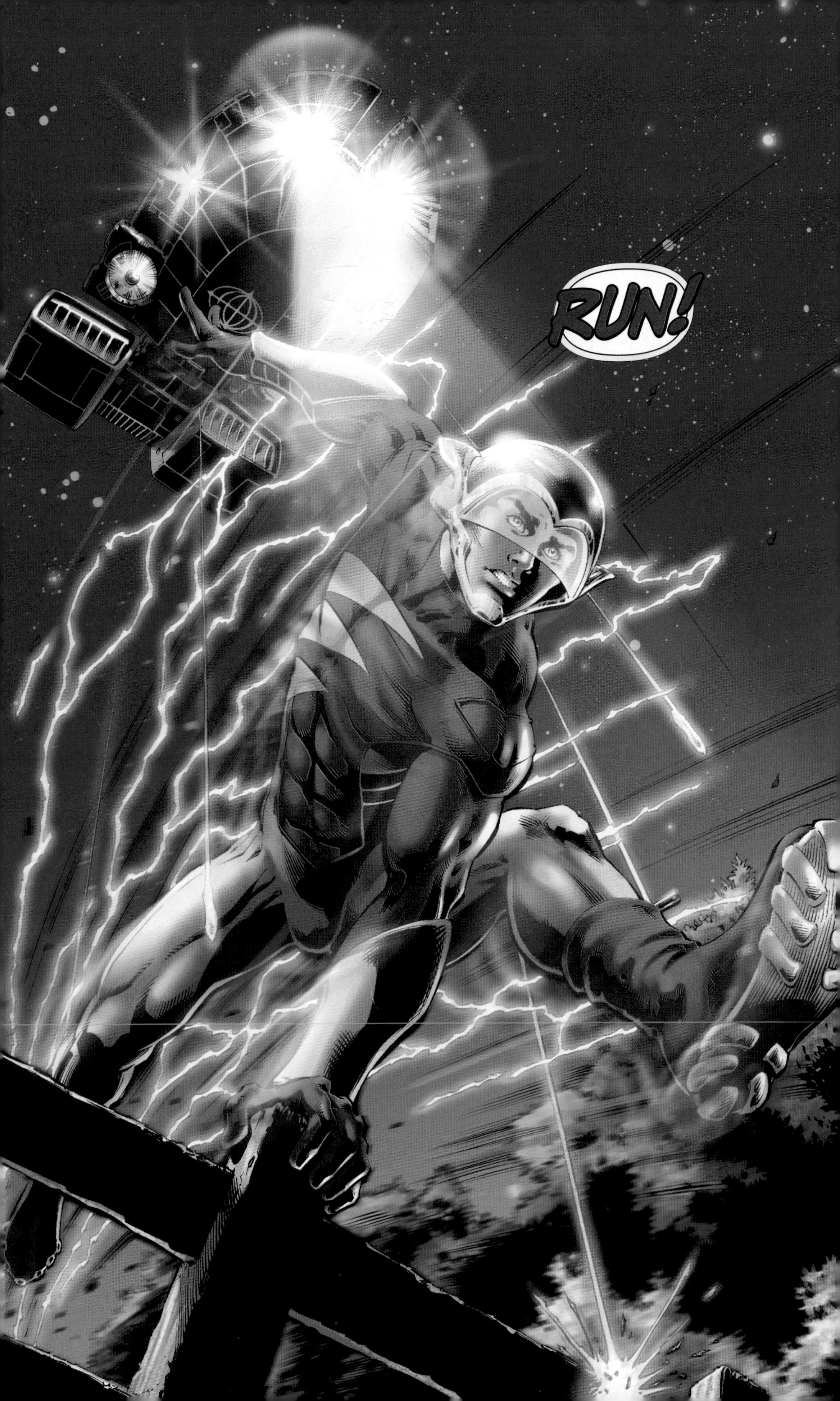
RUN!

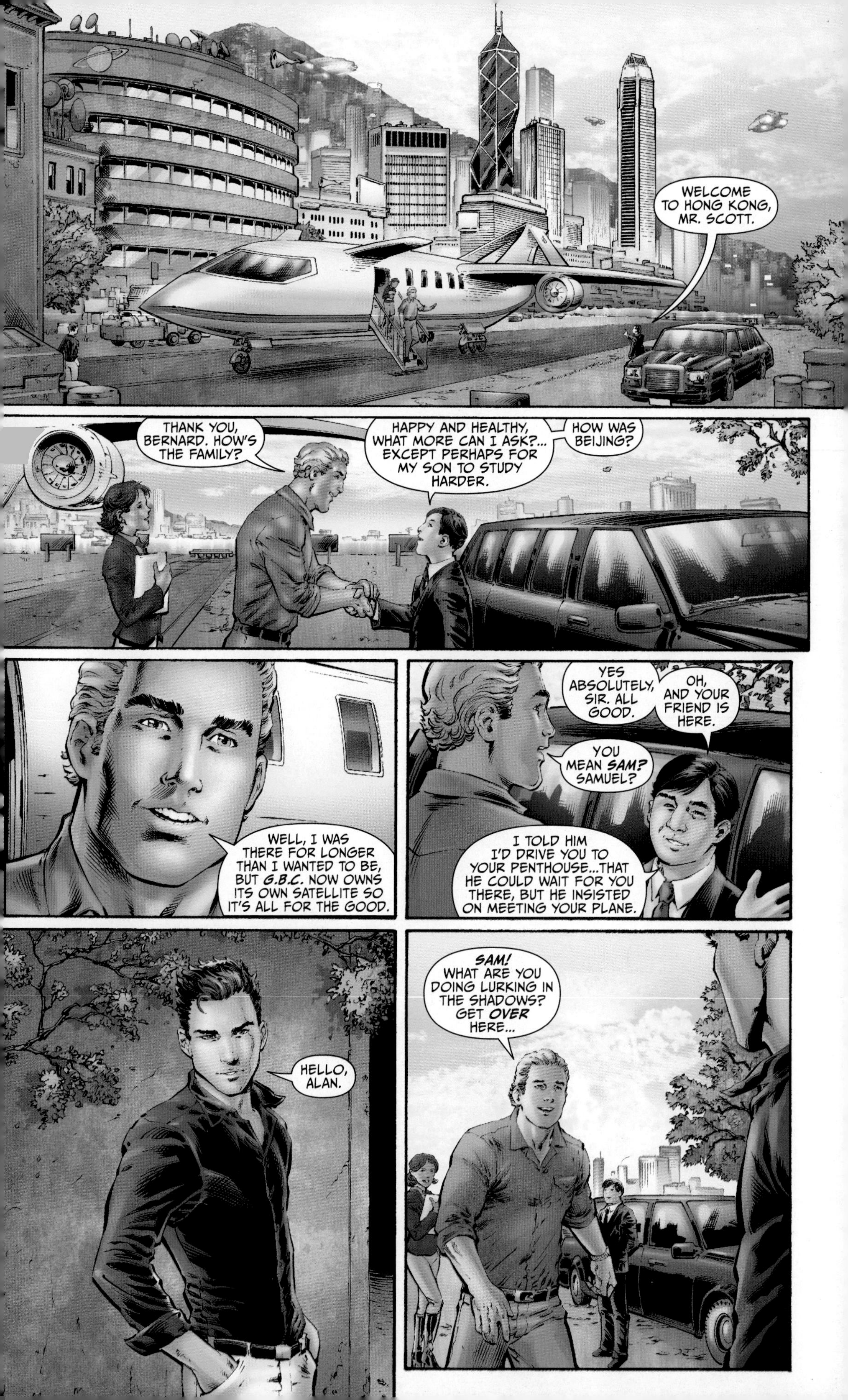
WELCOME TO HONG KONG, MR. SCOTT.
THANK YOU, BERNARD. HOW'S THE FAMILY?
HAPPY AND HEALTHY, WHAT MORE CAN I ASK?... EXCEPT PERHAPS FOR MY SON TO STUDY HARDER.
HOW WAS BEIJING?
WELL, I WAS THERE FOR LONGER THAN I WANTED TO BE, BUT G.B.C. NOW OWNS ITS OWN SATELLITE SO IT'S ALL FOR THE GOOD.
YES ABSOLUTELY, SIR. ALL GOOD.
OH, AND YOUR FRIEND IS HERE.
YOU MEAN SAM? SAMUEL?
I TOLD HIM I'D DRIVE YOU TO YOUR PENTHOUSE...THAT HE COULD WAIT FOR YOU THERE, BUT HE INSISTED ON MEETING YOUR PLANE.
HELLO, ALAN.
SAM! WHAT ARE YOU DOING LURKING IN THE SHADOWS? GET OVER HERE...

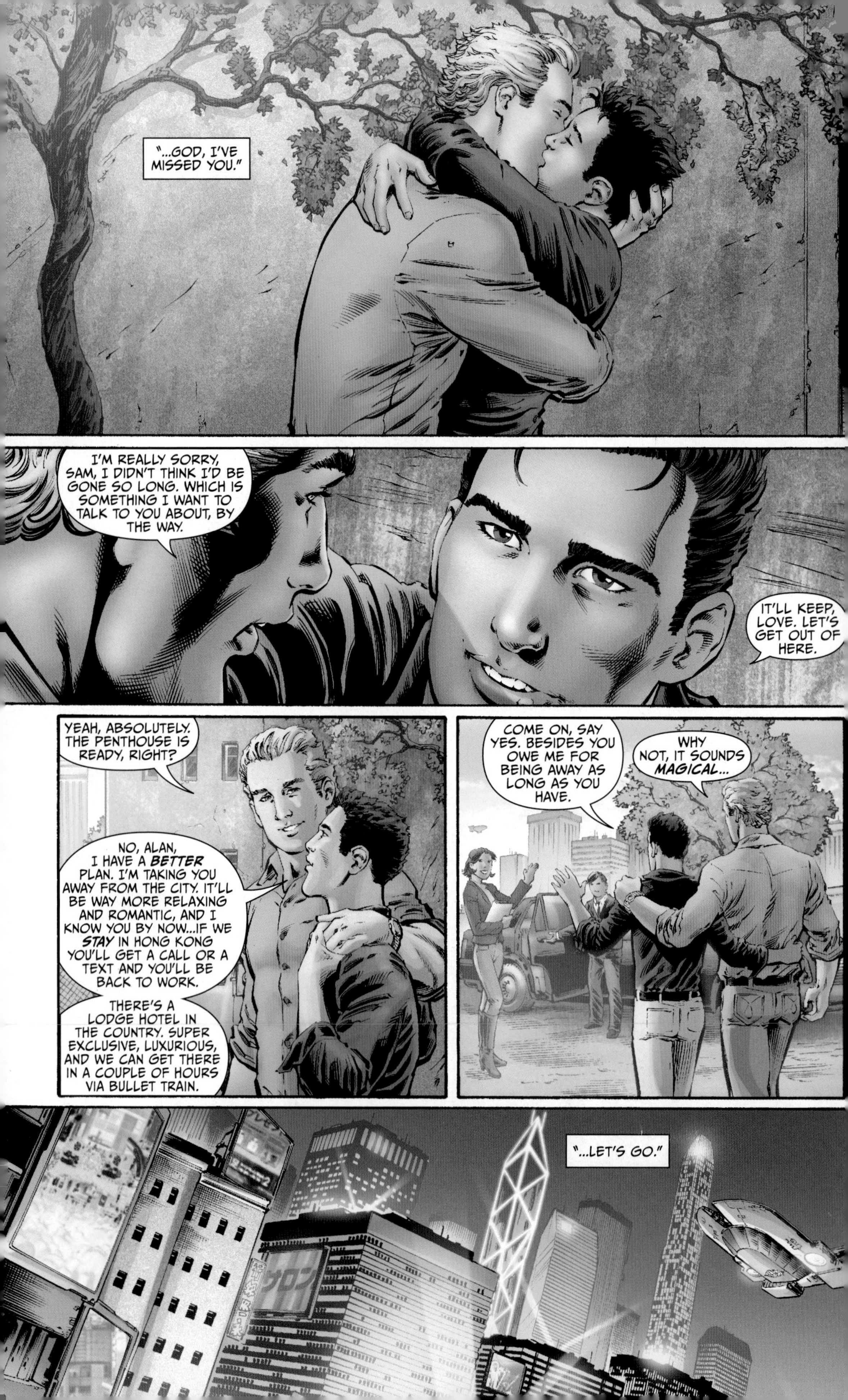
"...GOD, I'VE MISSED YOU."
I'M REALLY SORRY, SAM, I DIDN'T THINK I'D BE GONE SO LONG. WHICH IS SOMETHING I WANT TO TALK TO YOU ABOUT, BY THE WAY.
IT'LL KEEP, LOVE. LET'S GET OUT OF HERE.
YEAH, ABSOLUTELY. THE PENTHOUSE IS READY, RIGHT?
NO, ALAN, I HAVE A ***BETTER*** PLAN. I'M TAKING YOU AWAY FROM THE CITY. IT'LL BE WAY MORE RELAXING AND ROMANTIC, AND I KNOW YOU BY NOW...IF WE ***STAY*** IN HONG KONG YOU'LL GET A CALL OR A TEXT AND YOU'LL BE BACK TO WORK.
THERE'S A LODGE HOTEL IN THE COUNTRY. SUPER EXCLUSIVE, LUXURIOUS, AND WE CAN GET THERE IN A COUPLE OF HOURS VIA BULLET TRAIN.
COME ON, SAY YES. BESIDES YOU OWE ME FOR BEING AWAY AS LONG AS YOU HAVE.
WHY NOT, IT SOUNDS ***MAGICAL***...
"...LET'S GO."

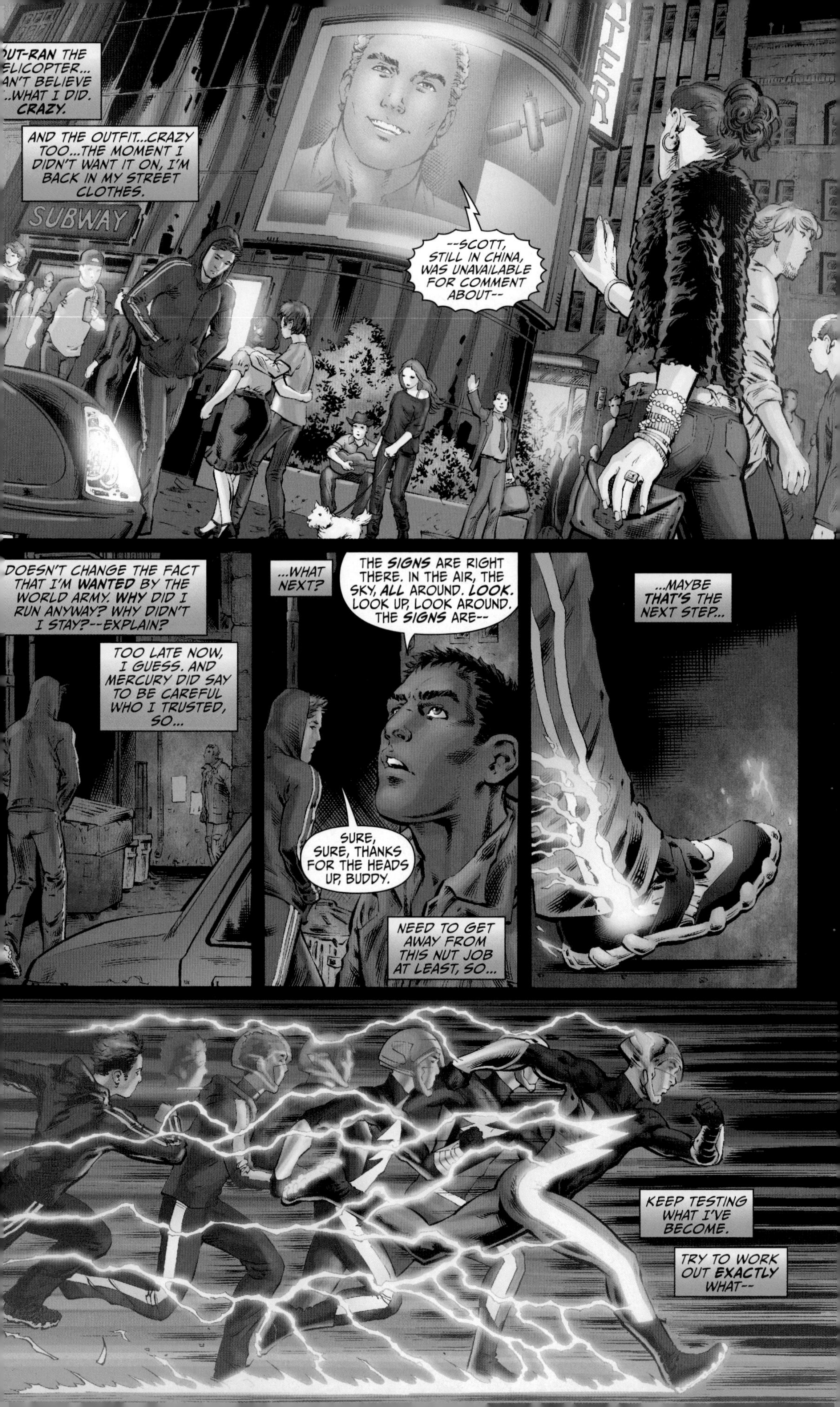

OUT-RAN THE HELICOPTER... CAN'T BELIEVE ...WHAT I DID. CRAZY.
AND THE OUTFIT...CRAZY TOO...THE MOMENT I DIDN'T WANT IT ON, I'M BACK IN MY STREET CLOTHES.
SUBWAY
--SCOTT, STILL IN CHINA, WAS UNAVAILABLE FOR COMMENT ABOUT--
DOESN'T CHANGE THE FACT THAT I'M WANTED BY THE WORLD ARMY. WHY DID I RUN ANYWAY? WHY DIDN'T I STAY?--EXPLAIN?
TOO LATE NOW, I GUESS. AND MERCURY DID SAY TO BE CAREFUL WHO I TRUSTED, SO...
...WHAT NEXT?
THE SIGNS ARE RIGHT THERE. IN THE AIR, THE SKY, ALL AROUND. LOOK. LOOK UP, LOOK AROUND. THE SIGNS ARE--
SURE, SURE, THANKS FOR THE HEADS UP, BUDDY.
NEED TO GET AWAY FROM THIS NUT JOB AT LEAST, SO...
...MAYBE THAT'S THE NEXT STEP...
KEEP TESTING WHAT I'VE BECOME.
TRY TO WORK OUT EXACTLY WHAT--

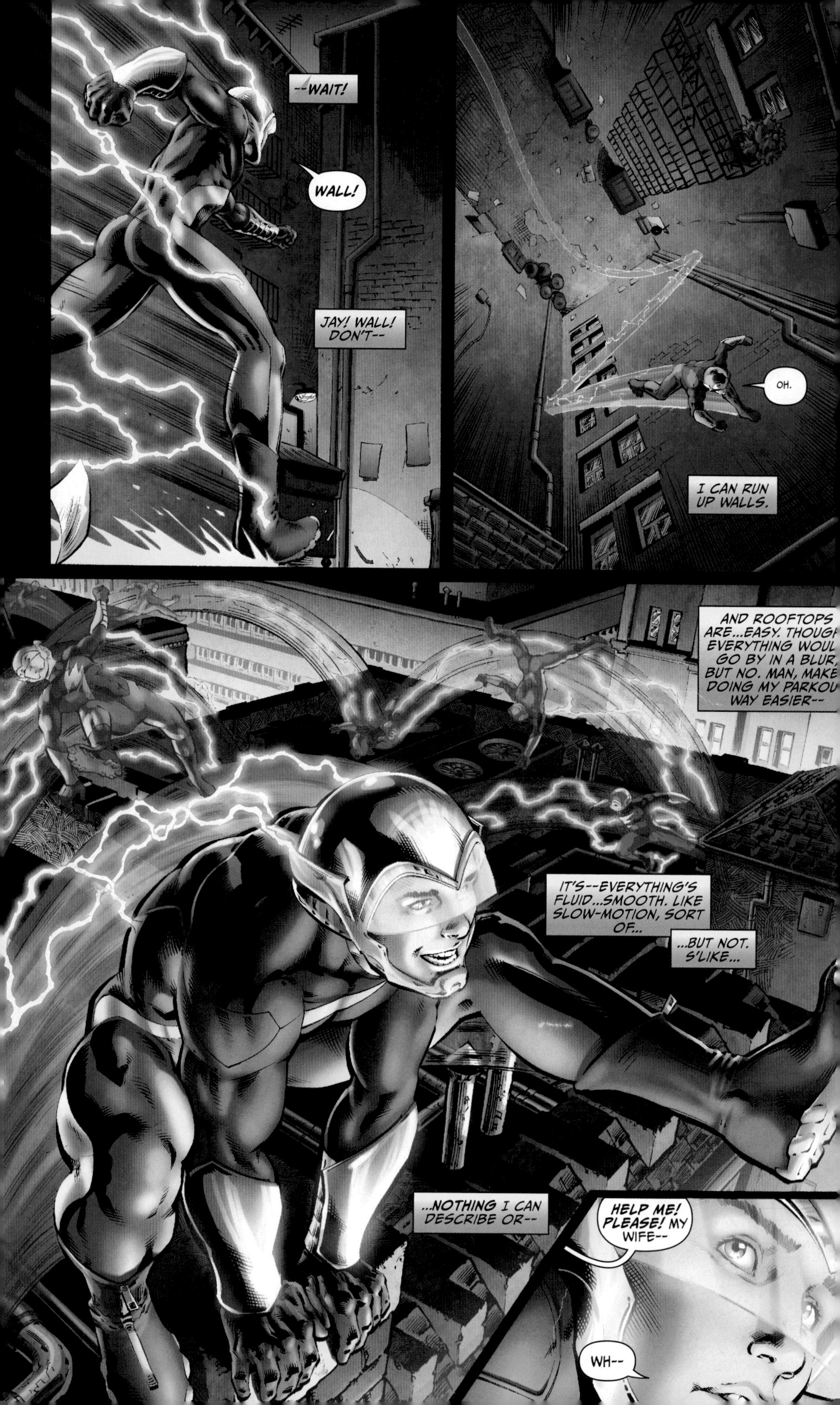
--WAIT!
WALL!
JAY! WALL! DON'T--
OH.
I CAN RUN UP WALLS.
AND ROOFTOPS ARE...EASY. THOUG EVERYTHING WOUL GO BY IN A BLUR, BUT NO. MAN, MAKE DOING MY PARKOU WAY EASIER--
IT'S--EVERYTHING'S FLUID...SMOOTH. LIKE SLOW-MOTION, SORT OF...
...BUT NOT. S'LIKE...
...NOTHING I CAN DESCRIBE OR--
HELP ME! PLEASE! MY WIFE--
WH--

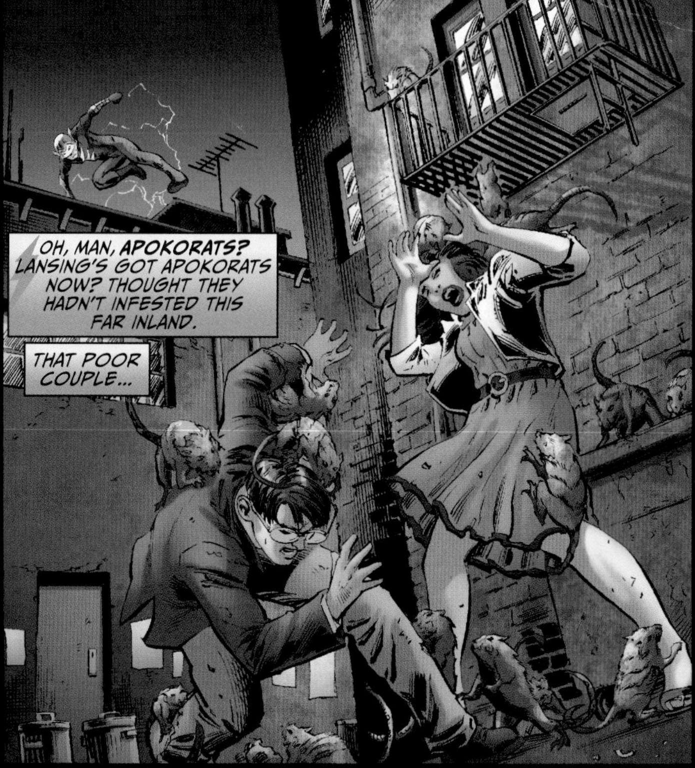
OH, MAN, APOKORATS? LANSING'S GOT APOKORATS NOW? THOUGHT THEY HADN'T INFESTED THIS FAR INLAND.
THAT POOR COUPLE...
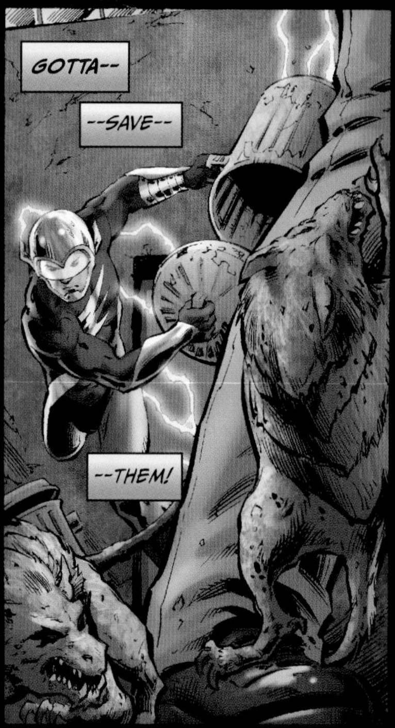
GOTTA--
--SAVE--
--THEM!
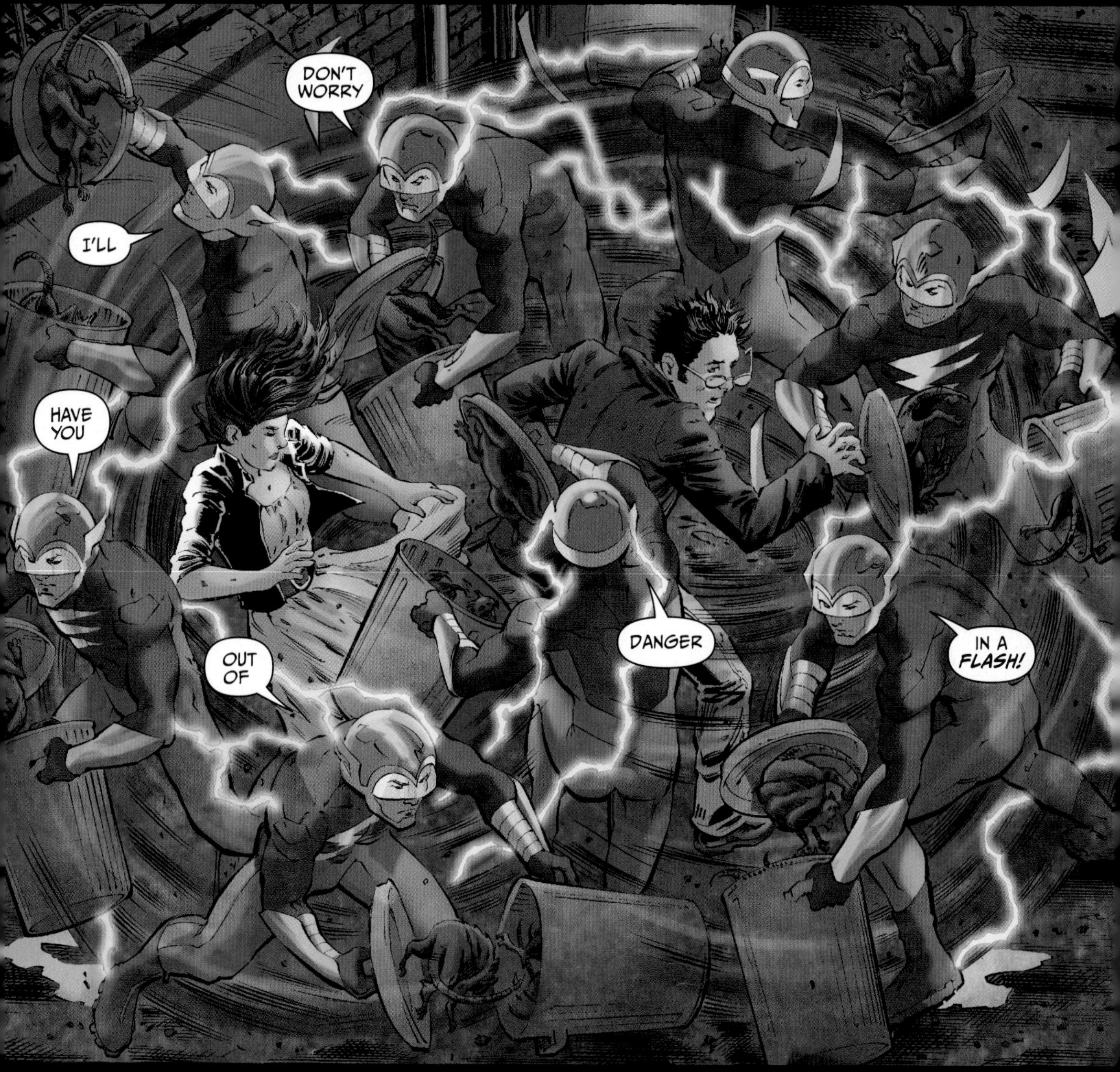
DON'T WORRY
I'LL
HAVE YOU
OUT OF
DANGER
IN A FLASH!

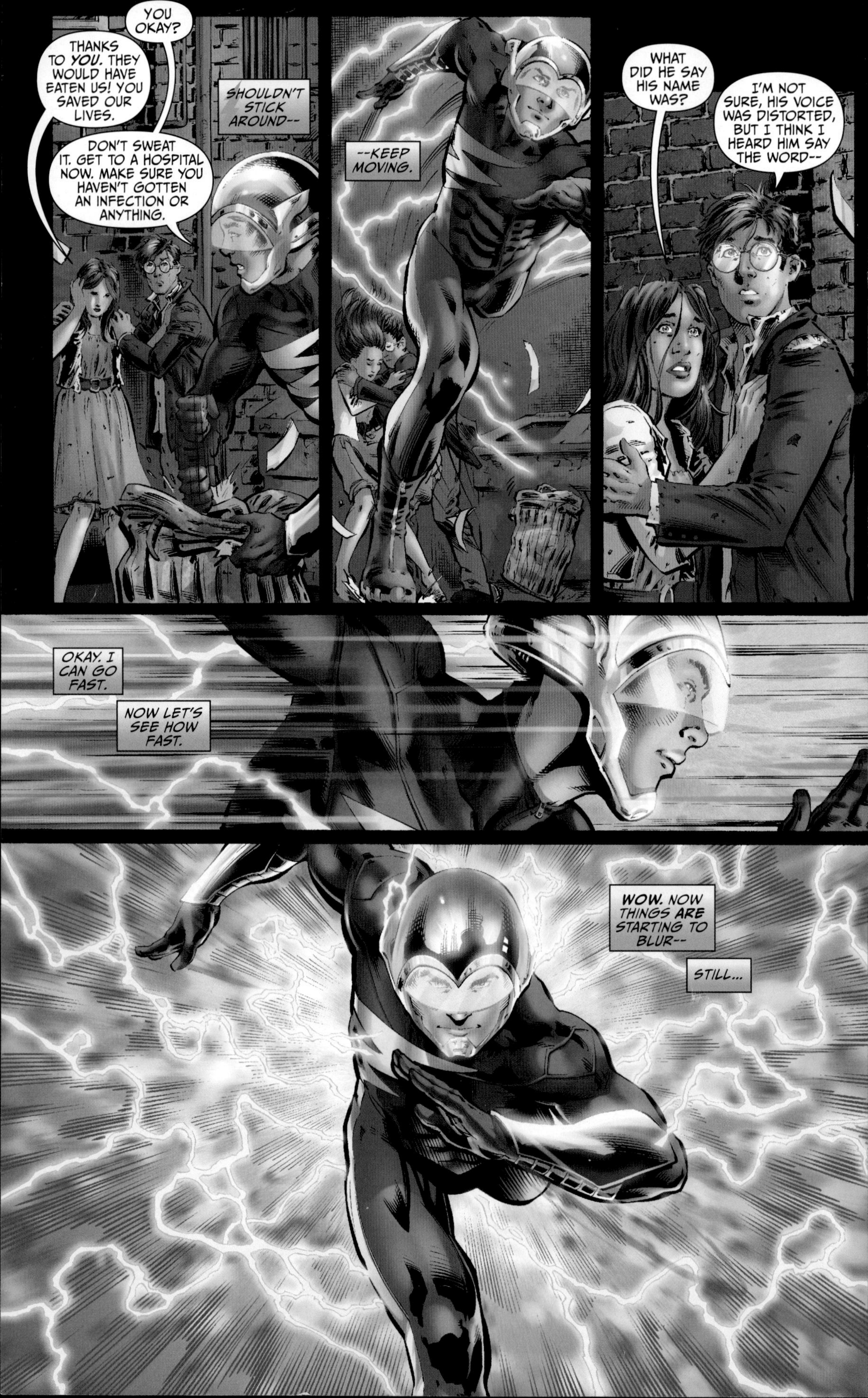
YOU OKAY?
THANKS TO *YOU.* THEY WOULD HAVE EATEN US! YOU SAVED OUR LIVES.
DON'T SWEAT IT. GET TO A HOSPITAL NOW. MAKE SURE YOU HAVEN'T GOTTEN AN INFECTION OR ANYTHING.
SHOULDN'T STICK AROUND--
--KEEP MOVING.
WHAT DID HE SAY HIS NAME WAS?
I'M NOT SURE, HIS VOICE WAS DISTORTED, BUT I THINK I HEARD HIM SAY THE WORD--
OKAY. I CAN GO FAST.
NOW LET'S SEE HOW FAST.
WOW. NOW THINGS **ARE** STARTING TO BLUR--
STILL...

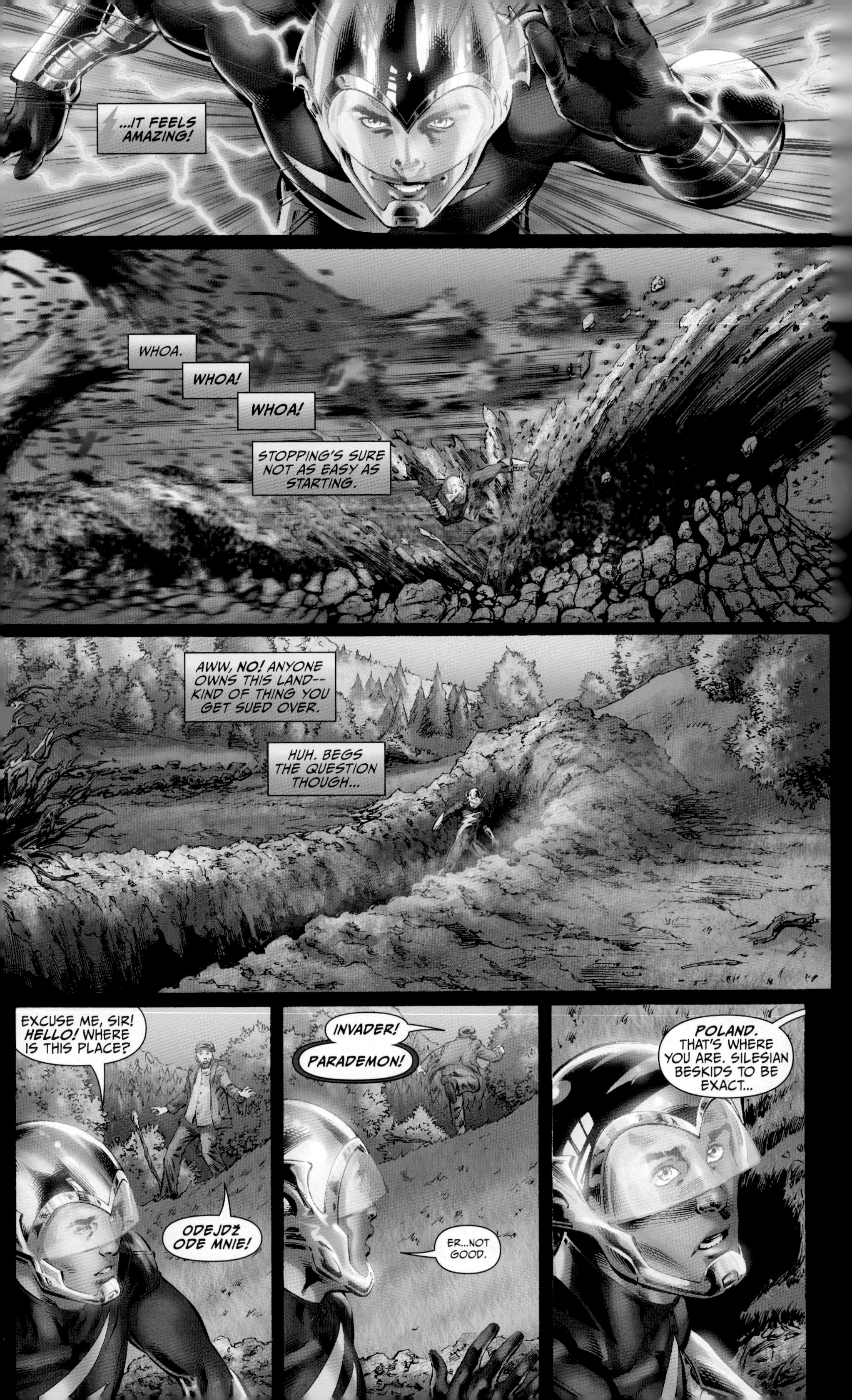
...IT FEELS AMAZING!
WHOA.
WHOA!
WHOA!
STOPPING'S SURE NOT AS EASY AS STARTING.
AWW, NO! ANYONE OWNS THIS LAND-- KIND OF THING YOU GET SUED OVER.
HUH. BEGS THE QUESTION THOUGH...
EXCUSE ME, SIR! HELLO! WHERE IS THIS PLACE?
ODEJDŹ ODE MNIE!
INVADER!
PARADEMON!
ER...NOT GOOD.
POLAND. THAT'S WHERE YOU ARE. SILESIAN BESKIDS TO BE EXACT...

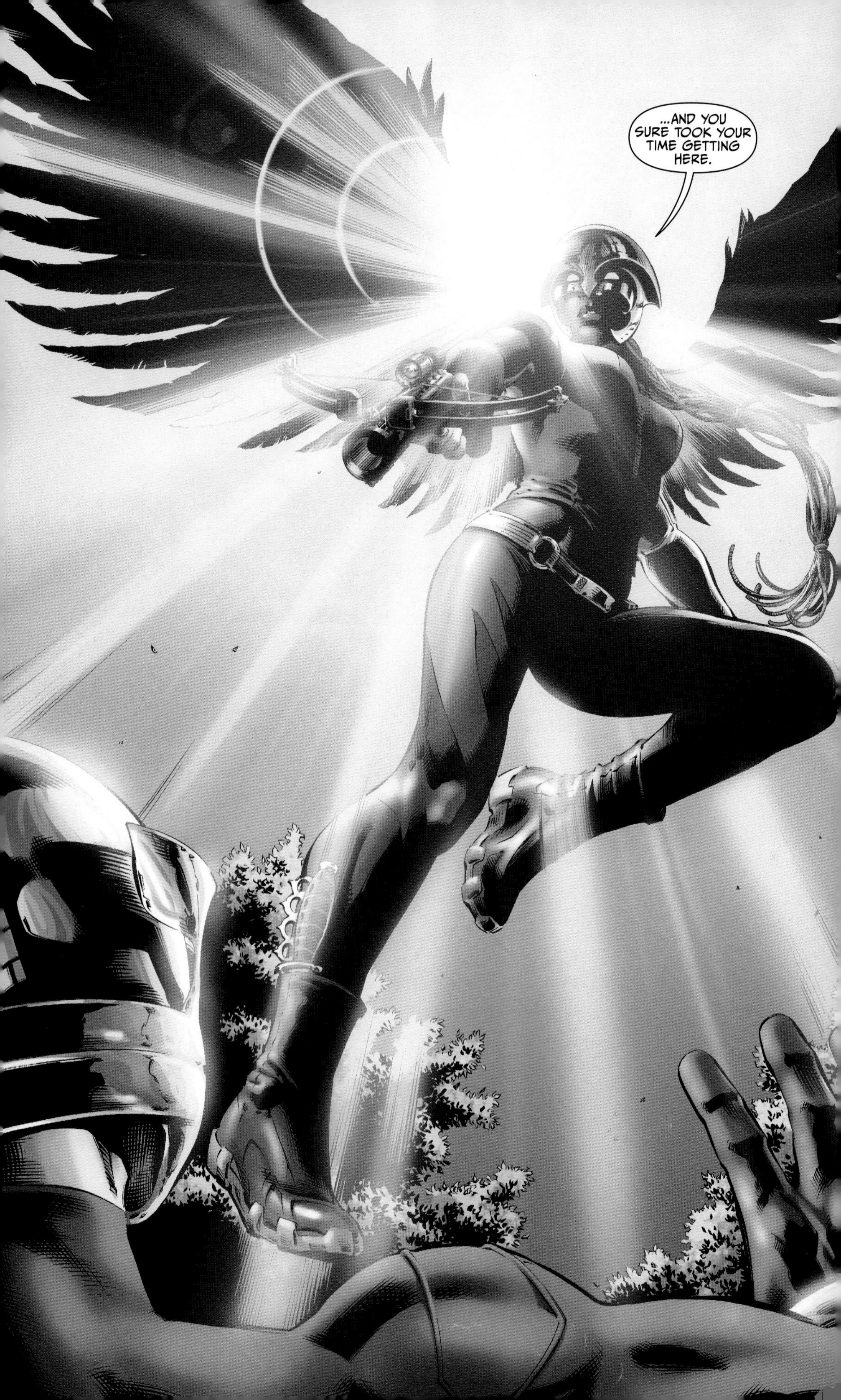
...AND YOU SURE TOOK YOUR TIME GETTING HERE.

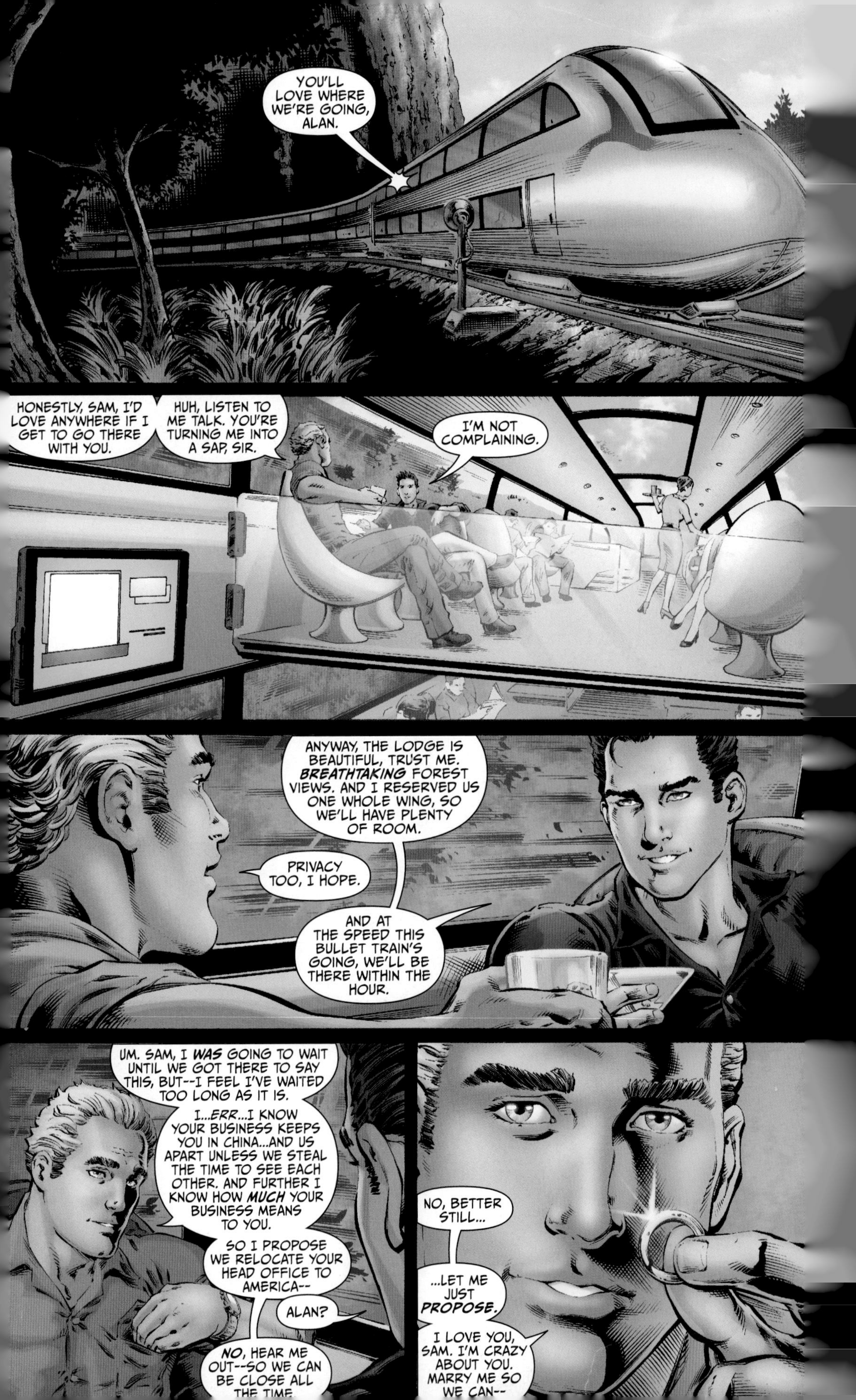
YOU'LL LOVE WHERE WE'RE GOING, ALAN.
HONESTLY, SAM, I'D LOVE ANYWHERE IF I GET TO GO THERE WITH YOU.
HUH, LISTEN TO ME TALK. YOU'RE TURNING ME INTO A SAP, SIR.
I'M NOT COMPLAINING.
ANYWAY, THE LODGE IS BEAUTIFUL, TRUST ME. BREATHTAKING FOREST VIEWS. AND I RESERVED US ONE WHOLE WING, SO WE'LL HAVE PLENTY OF ROOM.
PRIVACY TOO, I HOPE.
AND AT THE SPEED THIS BULLET TRAIN'S GOING, WE'LL BE THERE WITHIN THE HOUR.
UM. SAM, I WAS GOING TO WAIT UNTIL WE GOT THERE TO SAY THIS, BUT--I FEEL I'VE WAITED TOO LONG AS IT IS.
I...ERR...I KNOW YOUR BUSINESS KEEPS YOU IN CHINA...AND US APART UNLESS WE STEAL THE TIME TO SEE EACH OTHER. AND FURTHER I KNOW HOW MUCH YOUR BUSINESS MEANS TO YOU.
SO I PROPOSE WE RELOCATE YOUR HEAD OFFICE TO AMERICA--
ALAN?
NO, HEAR ME OUT--SO WE CAN BE CLOSE ALL THE TIME.
NO, BETTER STILL...
...LET ME JUST PROPOSE.
I LOVE YOU, SAM. I'M CRAZY ABOUT YOU. MARRY ME SO WE CAN--

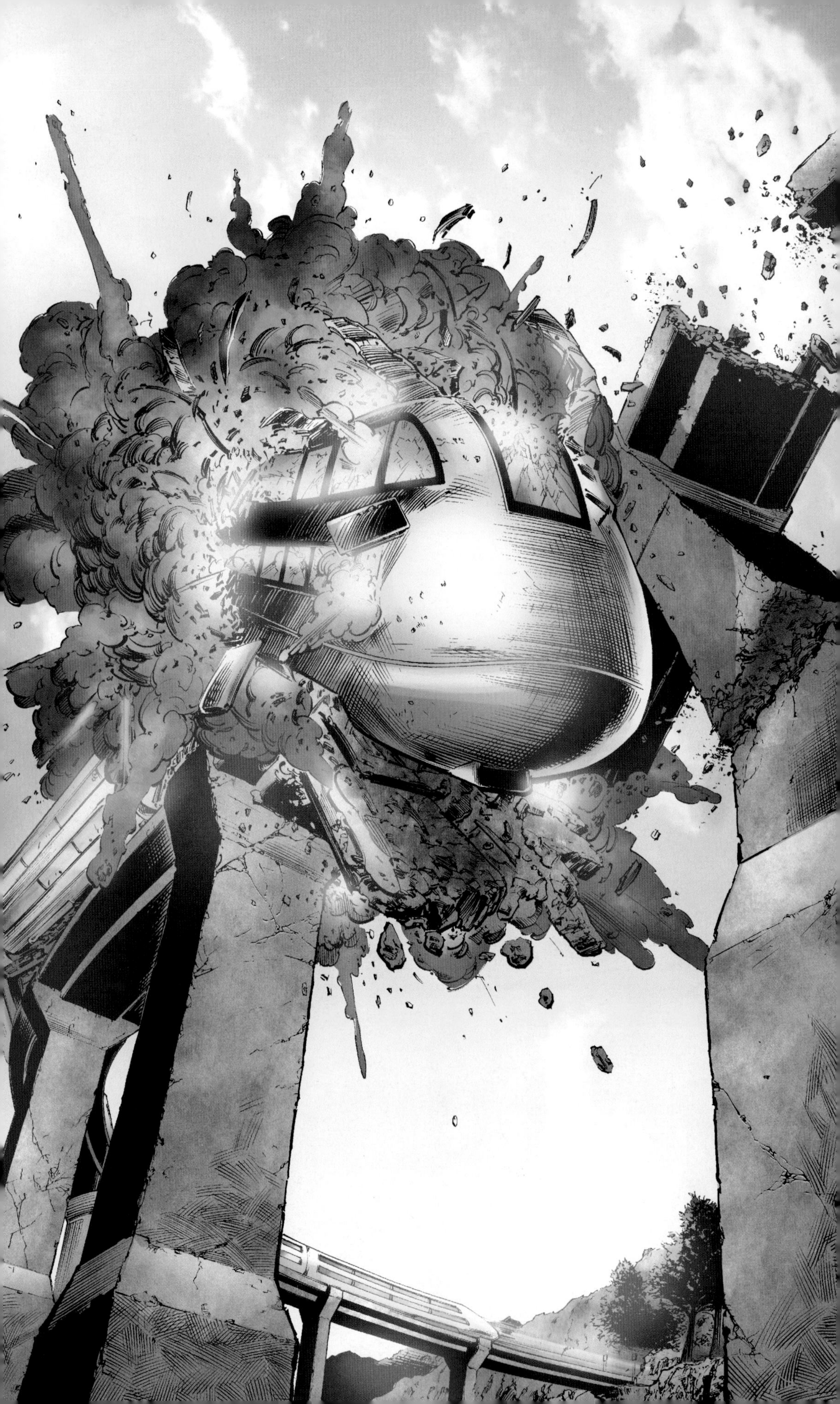

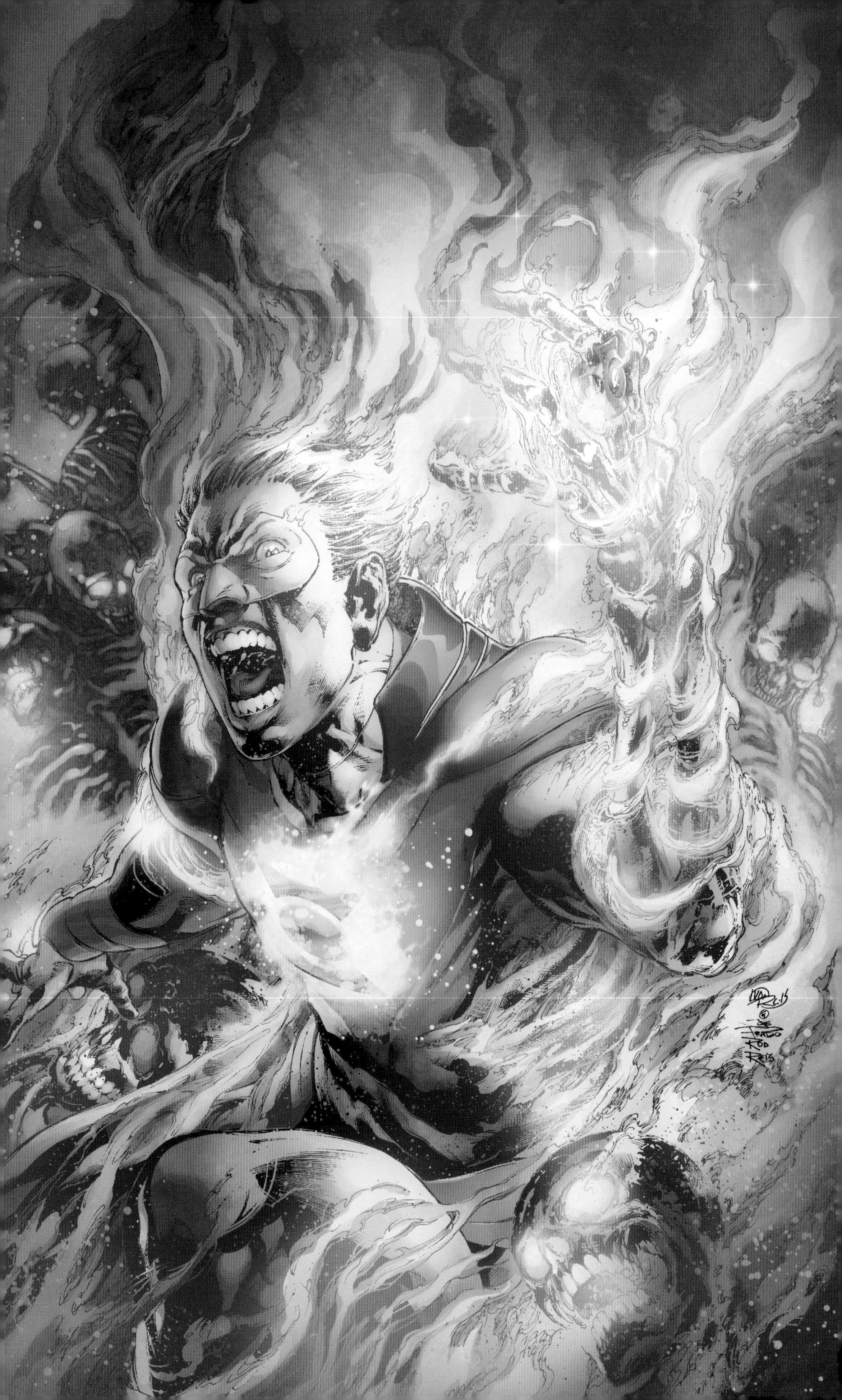

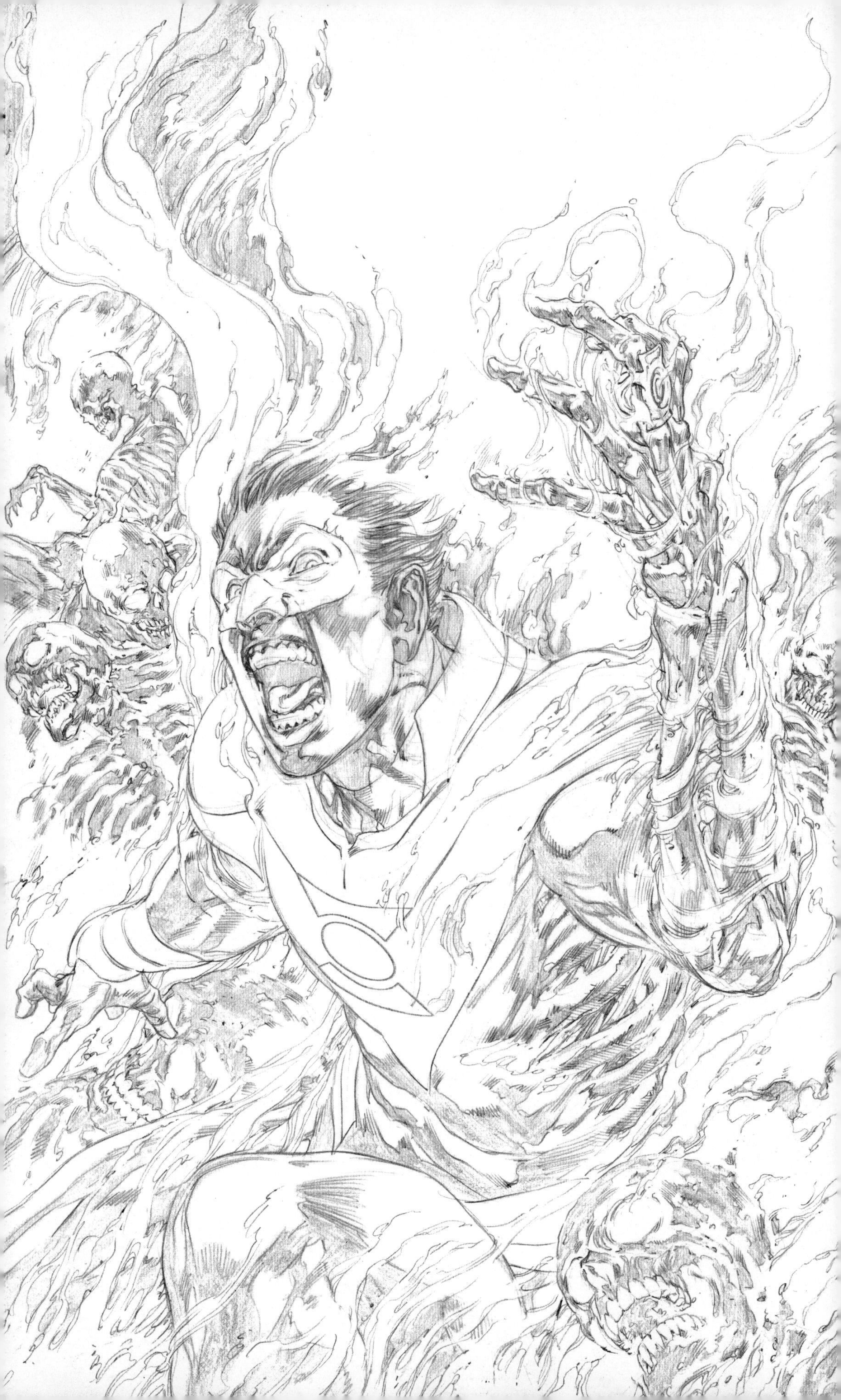

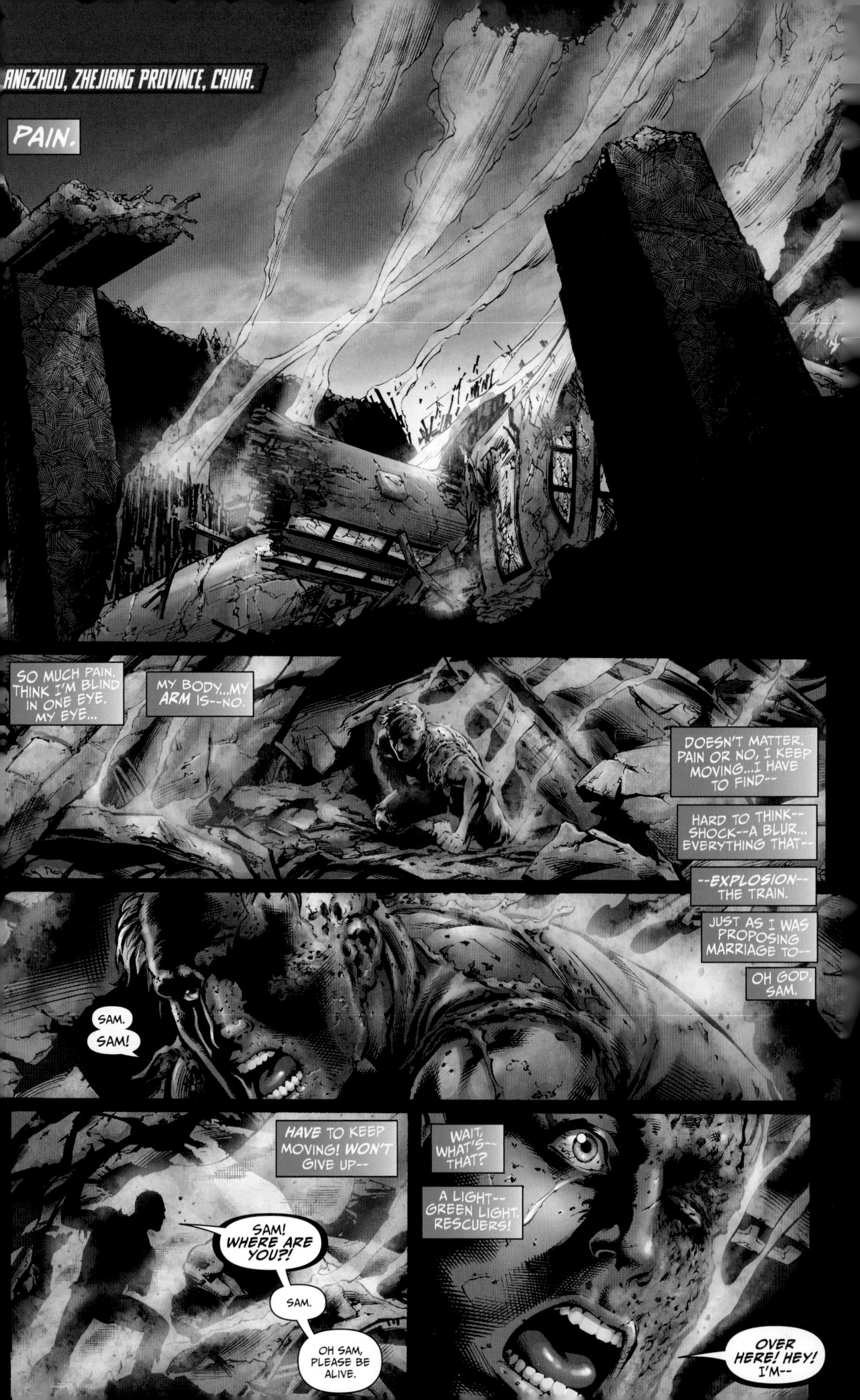
ANGZHOU, ZHEJIANG PROVINCE, CHINA.
PAIN.
SO MUCH PAIN. THINK I'M BLIND IN ONE EYE. MY EYE...
MY BODY...MY ARM IS--NO.
DOESN'T MATTER. PAIN OR NO, I KEEP MOVING...I HAVE TO FIND--
HARD TO THINK--SHOCK--A BLUR... EVERYTHING THAT--
--EXPLOSION-- THE TRAIN.
JUST AS I WAS PROPOSING MARRIAGE TO--
OH GOD, SAM.
SAM.
SAM!
HAVE TO KEEP MOVING! WON'T GIVE UP--
SAM! WHERE ARE YOU?!
SAM.
OH SAM, PLEASE BE ALIVE.
WAIT, WHAT'S--THAT?
A LIGHT--GREEN LIGHT. RESCUERS!
OVER HERE! HEY! I'M--

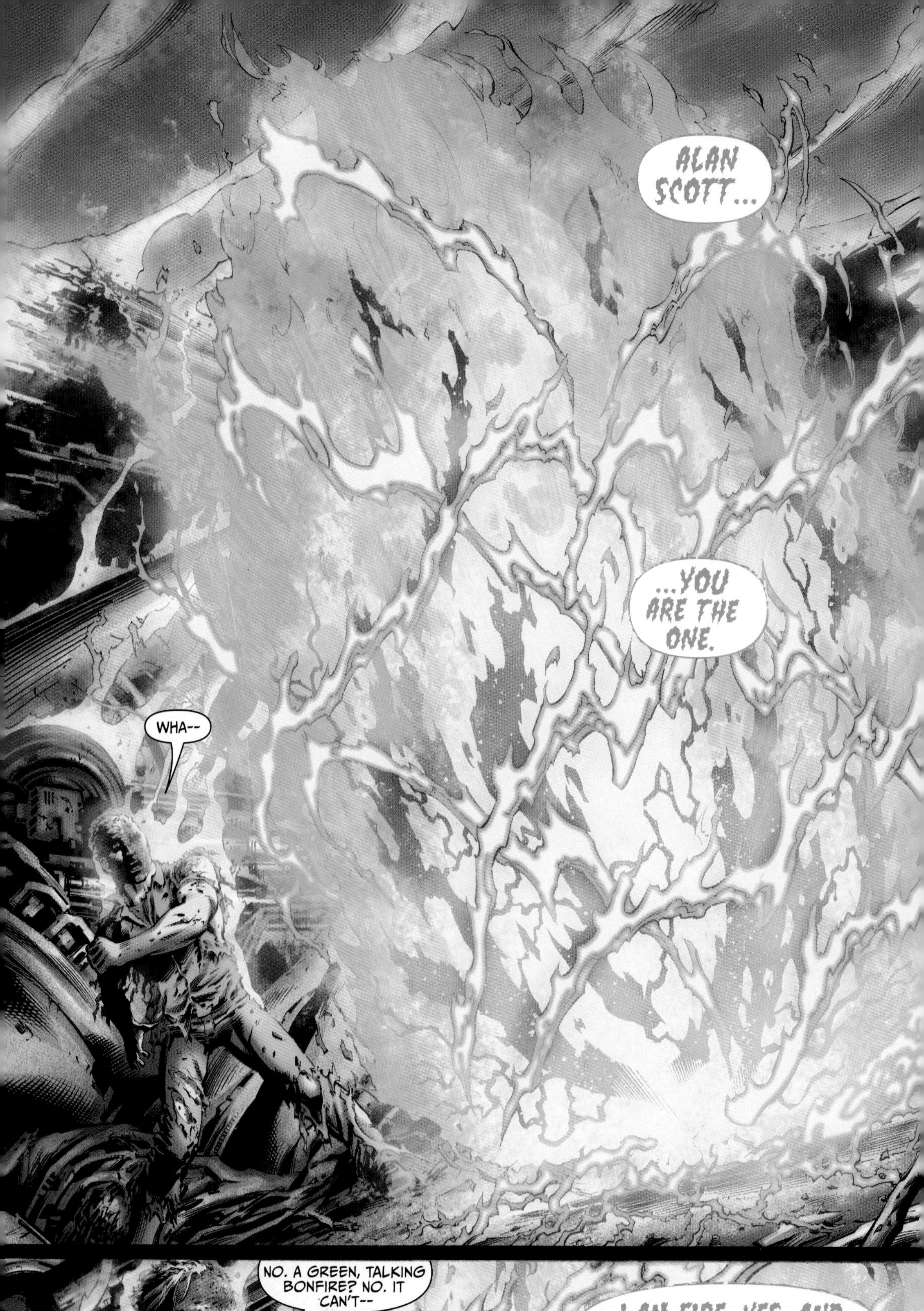
ALAN SCOTT...
...YOU ARE THE ONE.
WHA--

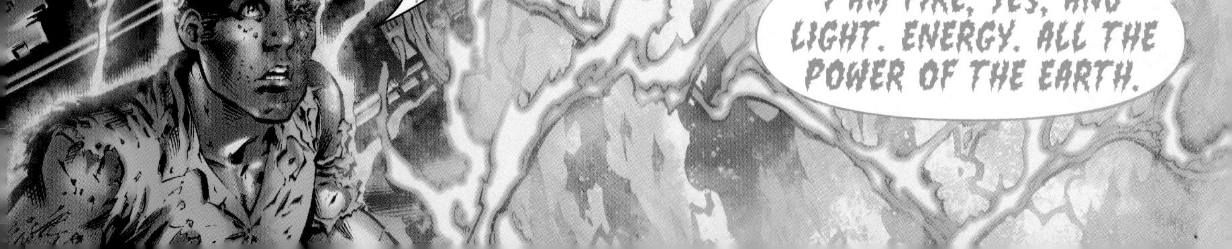
NO. A GREEN, TALKING BONFIRE? NO. IT CAN'T--
I AM FIRE, YES, AND LIGHT. ENERGY. ALL THE POWER OF THE EARTH.

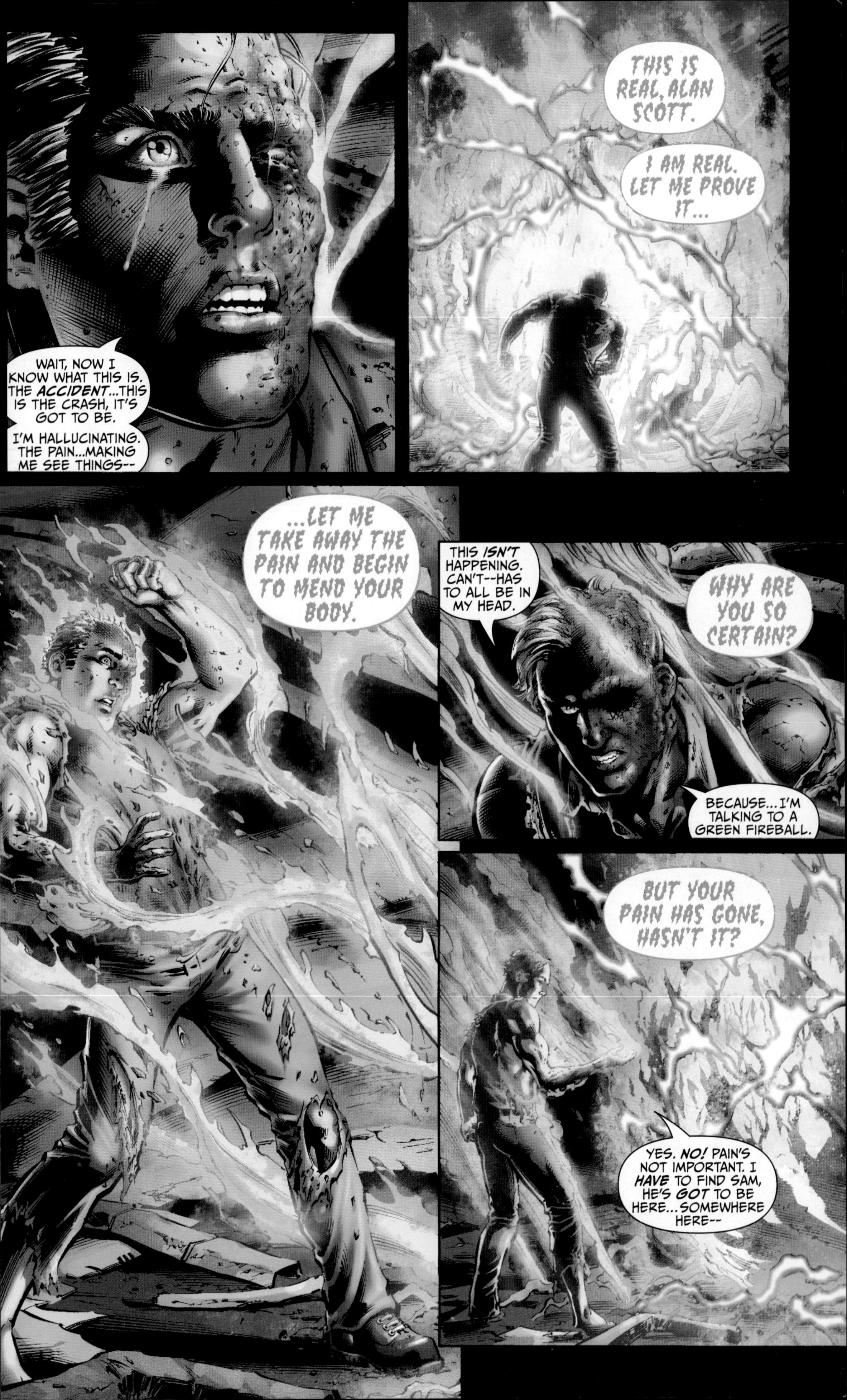

WAIT, NOW I KNOW WHAT THIS IS. THE ACCIDENT...THIS IS THE CRASH, IT'S GOT TO BE.
I'M HALLUCINATING. THE PAIN...MAKING ME SEE THINGS--
THIS IS REAL, ALAN SCOTT.
I AM REAL. LET ME PROVE IT...
...LET ME TAKE AWAY THE PAIN AND BEGIN TO MEND YOUR BODY.
THIS ISN'T HAPPENING. CAN'T--HAS TO ALL BE IN MY HEAD.
WHY ARE YOU SO CERTAIN?
BECAUSE...I'M TALKING TO A GREEN FIREBALL.
BUT YOUR PAIN HAS GONE, HASN'T IT?
YES. NO! PAIN'S NOT IMPORTANT. I HAVE TO FIND SAM, HE'S GOT TO BE HERE...SOMEWHERE HERE--

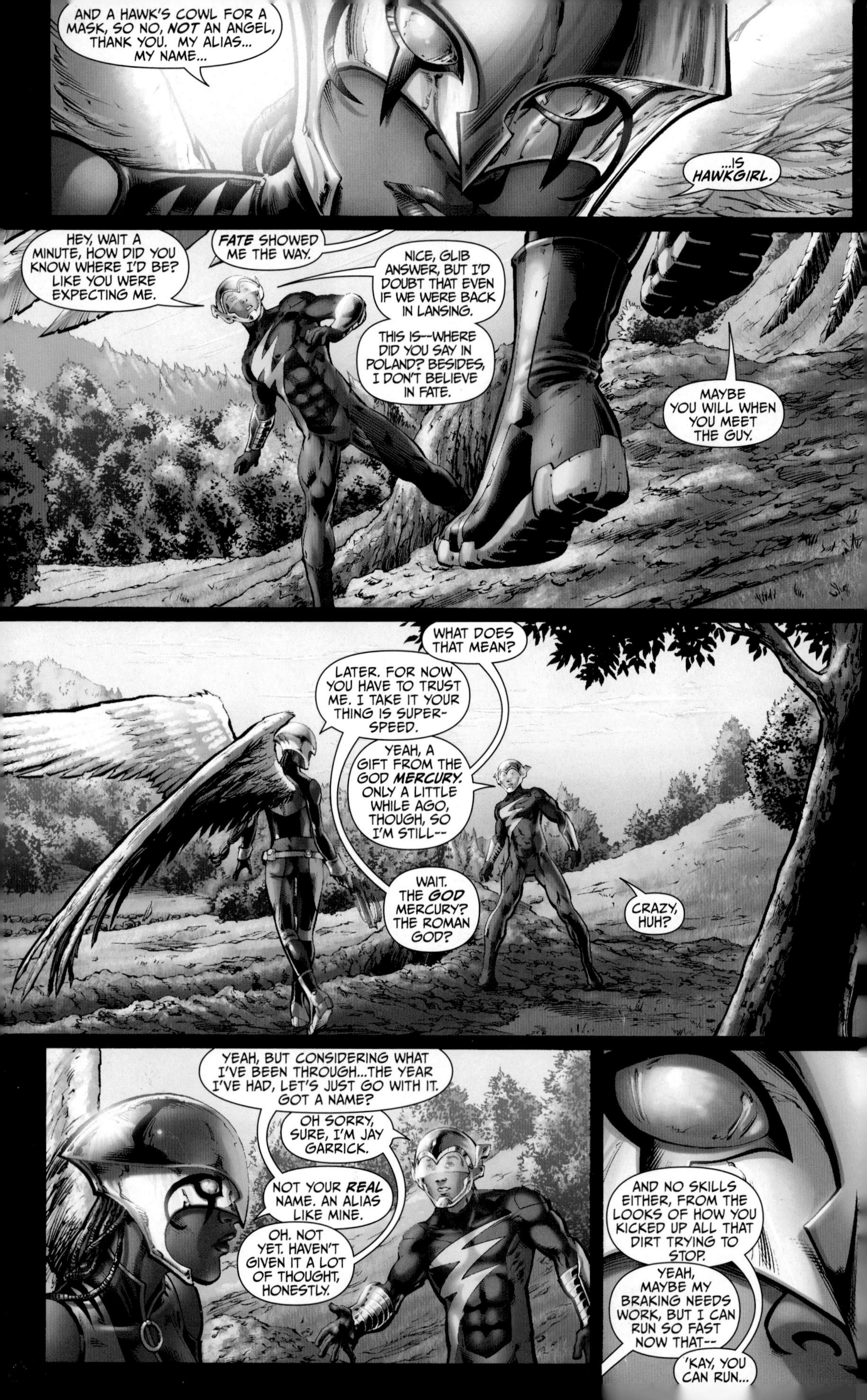

AND A HAWK'S COWL FOR A MASK, SO NO, *NOT* AN ANGEL, THANK YOU. MY ALIAS... MY NAME...
...IS *HAWKGIRL.*
HEY, WAIT A MINUTE, HOW DID YOU KNOW WHERE I'D BE? LIKE YOU WERE EXPECTING ME.
FATE SHOWED ME THE WAY.
NICE, GLIB ANSWER, BUT I'D DOUBT THAT EVEN IF WE WERE BACK IN LANSING.
THIS IS--WHERE DID YOU SAY IN POLAND? BESIDES, I DON'T BELIEVE IN FATE.
MAYBE YOU WILL WHEN YOU MEET THE GUY.
WHAT DOES THAT MEAN?
LATER. FOR NOW YOU HAVE TO TRUST ME. I TAKE IT YOUR THING IS SUPER-SPEED.
YEAH, A GIFT FROM THE GOD *MERCURY.* ONLY A LITTLE WHILE AGO, THOUGH, SO I'M STILL--
WAIT. THE *GOD* MERCURY? THE ROMAN GOD?
CRAZY, HUH?
YEAH, BUT CONSIDERING WHAT I'VE BEEN THROUGH...THE YEAR I'VE HAD, LET'S JUST GO WITH IT. GOT A NAME?
OH SORRY, SURE, I'M JAY GARRICK.
NOT YOUR *REAL* NAME. AN ALIAS LIKE MINE.
OH. NOT YET. HAVEN'T GIVEN IT A LOT OF THOUGHT, HONESTLY.
AND NO SKILLS EITHER, FROM THE LOOKS OF HOW YOU KICKED UP ALL THAT DIRT TRYING TO STOP.
YEAH, MAYBE MY BRAKING NEEDS WORK, BUT I CAN RUN SO FAST NOW THAT--
'KAY, YOU CAN RUN...

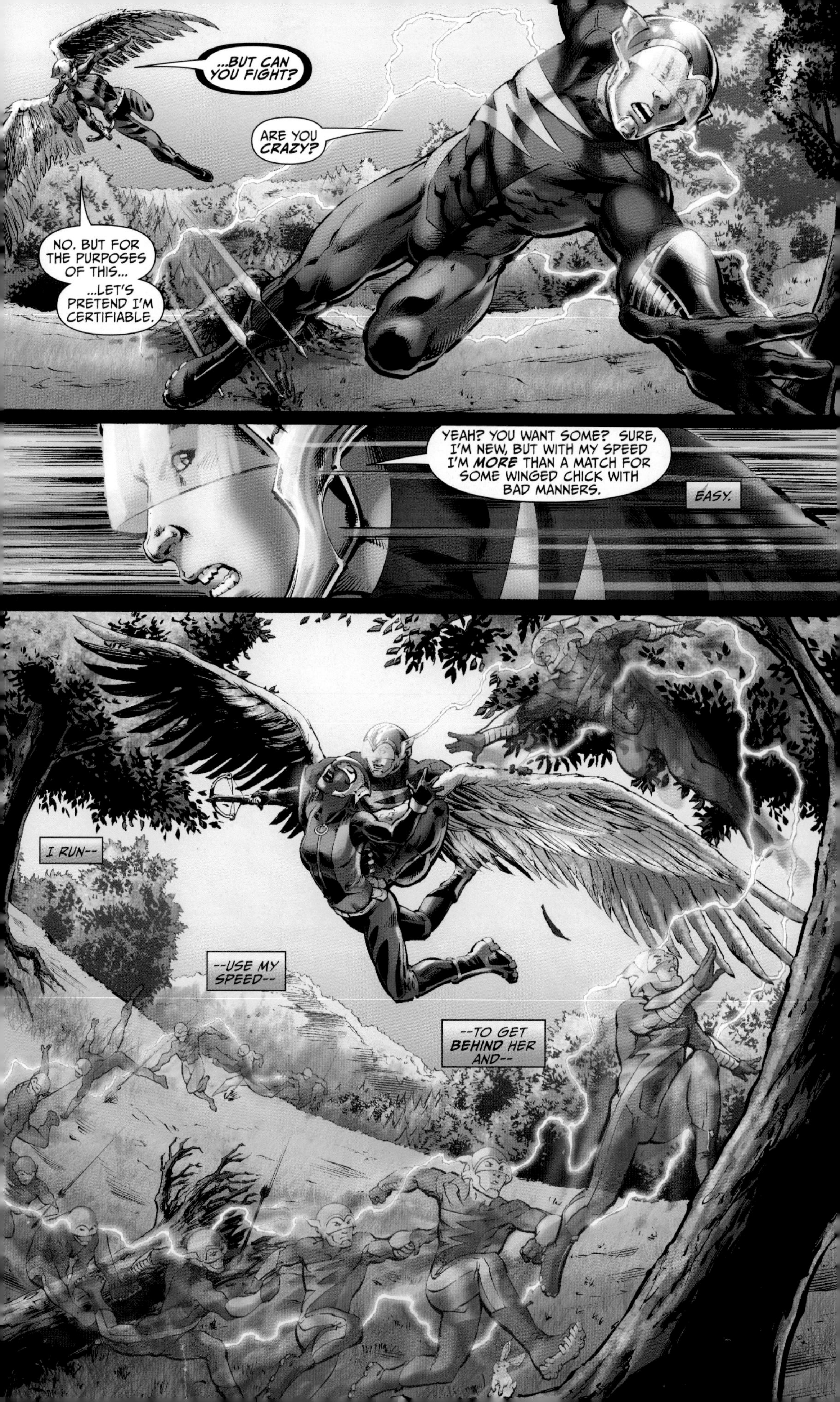
...BUT CAN YOU FIGHT?
ARE YOU *CRAZY?*
NO. BUT FOR THE PURPOSES OF THIS... ...LET'S PRETEND I'M CERTIFIABLE.
YEAH? YOU WANT SOME? SURE, I'M NEW, BUT WITH MY SPEED I'M *MORE* THAN A MATCH FOR SOME WINGED CHICK WITH BAD MANNERS.
EASY.
I RUN--
--USE MY SPEED--
--TO GET *BEHIND* HER AND--

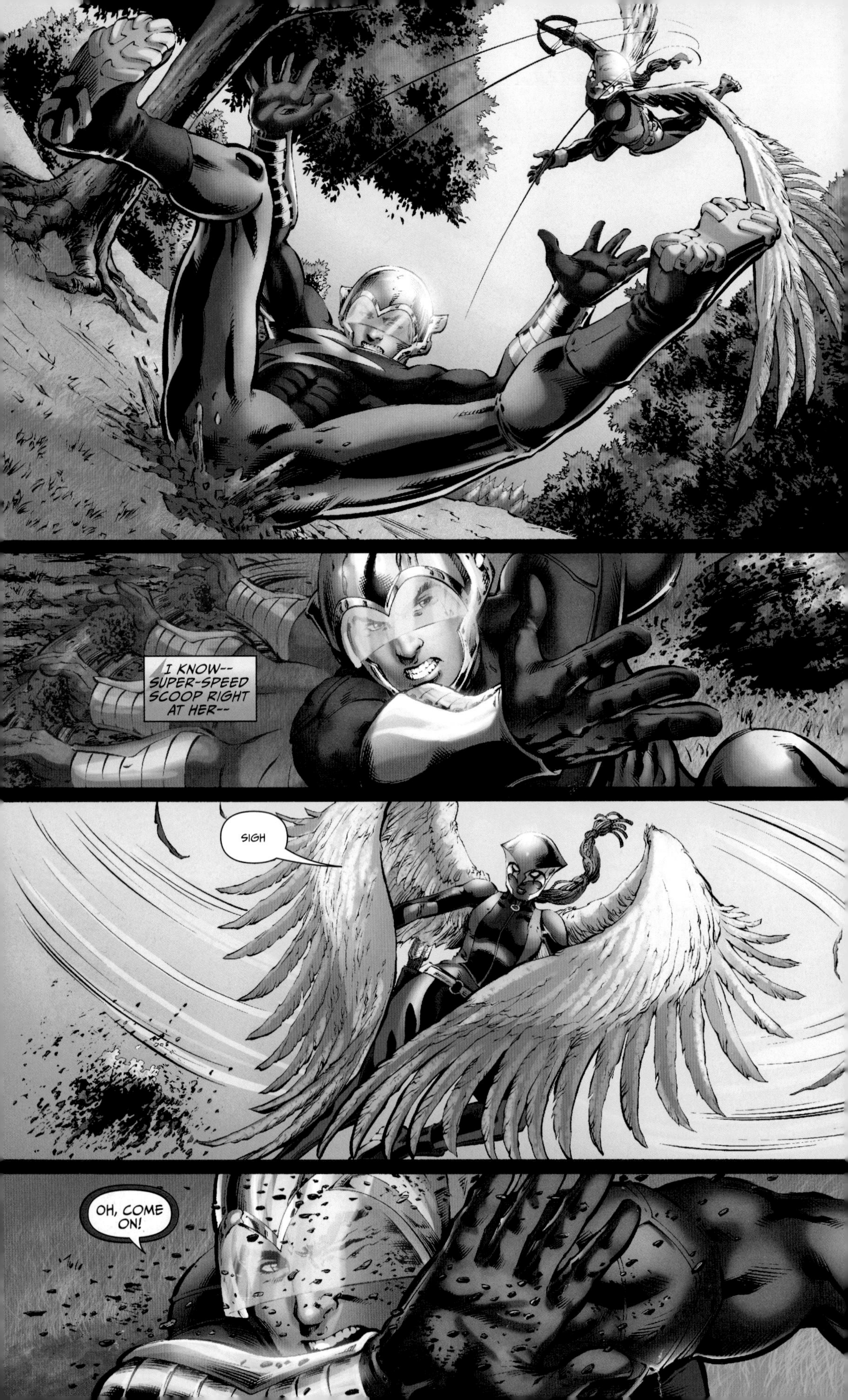
I KNOW--
SUPER-SPEED
SCOOP RIGHT
AT HER--
SIGH
OH, COME
ON!

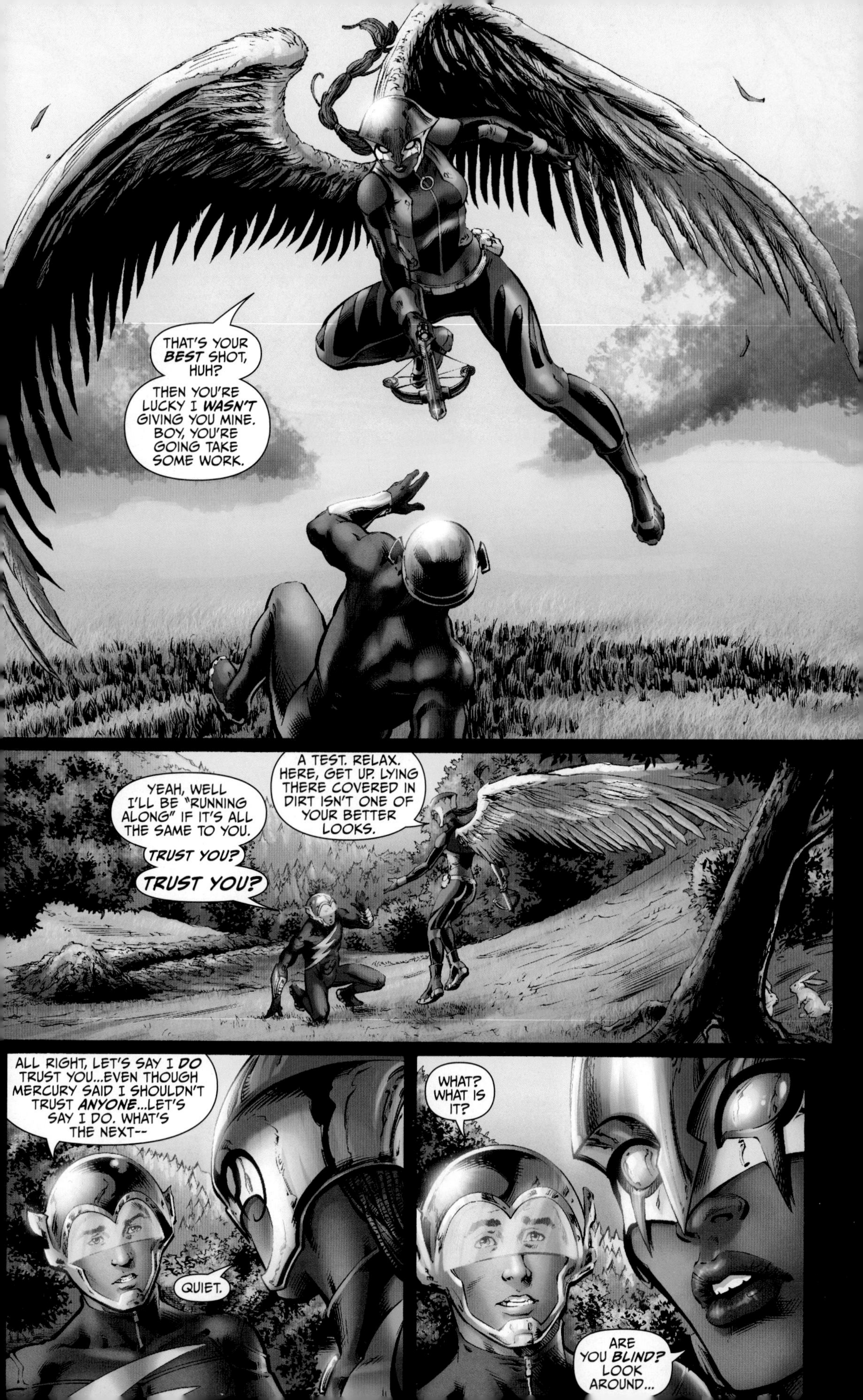
THAT'S YOUR BEST SHOT, HUH?
THEN YOU'RE LUCKY I WASN'T GIVING YOU MINE. BOY, YOU'RE GOING TAKE SOME WORK.
YEAH, WELL I'LL BE "RUNNING ALONG" IF IT'S ALL THE SAME TO YOU.
A TEST. RELAX. HERE, GET UP. LYING THERE COVERED IN DIRT ISN'T ONE OF YOUR BETTER LOOKS.
TRUST YOU?
TRUST YOU?
ALL RIGHT, LET'S SAY I DO TRUST YOU...EVEN THOUGH MERCURY SAID I SHOULDN'T TRUST ANYONE...LET'S SAY I DO. WHAT'S THE NEXT--
QUIET.
WHAT? WHAT IS IT?
ARE YOU BLIND? LOOK AROUND...

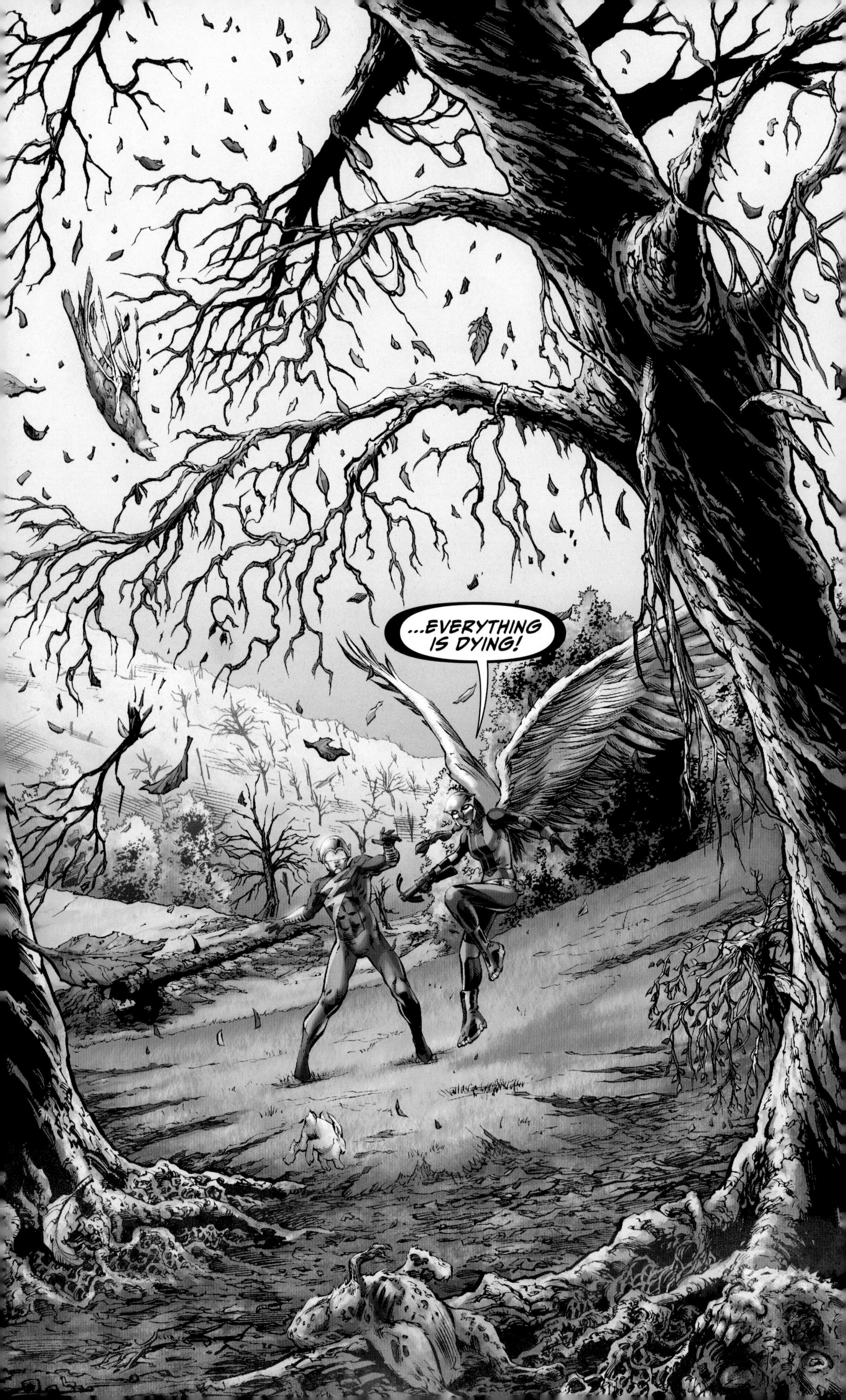
...EVERYTHING IS DYING!

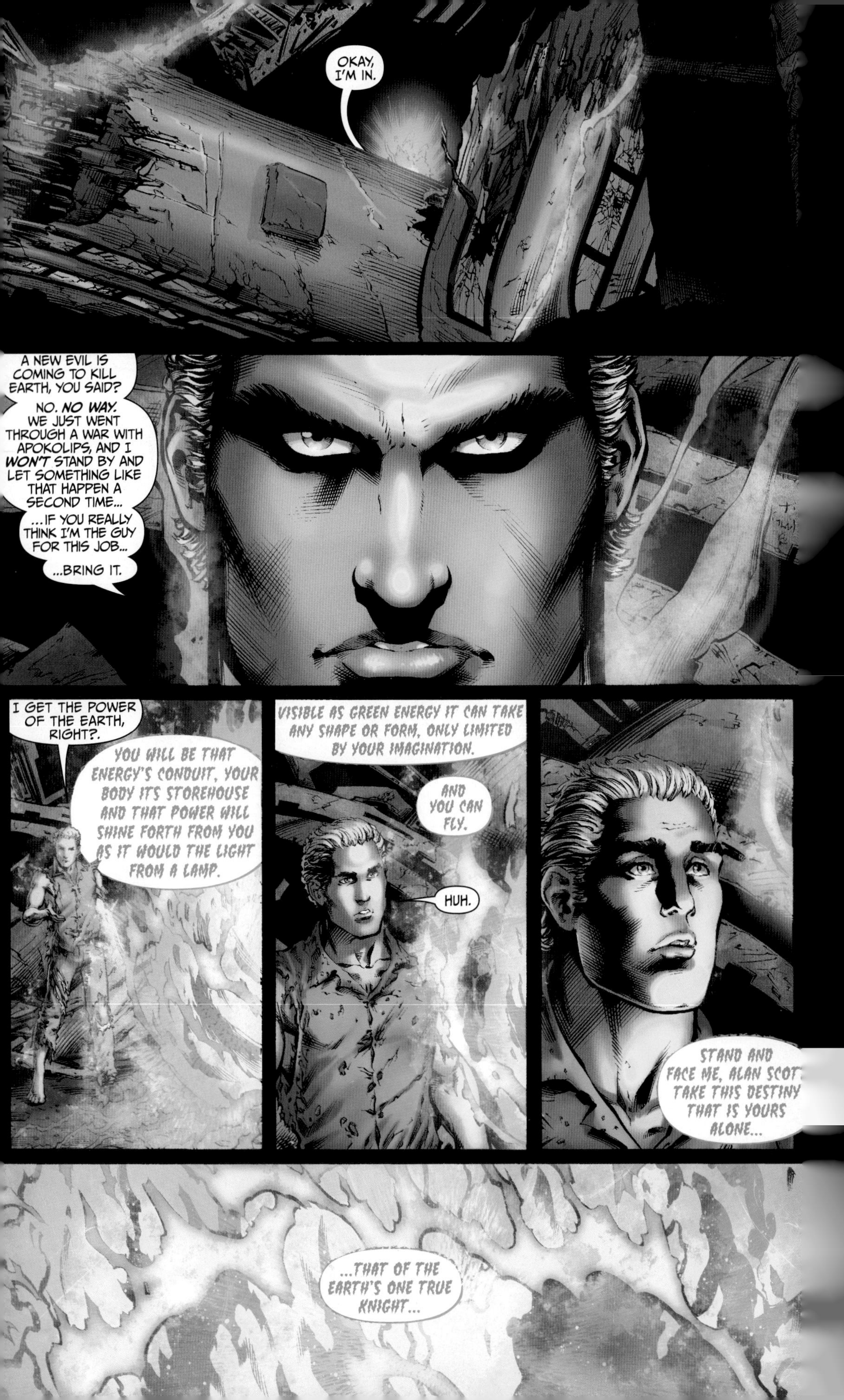
OKAY, I'M IN.
A NEW EVIL IS COMING TO KILL EARTH, YOU SAID?
NO. NO WAY. WE JUST WENT THROUGH A WAR WITH APOKOLIPS, AND I WON'T STAND BY AND LET SOMETHING LIKE THAT HAPPEN A SECOND TIME...
...IF YOU REALLY THINK I'M THE GUY FOR THIS JOB...
...BRING IT.
I GET THE POWER OF THE EARTH, RIGHT?.
YOU WILL BE THAT ENERGY'S CONDUIT, YOUR BODY ITS STOREHOUSE AND THAT POWER WILL SHINE FORTH FROM YOU AS IT WOULD THE LIGHT FROM A LAMP.
VISIBLE AS GREEN ENERGY IT CAN TAKE ANY SHAPE OR FORM, ONLY LIMITED BY YOUR IMAGINATION.
AND YOU CAN FLY.
HUH.
STAND AND FACE ME, ALAN SCOTT TAKE THIS DESTINY THAT IS YOURS ALONE...
...THAT OF THE EARTH'S ONE TRUE KNIGHT...

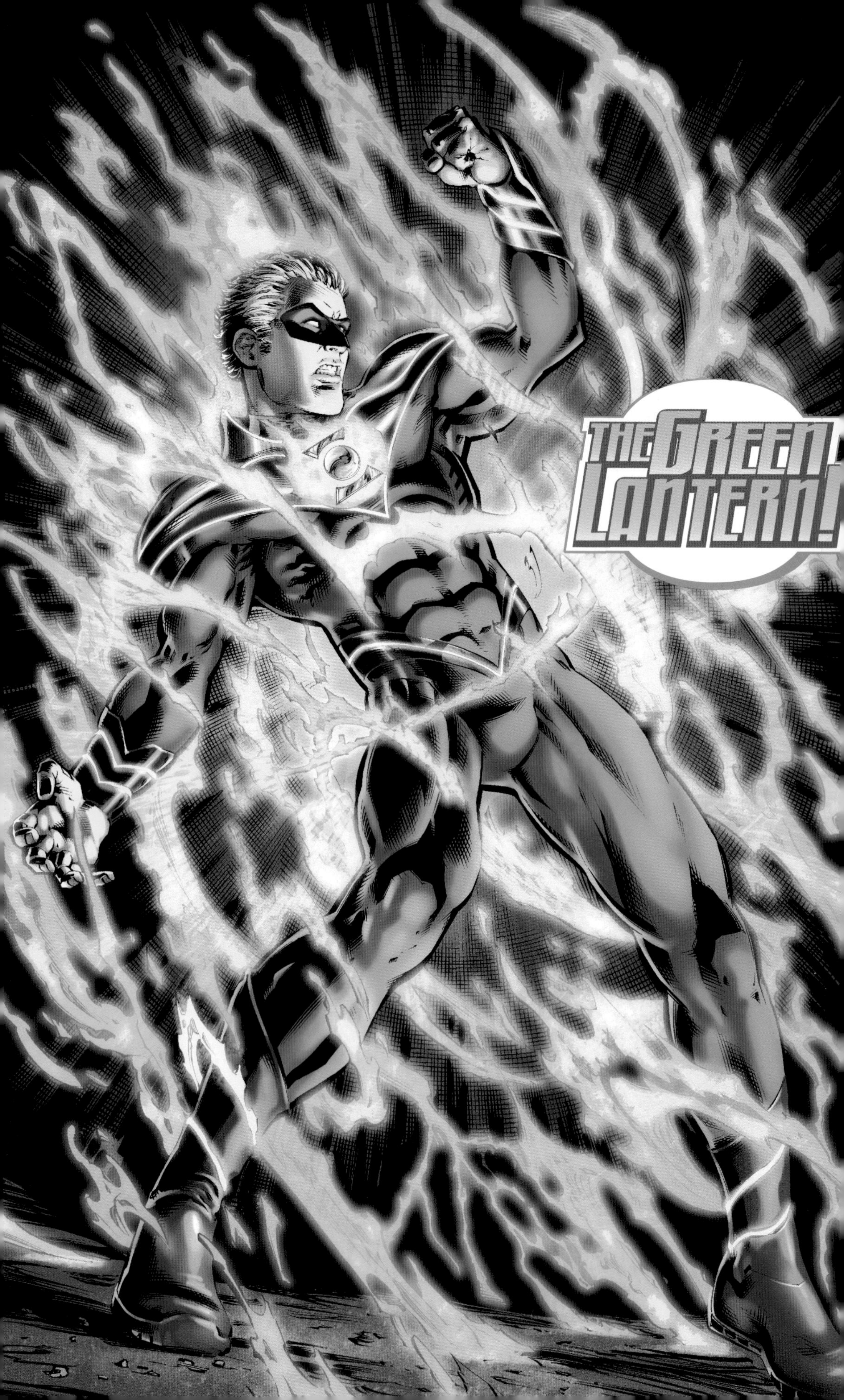
THE GREEN LANTERN!

... I GET A COSTUME TOO, APPARENTLY.

YOUR DOING. EVEN AS YOU TOOK ON THE MANTLE, YOUR MIND...SOME PART OF IT, CHOSE THIS, AND TRUTHFULLY THAT'S FAR FROM UNWISE...

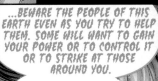

...BEWARE THE PEOPLE OF THIS EARTH EVEN AS YOU TRY TO HELP THEM. SOME WILL WANT TO GAIN YOUR POWER OR TO CONTROL IT OR TO STRIKE AT THOSE AROUND YOU.

BETTER YOU DO TAKE AN ALIAS TO CONCEAL WHO YOU ARE.

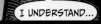

I UNDERSTAND...

"...BE CAREFUL OF MY ENEMIES."

VIRGINIA.

THE GREEN...

...THE GREEN HAS FOUND ITS CHAMPION.

AND SO I MUST AWAKEN...

...IN THE NAME OF THE GREY I MUST ARISE.

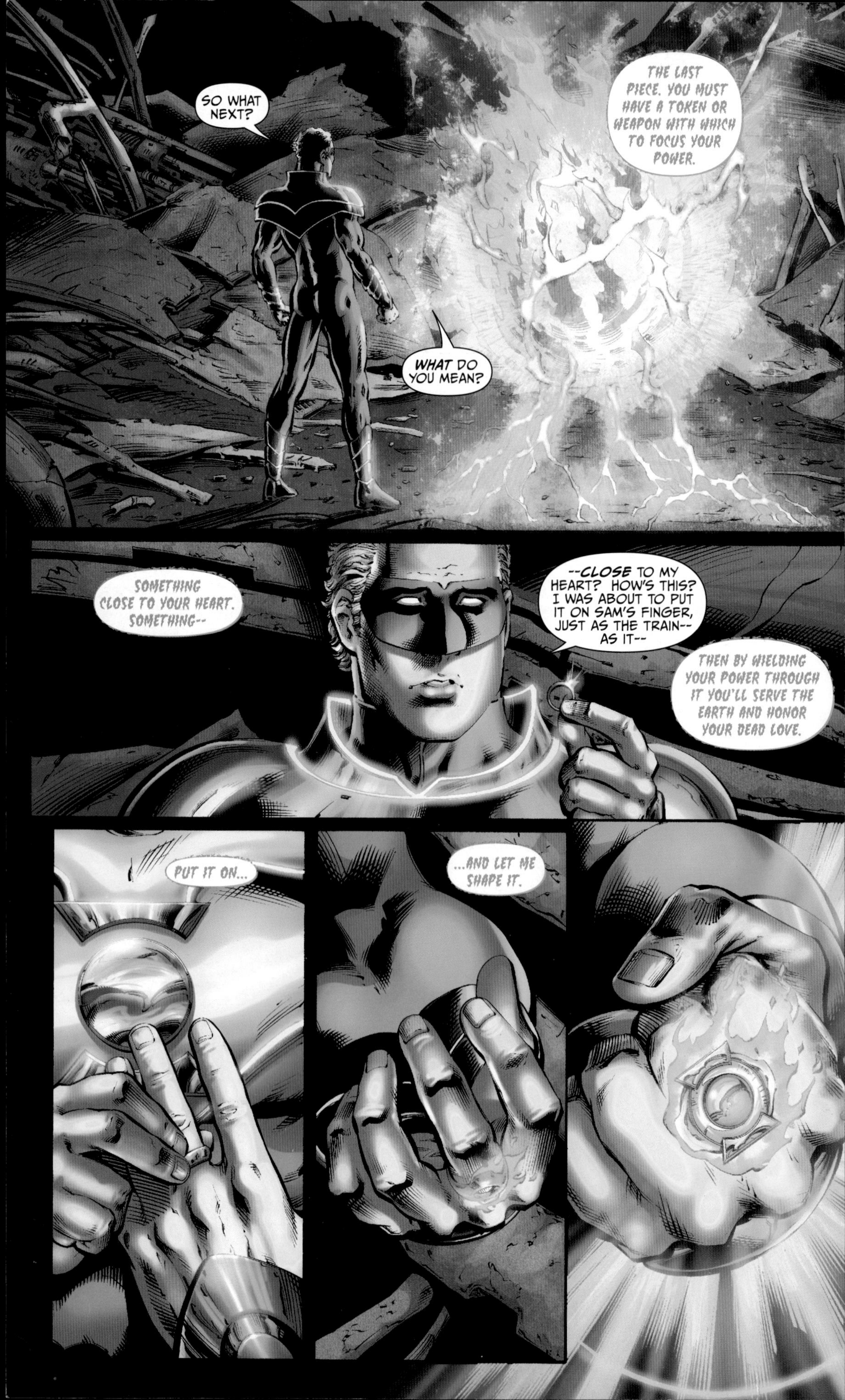
SO WHAT NEXT?
THE LAST PIECE. YOU MUST HAVE A TOKEN OR WEAPON WITH WHICH TO FOCUS YOUR POWER.
WHAT DO YOU MEAN?
SOMETHING CLOSE TO YOUR HEART. SOMETHING--
--CLOSE TO MY HEART? HOW'S THIS? I WAS ABOUT TO PUT IT ON SAM'S FINGER, JUST AS THE TRAIN--AS IT--
THEN BY WIELDING YOUR POWER THROUGH IT YOU'LL SERVE THE EARTH AND HONOR YOUR DEAD LOVE.
PUT IT ON...
...AND LET ME SHAPE IT.

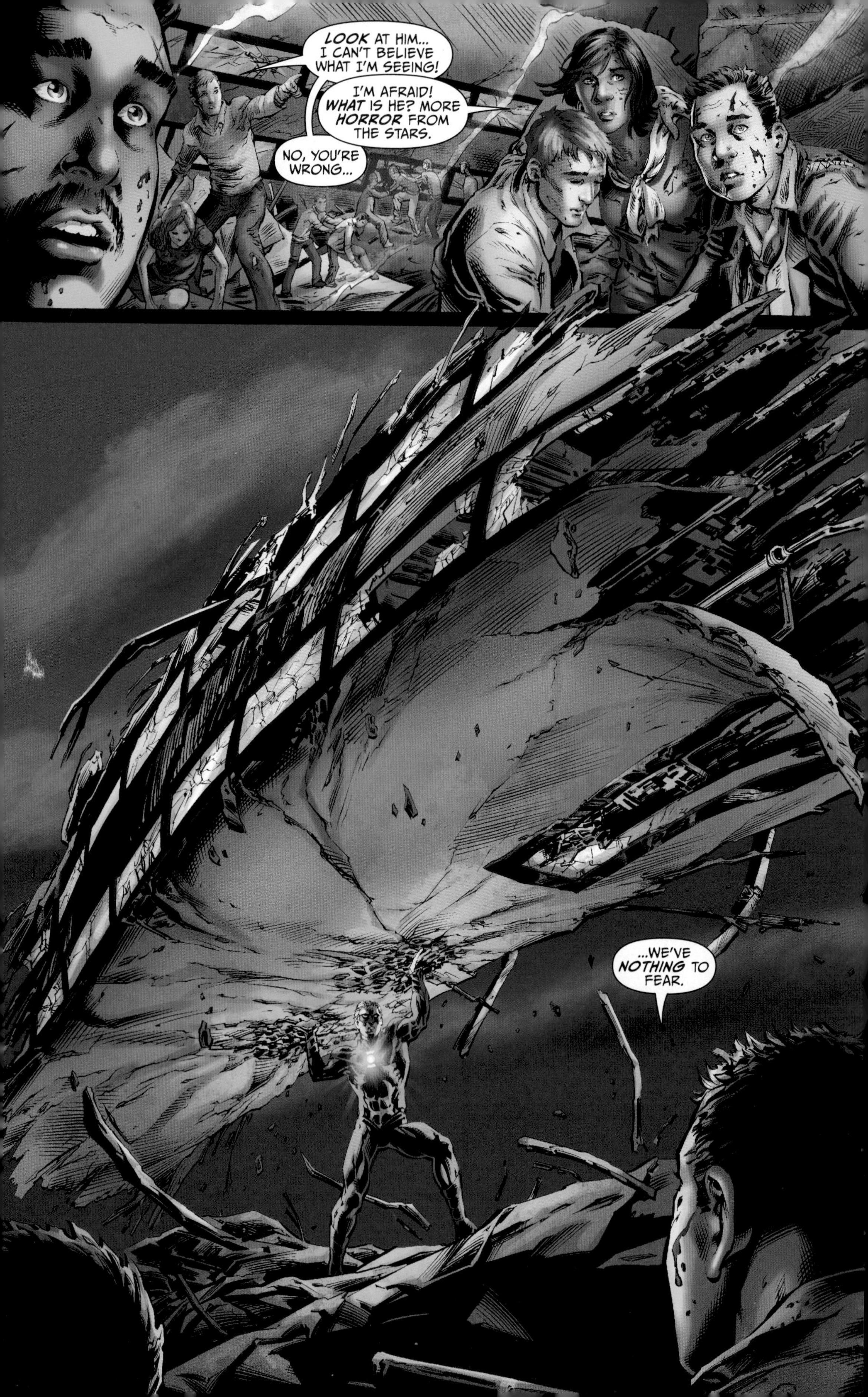
LOOK AT HIM... I CAN'T BELIEVE WHAT I'M SEEING!
I'M AFRAID! WHAT IS HE? MORE HORROR FROM THE STARS.
NO, YOU'RE WRONG...
...WE'VE NOTHING TO FEAR.

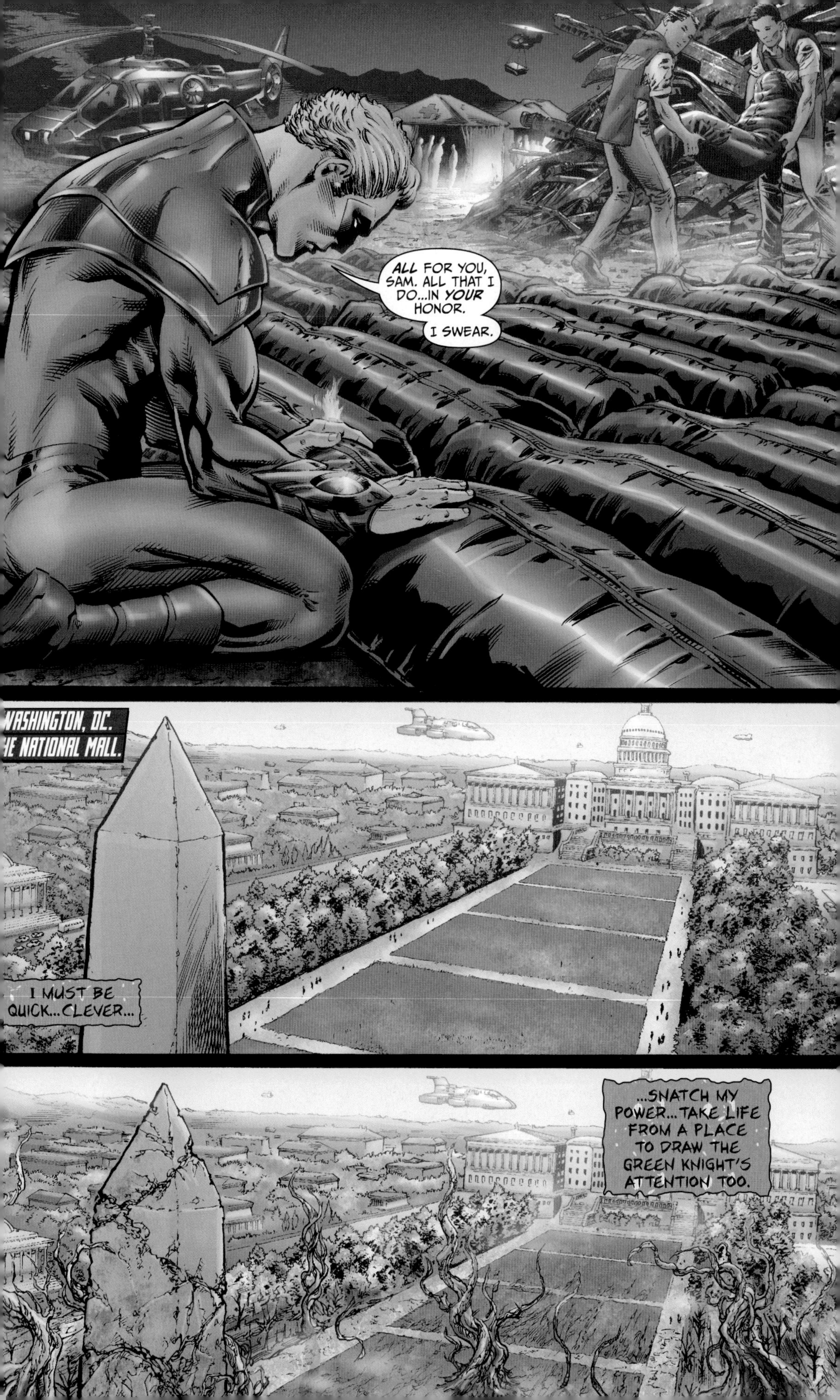
ALL FOR YOU, SAM. ALL THAT I DO...IN YOUR HONOR.
I SWEAR.
WASHINGTON, DC. THE NATIONAL MALL.
I MUST BE QUICK...CLEVER...
...SNATCH MY POWER...TAKE LIFE FROM A PLACE TO DRAW THE GREEN KNIGHT'S ATTENTION TOO.

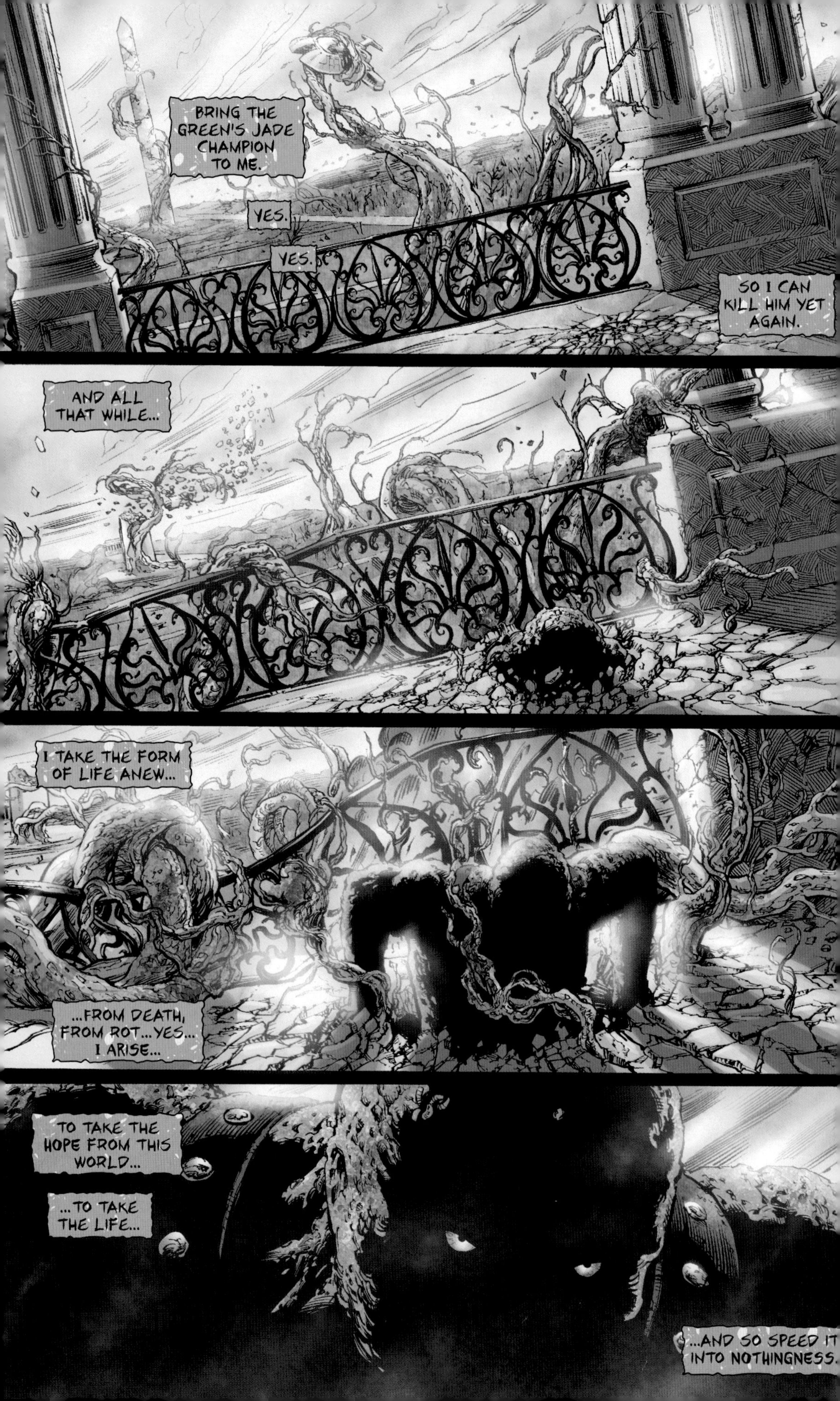
BRING THE GREEN'S JADE CHAMPION TO ME.
YES.
YES.
SO I CAN KILL HIM YET AGAIN.
AND ALL THAT WHILE...
I TAKE THE FORM OF LIFE ANEW...
...FROM DEATH, FROM ROT...YES... I ARISE...
TO TAKE THE HOPE FROM THIS WORLD...
...TO TAKE THE LIFE...
...AND SO SPEED IT INTO NOTHINGNESS.

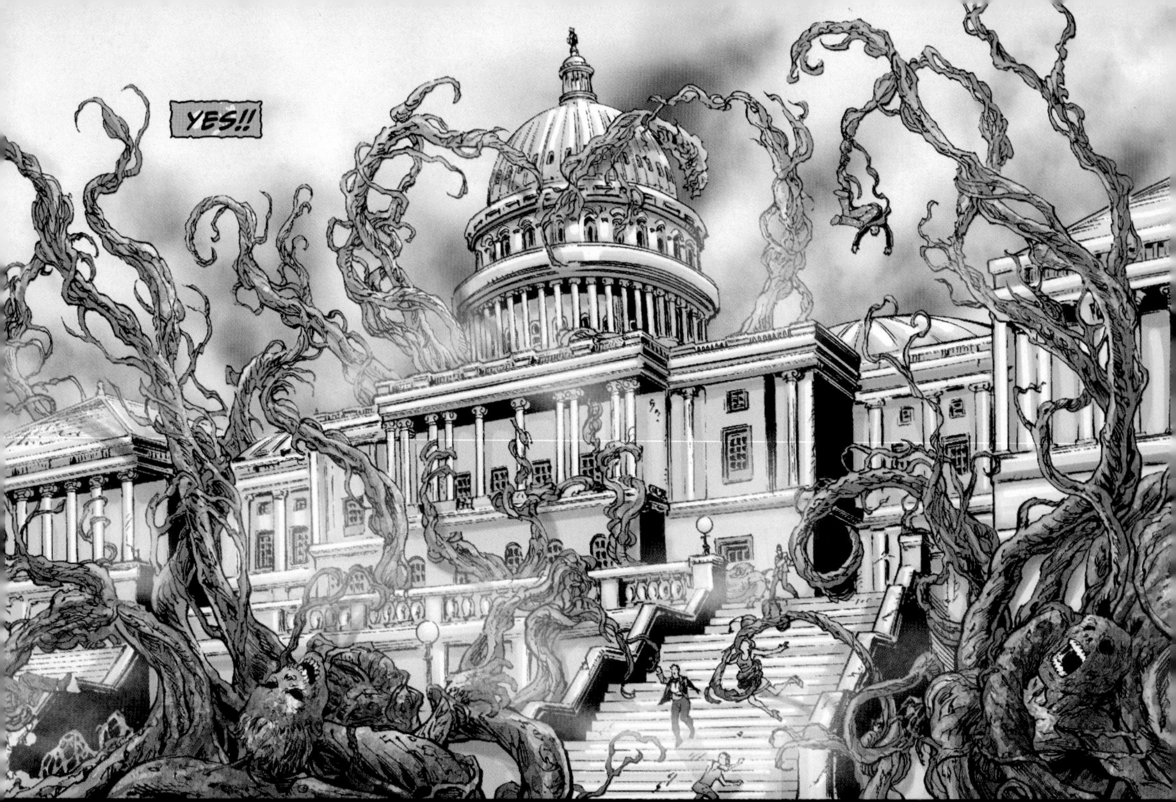
YES!!

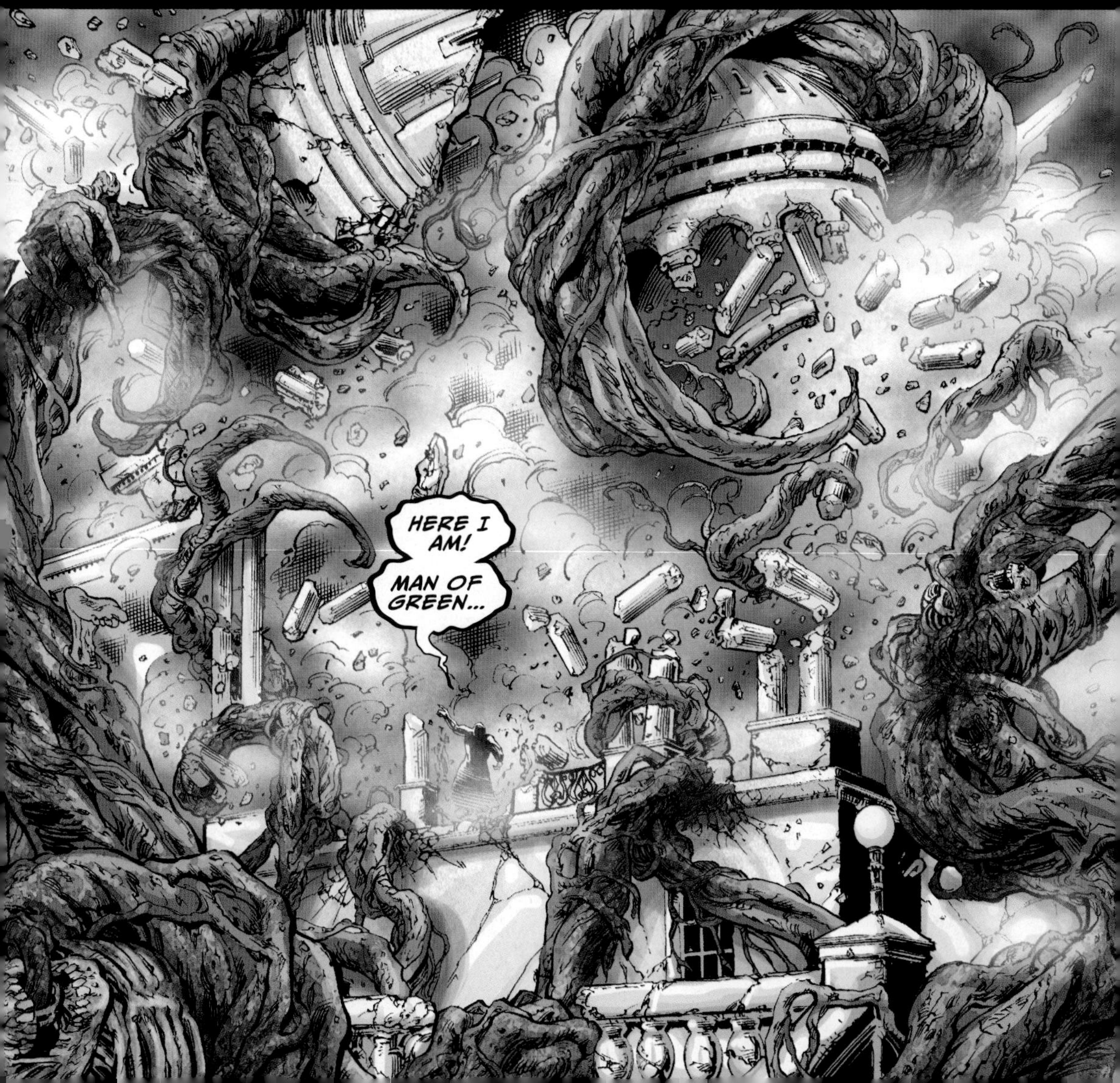
HERE I AM!
MAN OF GREEN...

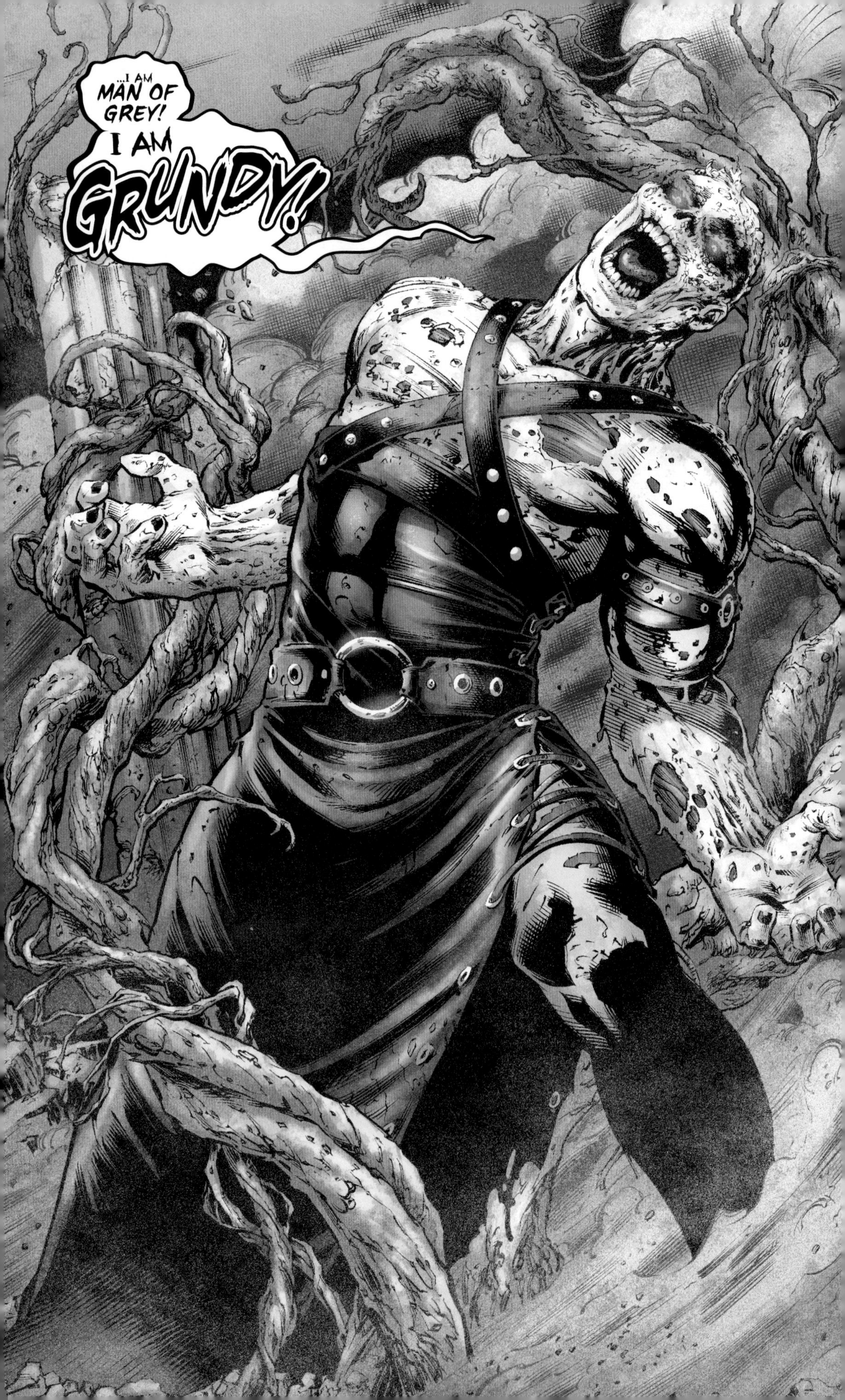
...I AM MAN OF GREY!
I AM GRUNDY!

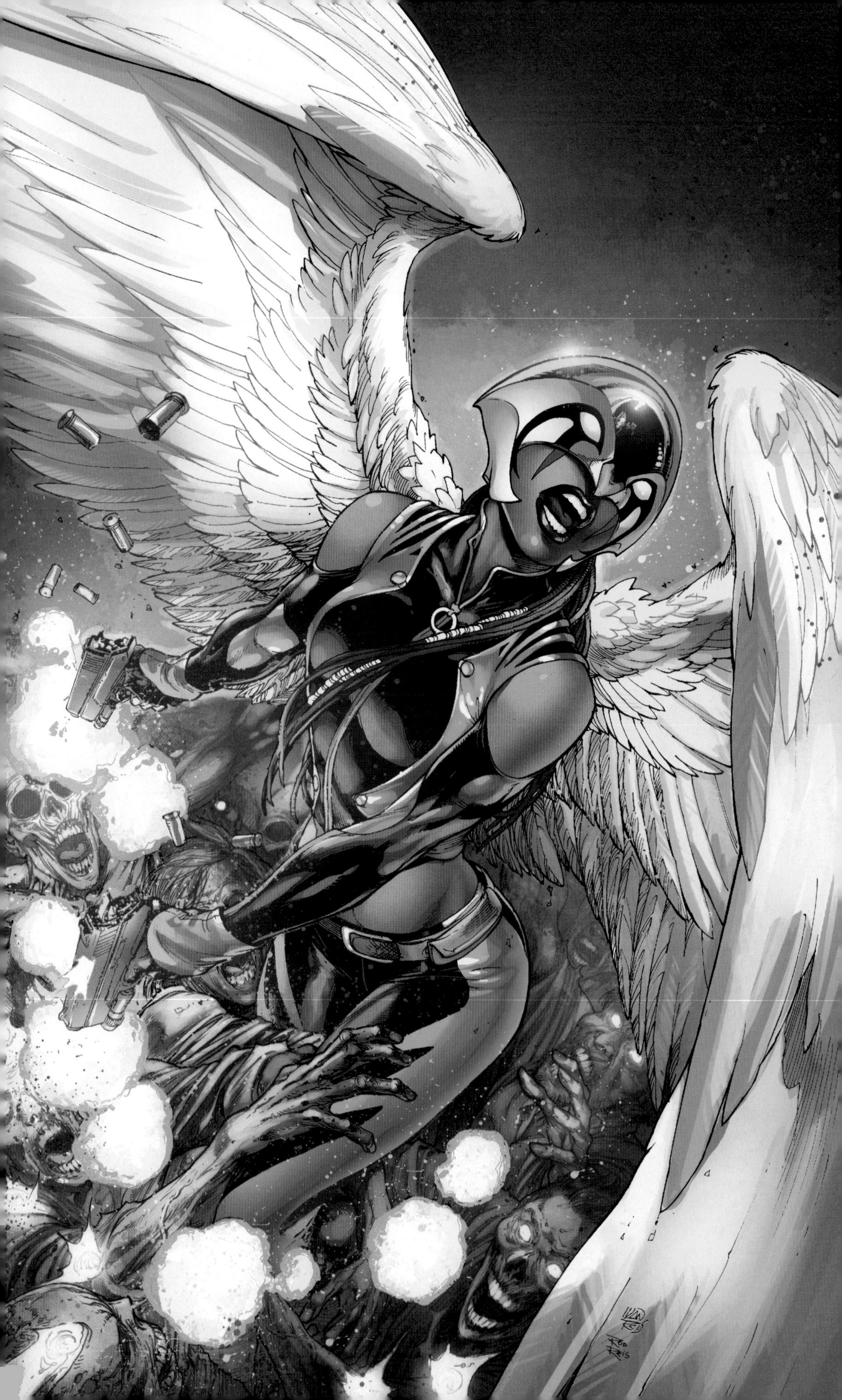

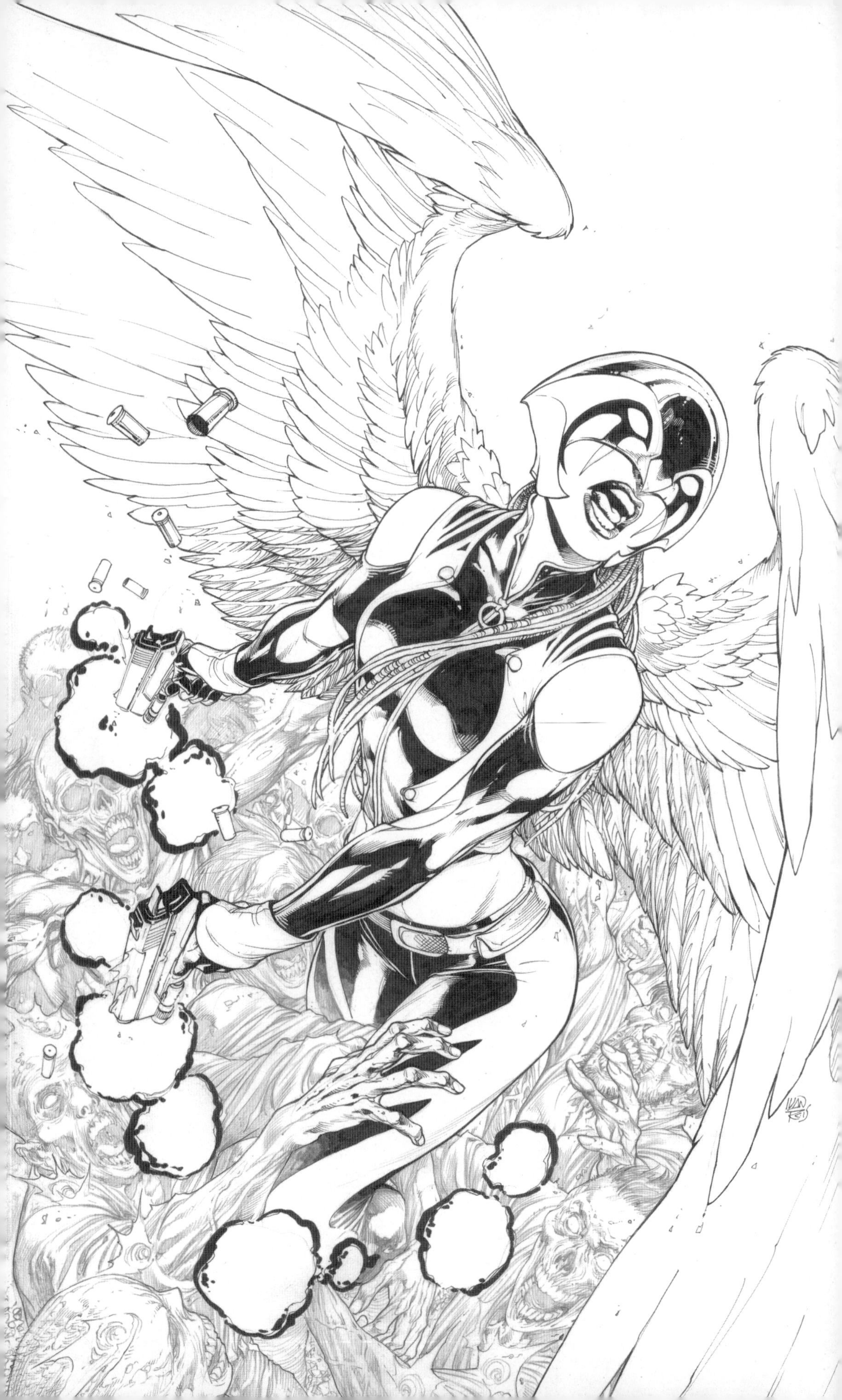

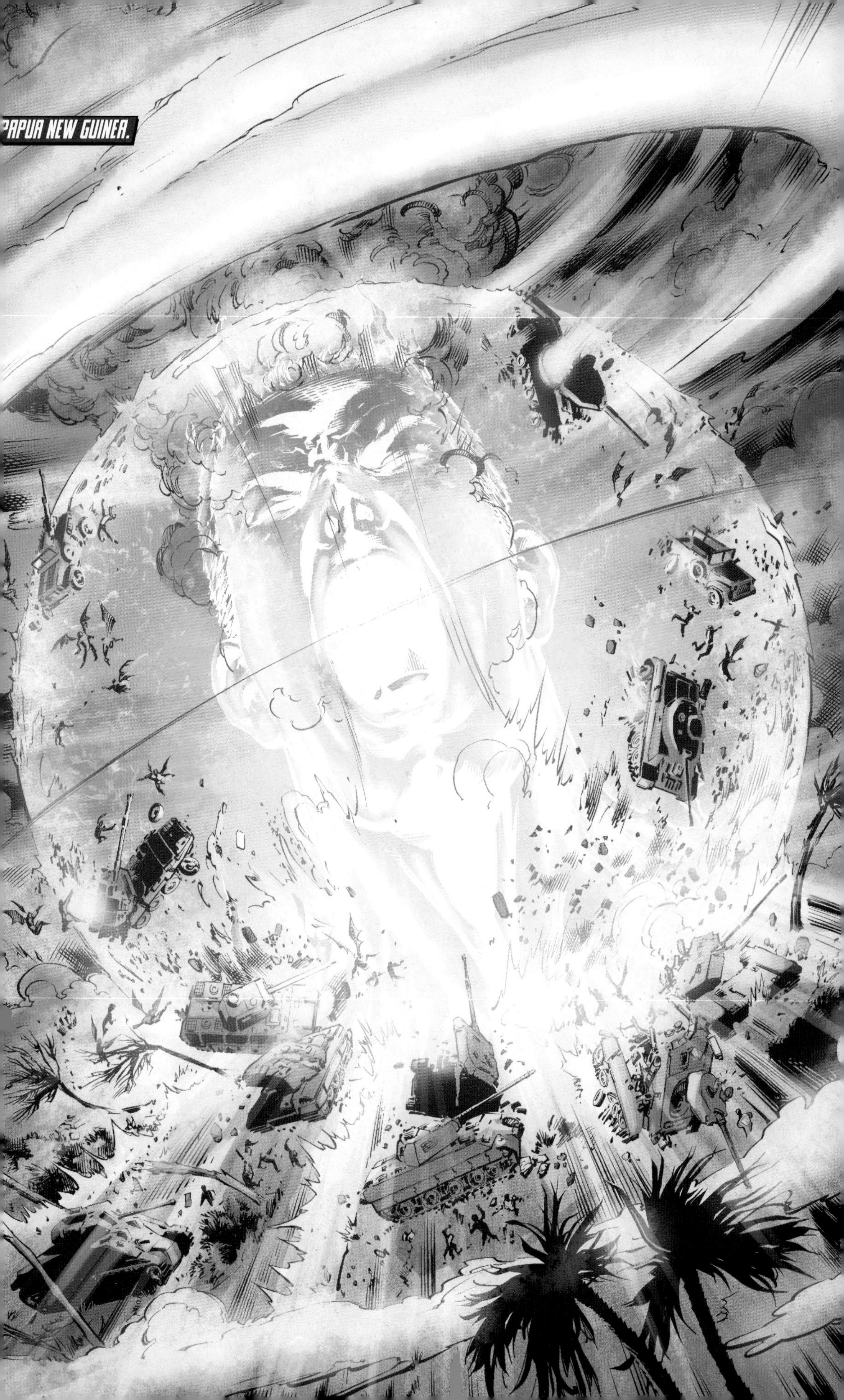
PAPUA NEW GUINEA.

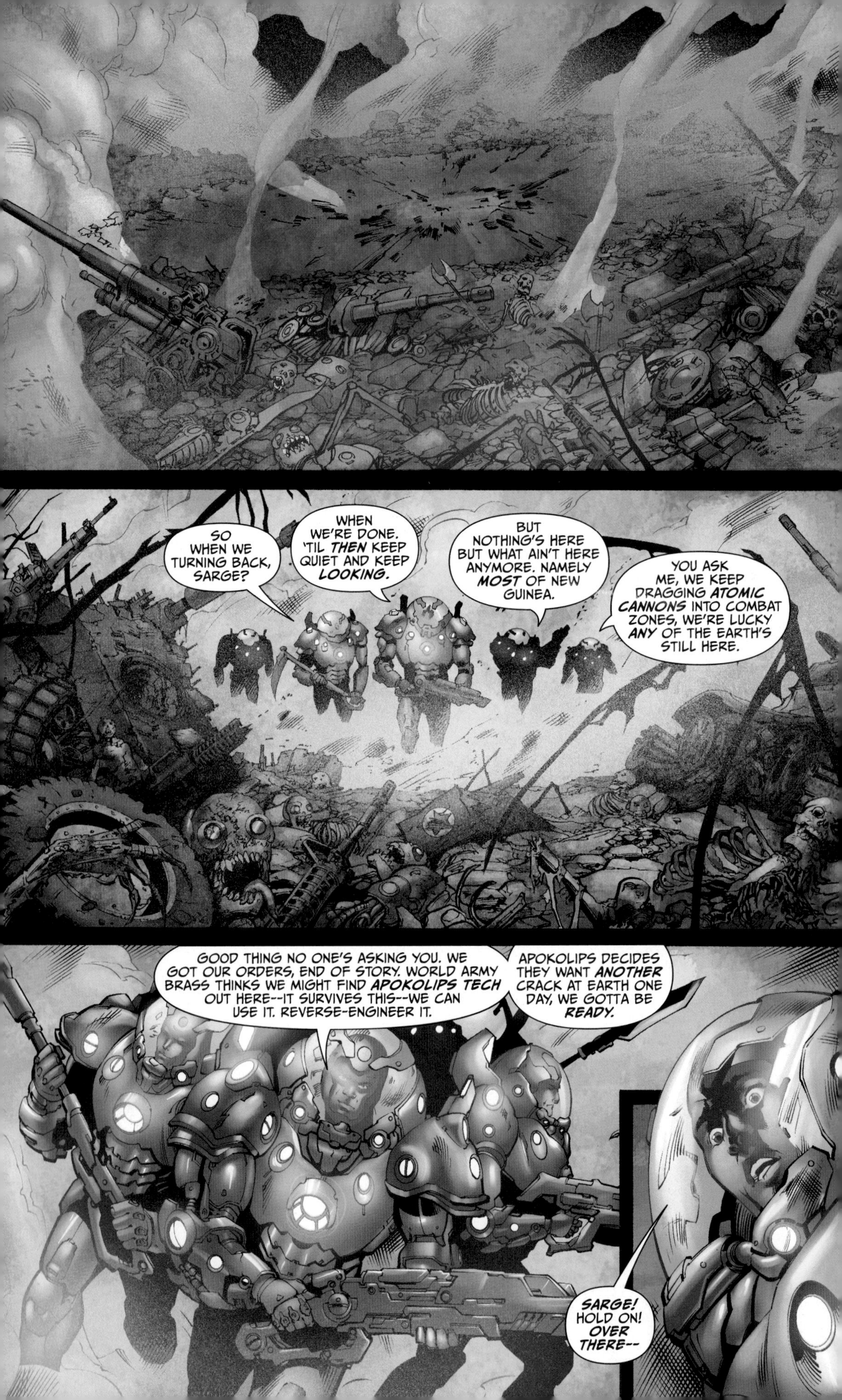
SO WHEN WE TURNING BACK, SARGE?
WHEN WE'RE DONE. 'TIL *THEN* KEEP QUIET AND KEEP *LOOKING.*
BUT NOTHING'S HERE BUT WHAT AIN'T HERE ANYMORE. NAMELY *MOST* OF NEW GUINEA.
YOU ASK ME, WE KEEP DRAGGING *ATOMIC CANNONS* INTO COMBAT ZONES, WE'RE LUCKY *ANY* OF THE EARTH'S STILL HERE.
GOOD THING NO ONE'S ASKING YOU. WE GOT OUR ORDERS, END OF STORY. WORLD ARMY BRASS THINKS WE MIGHT FIND *APOKOLIPS TECH* OUT HERE--IT SURVIVES THIS--WE CAN USE IT. REVERSE-ENGINEER IT.
APOKOLIPS DECIDES THEY WANT *ANOTHER* CRACK AT EARTH ONE DAY, WE GOTTA BE *READY.*
SARGE! HOLD ON! *OVER THERE--*

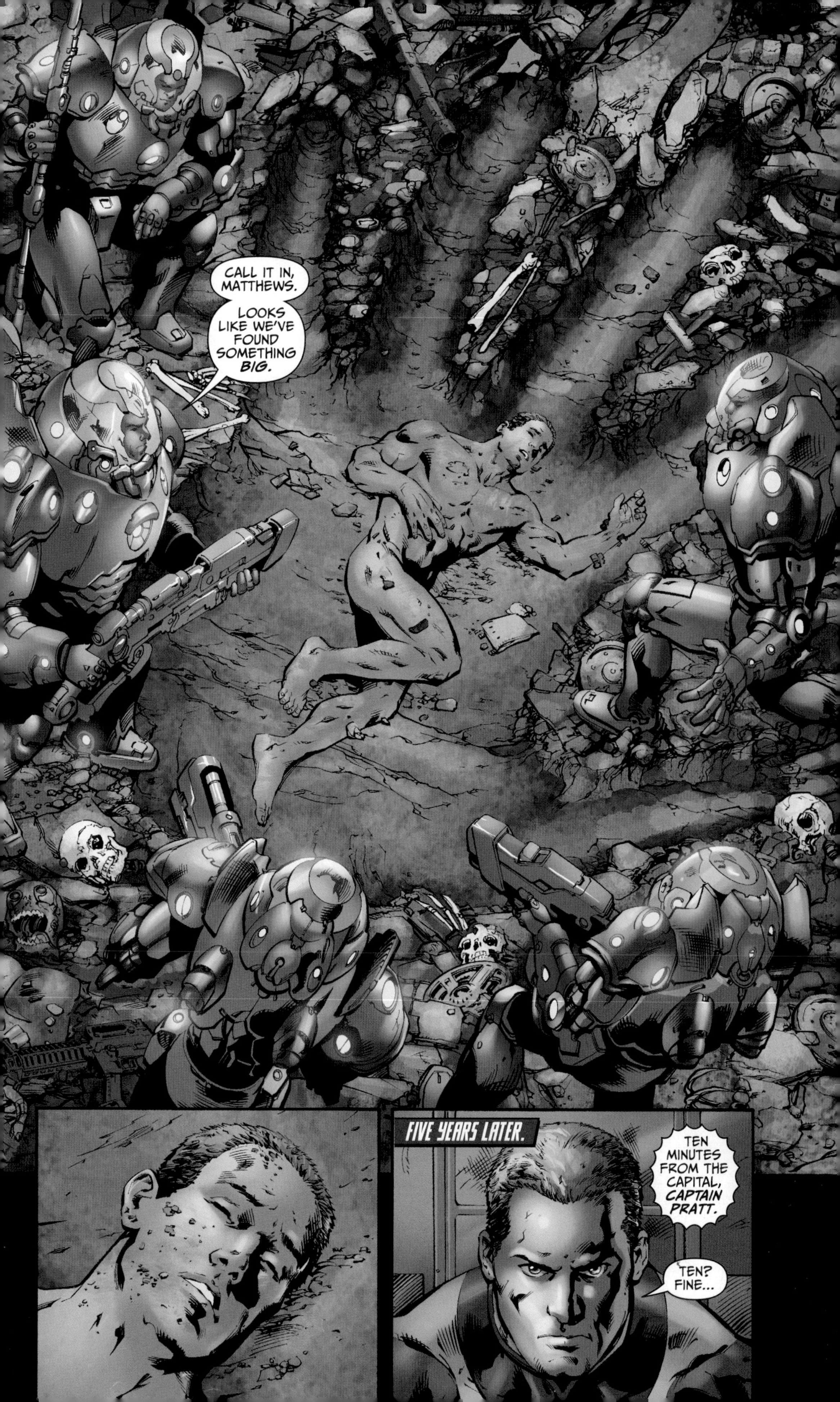
CALL IT IN, MATTHEWS.
LOOKS LIKE WE'VE FOUND SOMETHING BIG.
FIVE YEARS LATER.
TEN MINUTES FROM THE CAPITAL, CAPTAIN PRATT.
TEN? FINE...

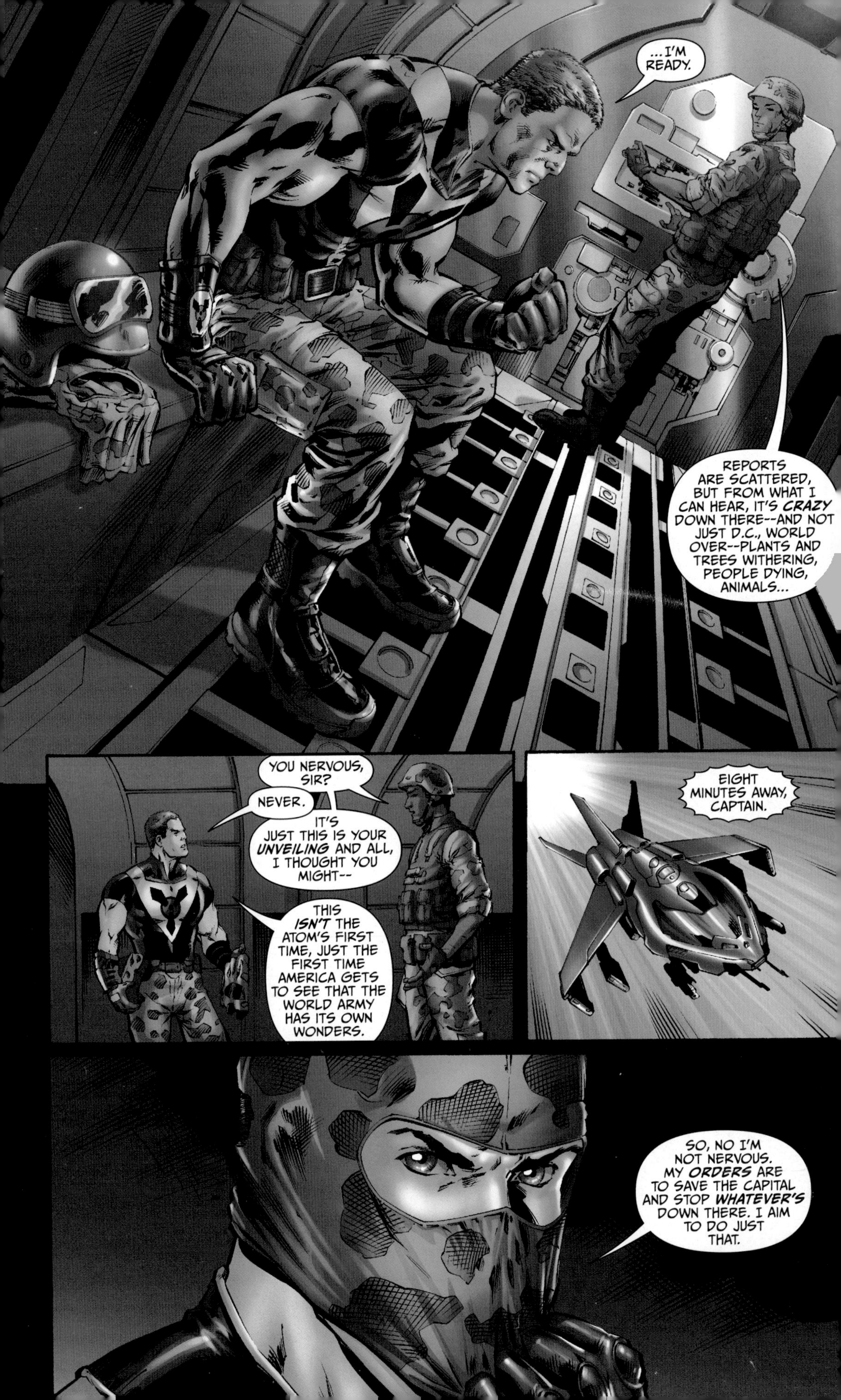
...I'M READY.
REPORTS ARE SCATTERED, BUT FROM WHAT I CAN HEAR, IT'S *CRAZY* DOWN THERE--AND NOT JUST D.C., WORLD OVER--PLANTS AND TREES WITHERING, PEOPLE DYING, ANIMALS...
YOU NERVOUS, SIR?
NEVER.
IT'S JUST THIS IS YOUR *UNVEILING* AND ALL, I THOUGHT YOU MIGHT--
THIS *ISN'T* THE ATOM'S FIRST TIME, JUST THE FIRST TIME AMERICA GETS TO SEE THAT THE WORLD ARMY HAS ITS OWN WONDERS.
EIGHT MINUTES AWAY, CAPTAIN.
SO, NO I'M NOT NERVOUS. MY *ORDERS* ARE TO SAVE THE CAPITAL AND STOP *WHATEVER'S* DOWN THERE. I AIM TO DO JUST THAT.

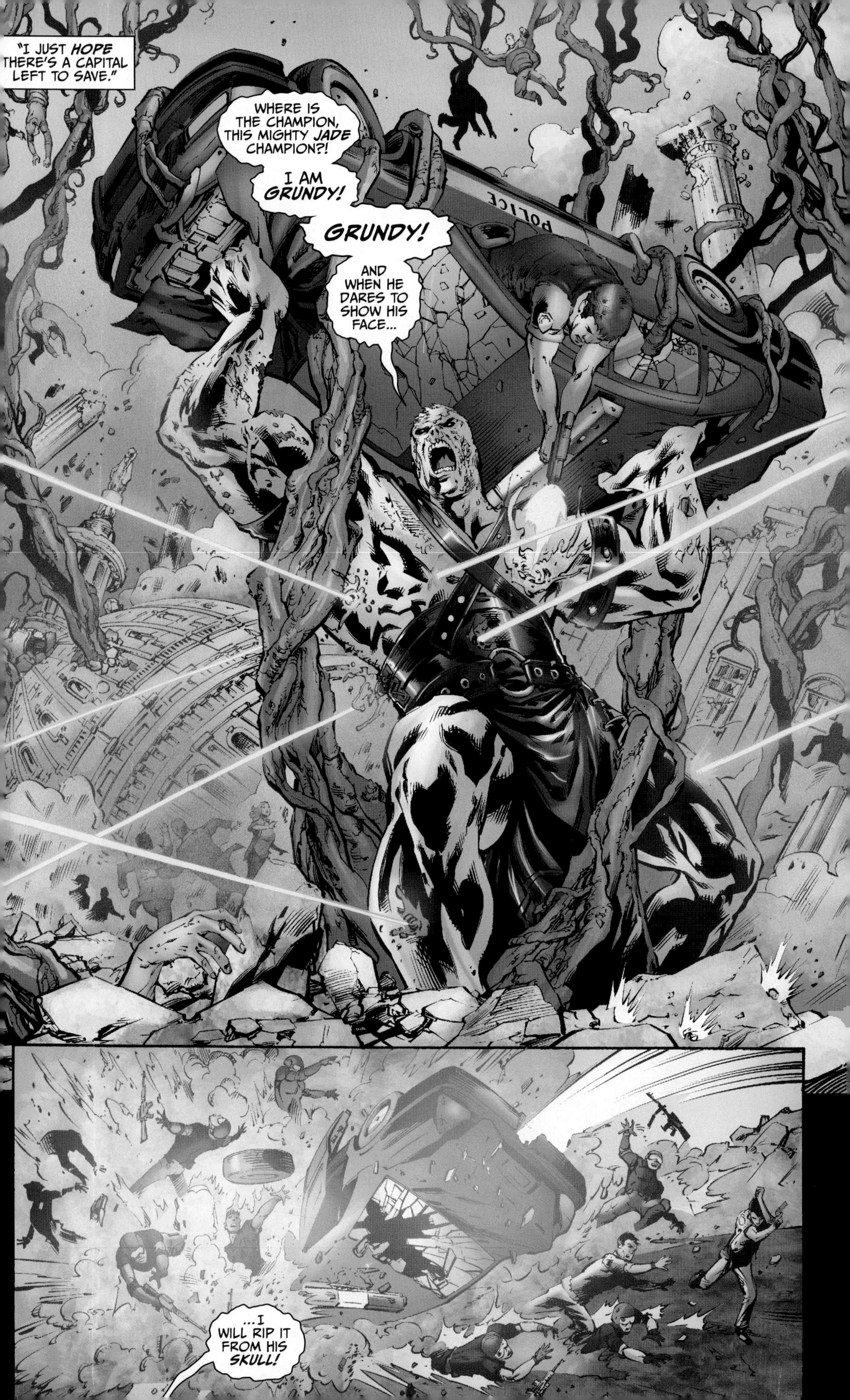
"I JUST *HOPE* THERE'S A CAPITAL LEFT TO SAVE."
WHERE IS THE CHAMPION, THIS MIGHTY *JADE* CHAMPION?!
I AM *GRUNDY!*
GRUNDY!
AND WHEN HE DARES TO SHOW HIS FACE...
POLICE
...I WILL RIP IT FROM HIS *SKULL!*

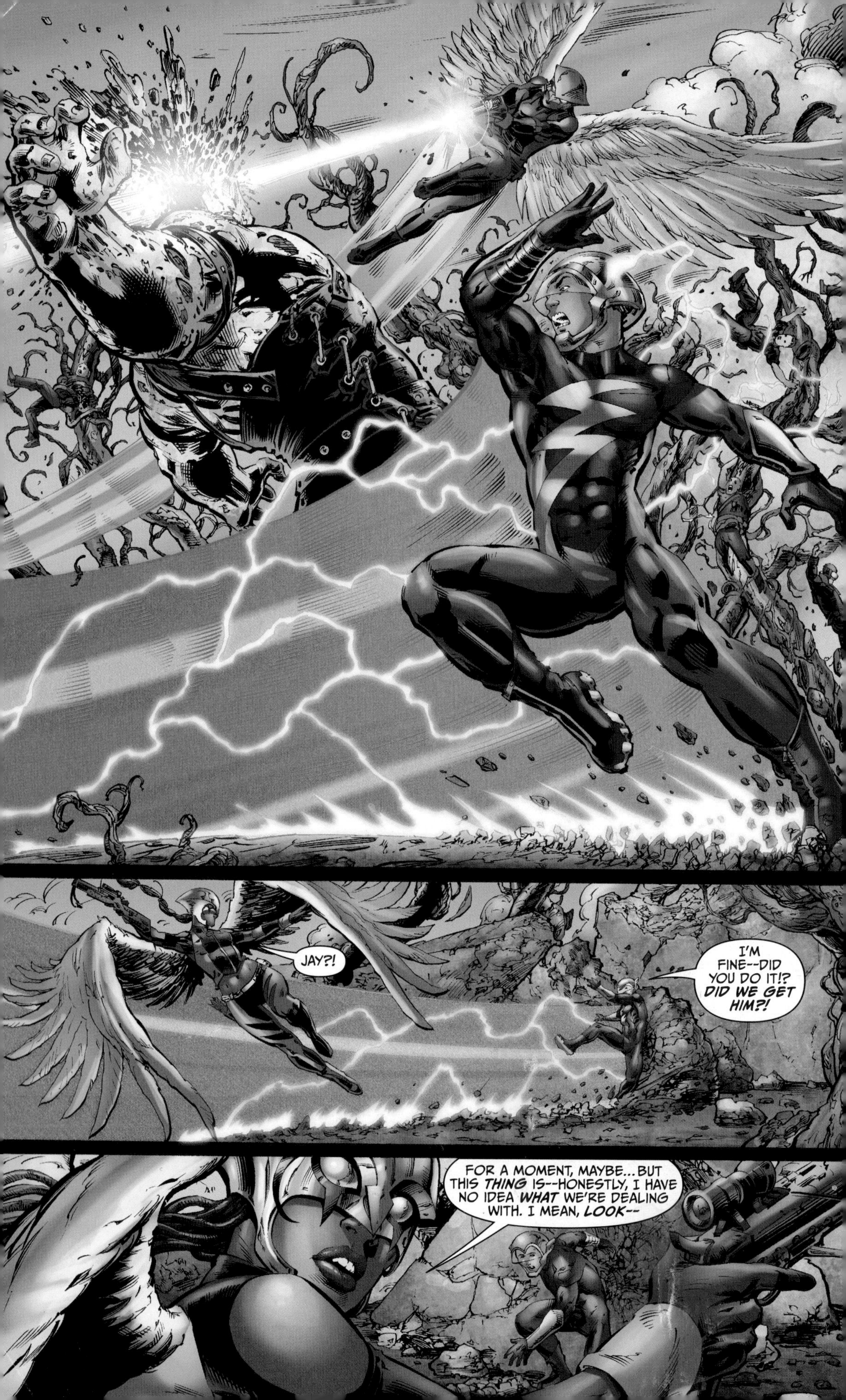
JAY?!
I'M FINE--DID YOU DO IT!? DID WE GET HIM?!
FOR A MOMENT, MAYBE...BUT THIS THING IS--HONESTLY, I HAVE NO IDEA WHAT WE'RE DEALING WITH. I MEAN, LOOK--

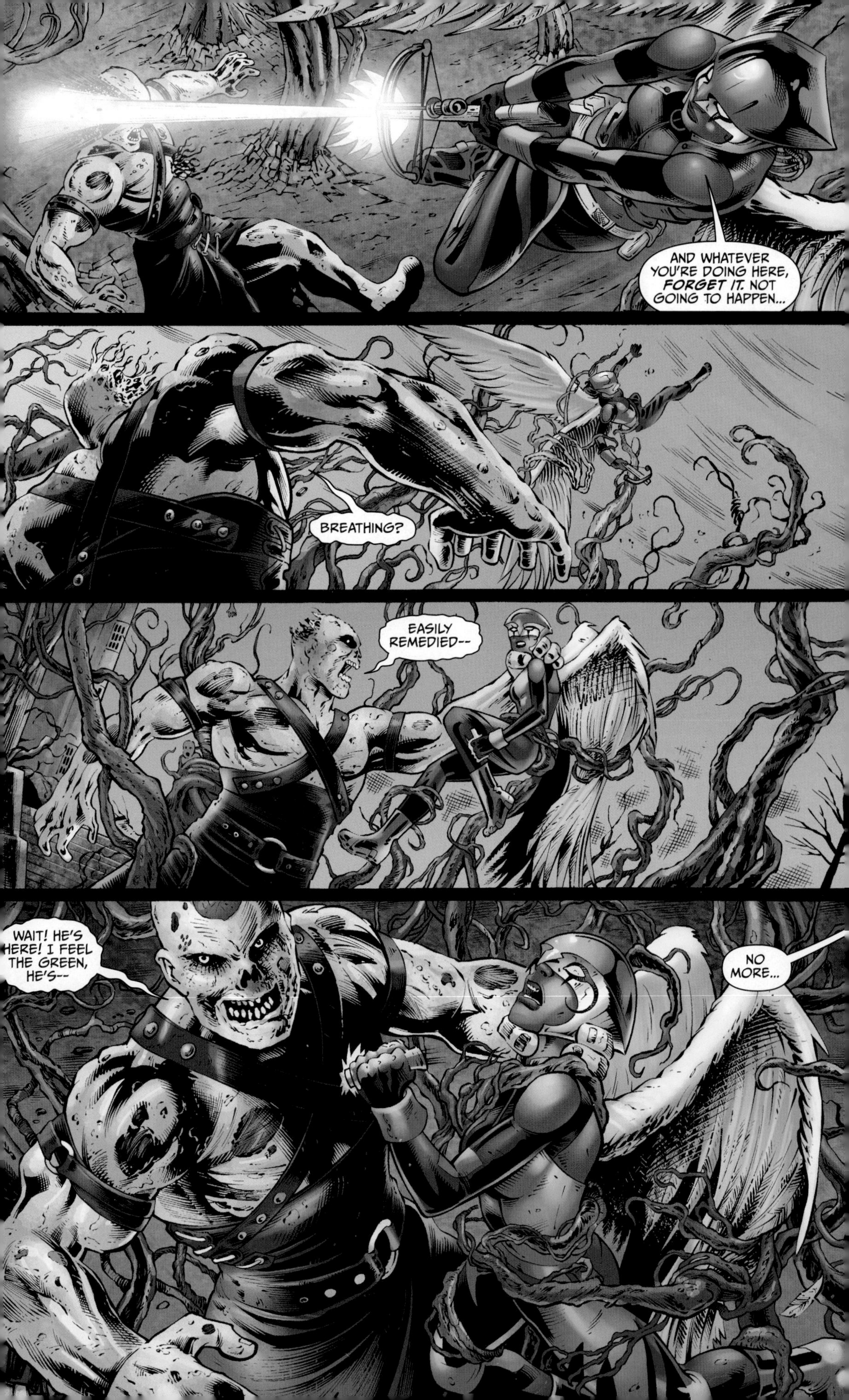
AND WHATEVER YOU'RE DOING HERE, **FORGET IT.** NOT GOING TO HAPPEN...
BREATHING?
EASILY REMEDIED--
WAIT! HE'S HERE! I FEEL THE GREEN, HE'S--
NO MORE...

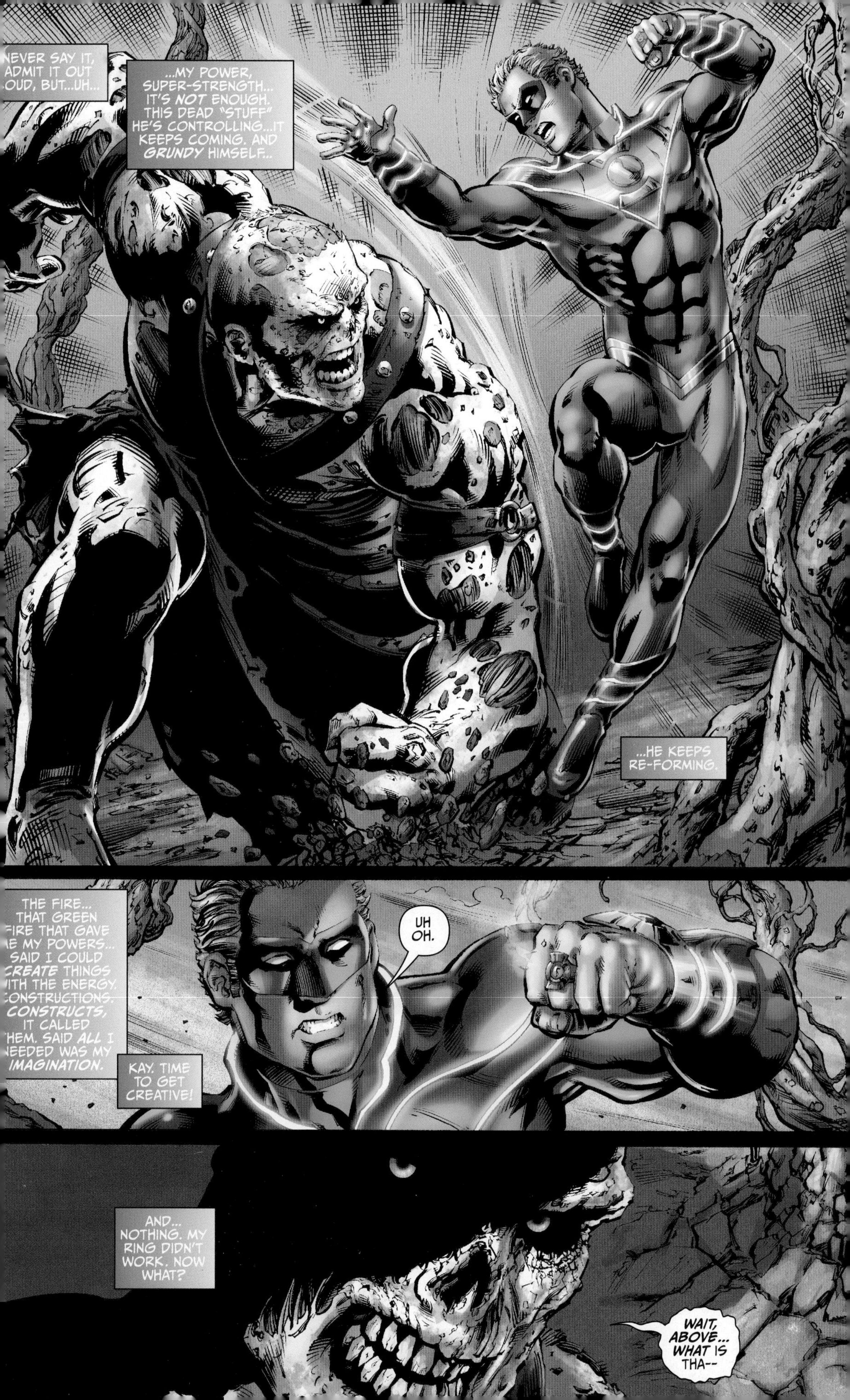
NEVER SAY IT, ADMIT IT OUT LOUD, BUT...UH...
...MY POWER, SUPER-STRENGTH... IT'S NOT ENOUGH. THIS DEAD "STUFF" HE'S CONTROLLING...IT KEEPS COMING. AND GRUNDY HIMSELF...
...HE KEEPS RE-FORMING.
THE FIRE... THAT GREEN FIRE THAT GAVE ME MY POWERS... SAID I COULD CREATE THINGS WITH THE ENERGY. CONSTRUCTIONS. CONSTRUCTS, IT CALLED THEM. SAID ALL I NEEDED WAS MY IMAGINATION.
KAY. TIME TO GET CREATIVE!
UH OH.
AND... NOTHING. MY RING DIDN'T WORK. NOW WHAT?
WAIT, ABOVE... WHAT IS THA--

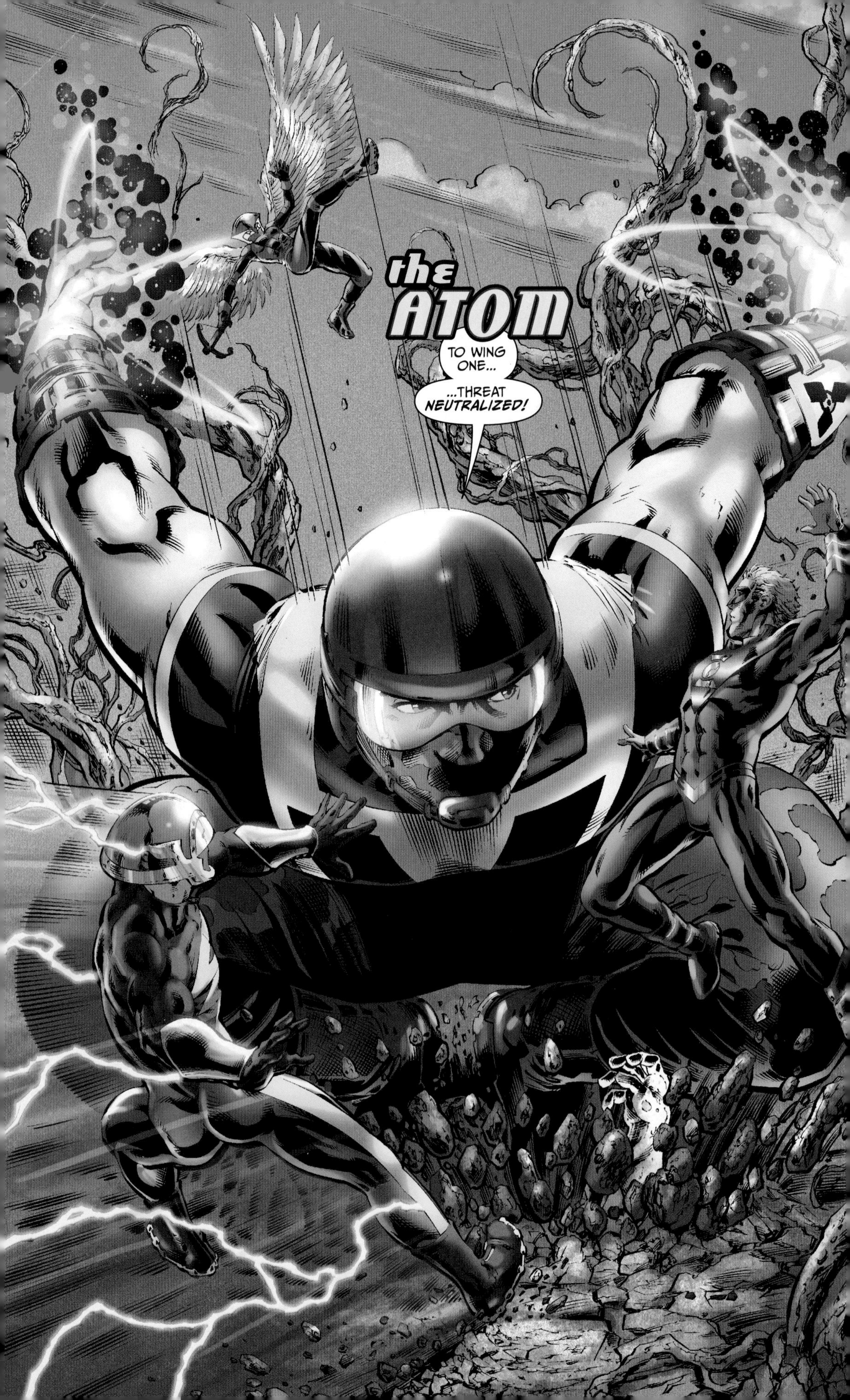
the ATOM
TO WING ONE...
...THREAT NEUTRALIZED!

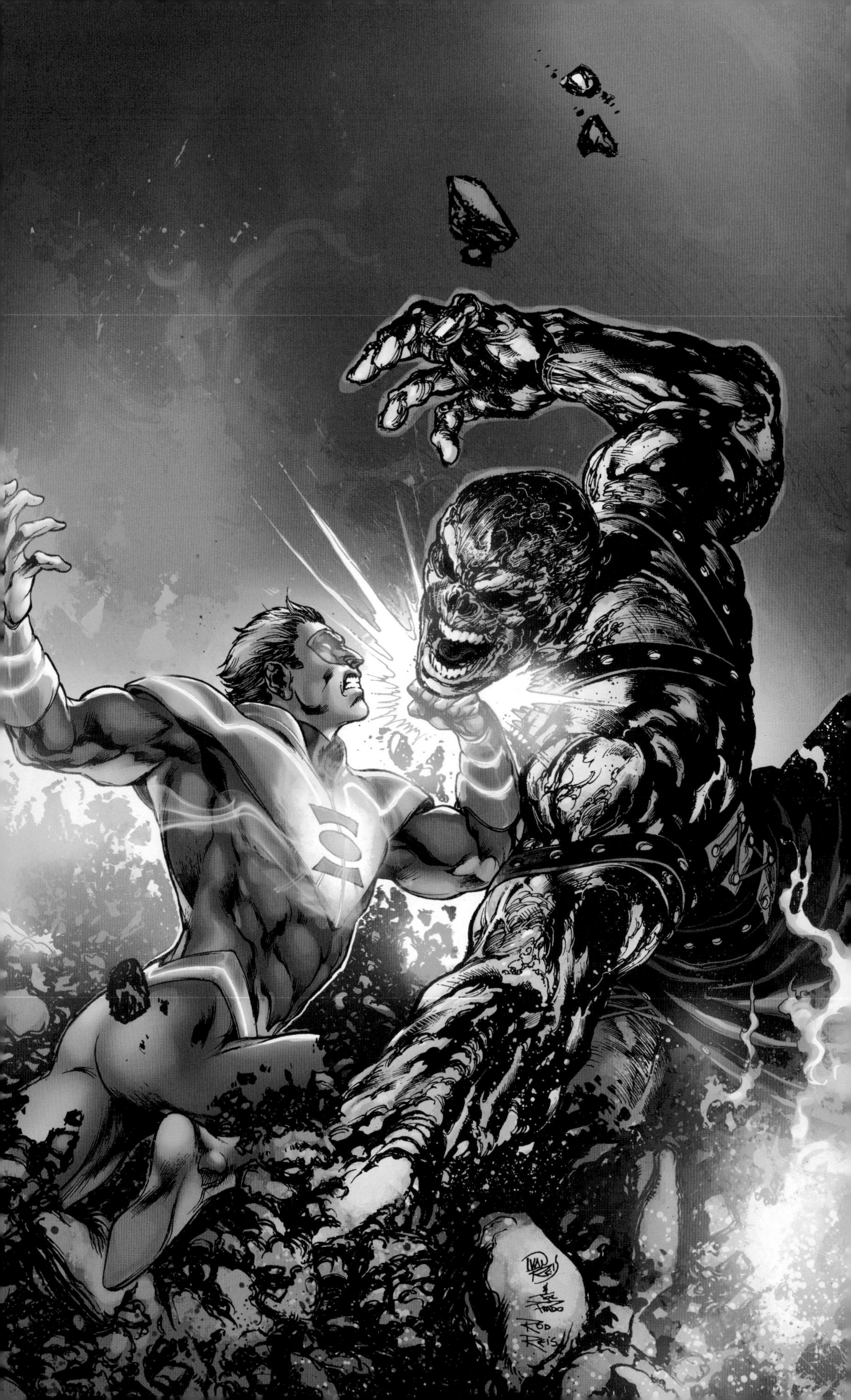

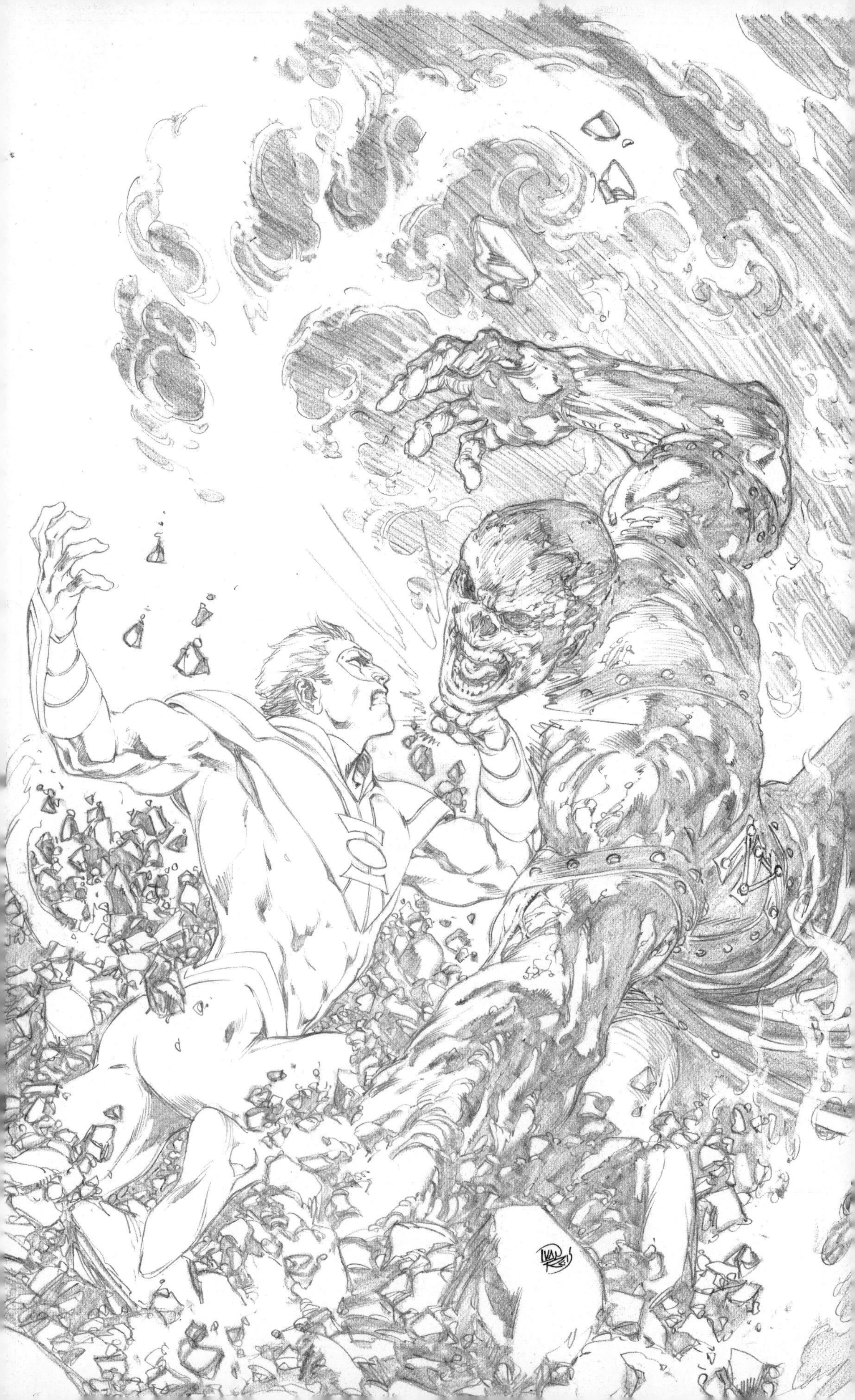

DODDS REPORTING. LIGHTFOOT IS SECURE. EN ROUTE TO BUNKER.

COMMANDER DODDS AND HIS "SANDMEN" COME THROUGH AGAIN.

YES. HANDY FELLOW, DODDS.

OF COURSE HIS BEING CANADIAN AND SAVING THE PRESIDENT...THE PRESS CORPS WILL LOVE THAT.

WELL, WORLD ARMY MEANS WE'RE ALL IN THIS TOGETHER, GENERAL, AND HER SECURITY DETAIL CERTAINLY WASN'T UP TO THE TASK OF PROTECTING HER. NOT AGAINST THAT ANYWAY.

STILL, GETTING THE PRESIDENT TUCKED AWAY SAFELY DOESN'T HELP ASCERTAIN WHAT "THAT" IS, EXACTLY. WHAT IN GOD'S NAME IS GOING ON IN WASHINGTON, KHAN?

NUKE D.C.? HOLD ON! GENTLEMEN OF THE WORLD COUNCIL...

...WE'RE STILL TRYING TO MAKE SENSE OF THE SITUATION, BUT--

YOU'RE COMMANDER OF SENTINEL, KHAN... WORLD ARMY INTEL. WE EXPECT YOU TO HAVE ALREADY MADE SENSE OF IT.

CHIEF MARSHAL VODCHENKO, WITH ALL DUE RESPECT...

...SHUT YOUR MOUTH AND LISTEN TO ME.

THIS IS WHAT WE KNOW. THE WORLD IS DYING. OUR SCIENTISTS HAVE THE CLOCK AT INSIDE TWO DAYS BEFORE THE EARTH PERISHES THROUGH THE DESTRUCTION OF ALL PLANT LIFE, MEANING NO OXYGEN PRODUCTION.

THE CAUSE OF THIS DESTRUCTION APPEARS TO BE THE CREATURE IN D.C....

...GRUNDY. HE DRAWS POWER FROM DYING THINGS AND THEN CONTROLS THEM WHEN DEAD. SUPER STRONG TOO.

BUT THERE'S MORE, GENTLEMEN. ALMOST IMMEDIATELY UPON GRUNDY'S APPEARANCE, HE WAS ATTACKED... COUNTERATTACKED I SHOULD SAY...

...APPARENTLY BY NEW WONDERS.

LIKE SUPERMAN?

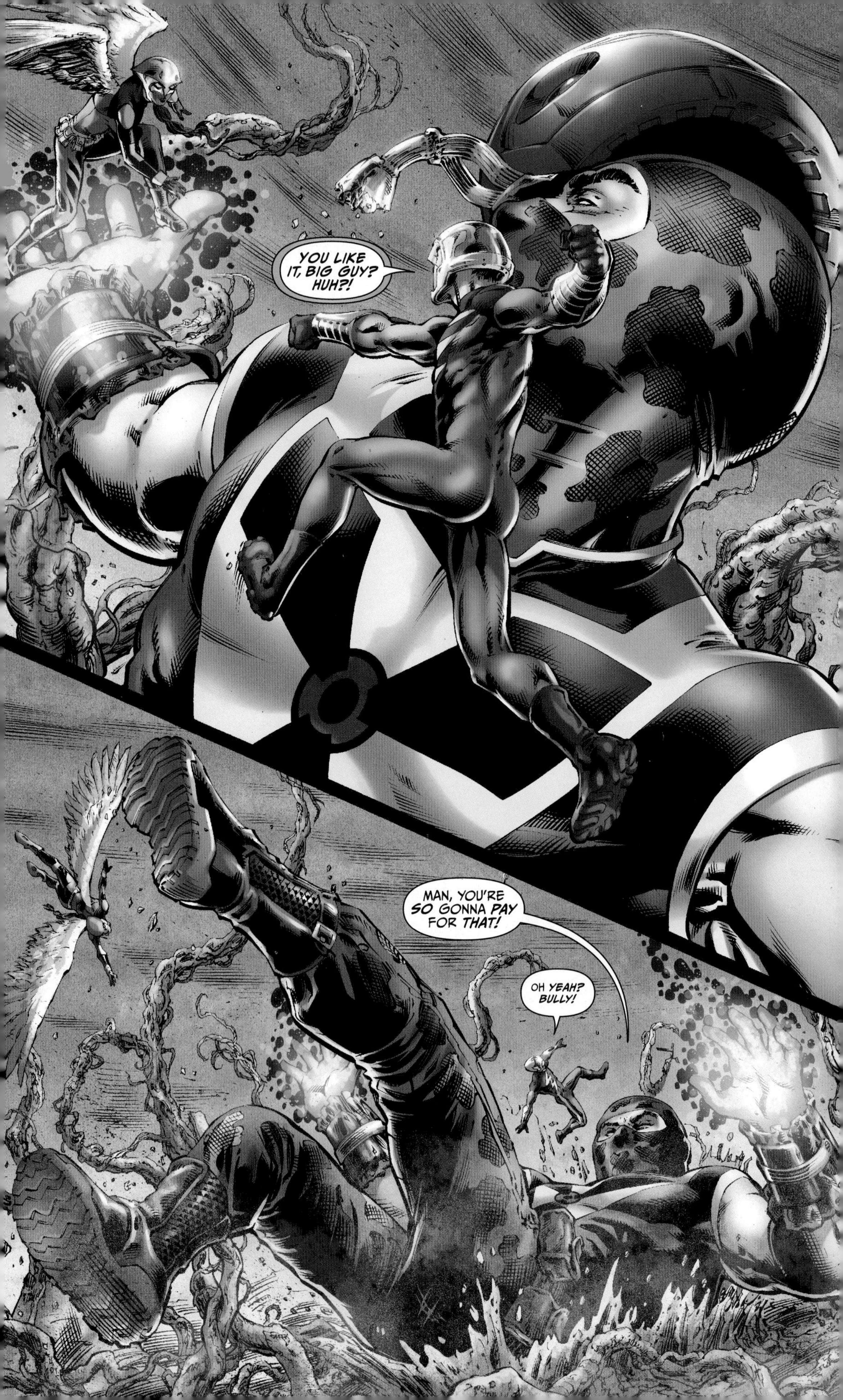
YOU LIKE IT, BIG GUY? HUH?!
MAN, YOU'RE SO GONNA PAY FOR THAT!
OH YEAH? BULLY!

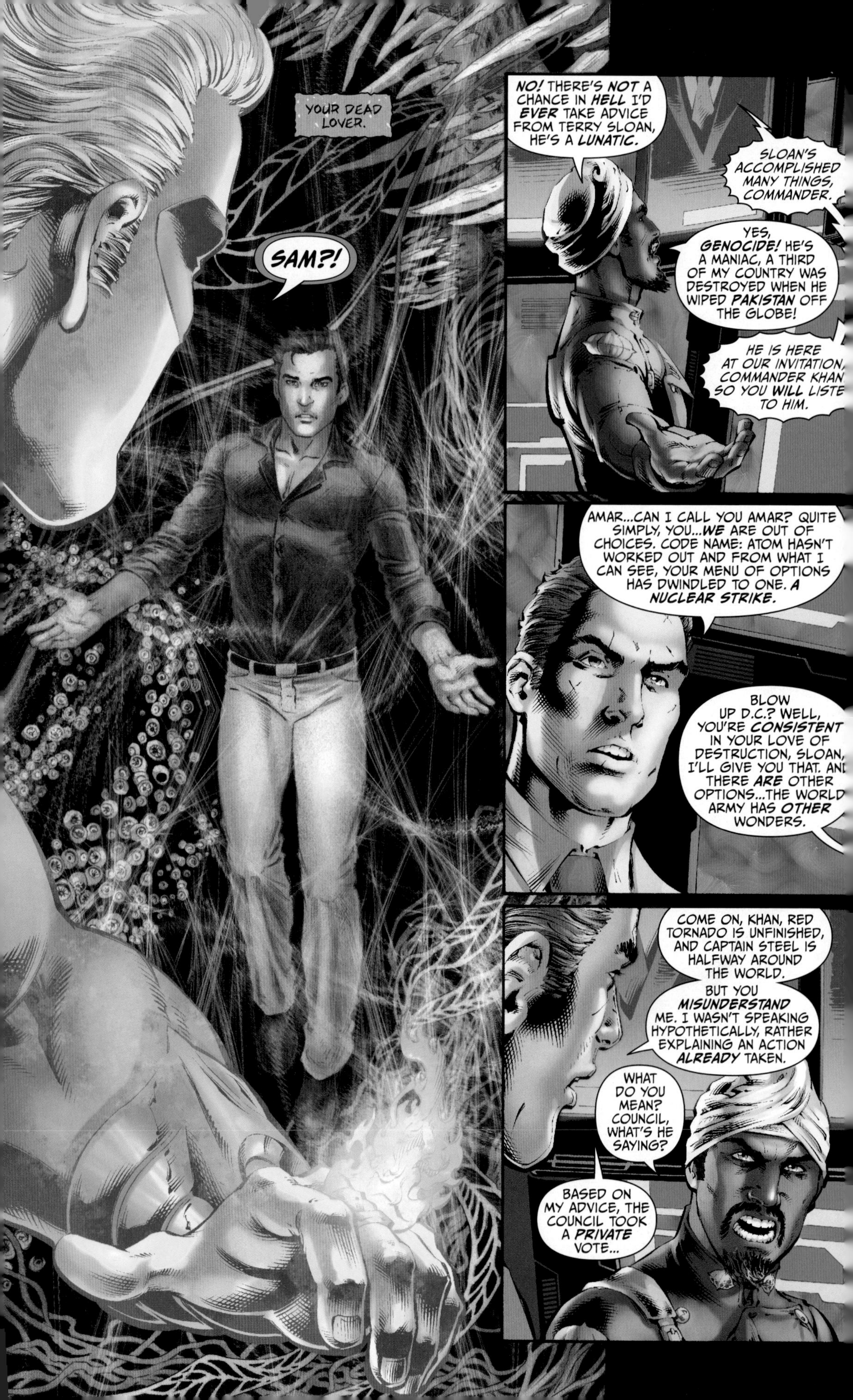
YOUR DEAD LOVER.
SAM?!
NO! THERE'S NOT A CHANCE IN HELL I'D EVER TAKE ADVICE FROM TERRY SLOAN, HE'S A LUNATIC.
SLOAN'S ACCOMPLISHED MANY THINGS, COMMANDER.
YES, GENOCIDE! HE'S A MANIAC, A THIRD OF MY COUNTRY WAS DESTROYED WHEN HE WIPED PAKISTAN OFF THE GLOBE!
HE IS HERE AT OUR INVITATION, COMMANDER KHAN SO YOU WILL LISTE TO HIM.
AMAR...CAN I CALL YOU AMAR? QUITE SIMPLY, YOU...WE ARE OUT OF CHOICES. CODE NAME: ATOM HASN'T WORKED OUT AND FROM WHAT I CAN SEE, YOUR MENU OF OPTIONS HAS DWINDLED TO ONE. A NUCLEAR STRIKE.
BLOW UP D.C.? WELL, YOU'RE CONSISTENT IN YOUR LOVE OF DESTRUCTION, SLOAN, I'LL GIVE YOU THAT. ANI THERE ARE OTHER OPTIONS...THE WORLD ARMY HAS OTHER WONDERS.
COME ON, KHAN, RED TORNADO IS UNFINISHED, AND CAPTAIN STEEL IS HALFWAY AROUND THE WORLD.
BUT YOU MISUNDERSTAND ME. I WASN'T SPEAKING HYPOTHETICALLY, RATHER EXPLAINING AN ACTION ALREADY TAKEN.
WHAT DO YOU MEAN? COUNCIL, WHAT'S HE SAYING?
BASED ON MY ADVICE, THE COUNCIL TOOK A PRIVATE VOTE...

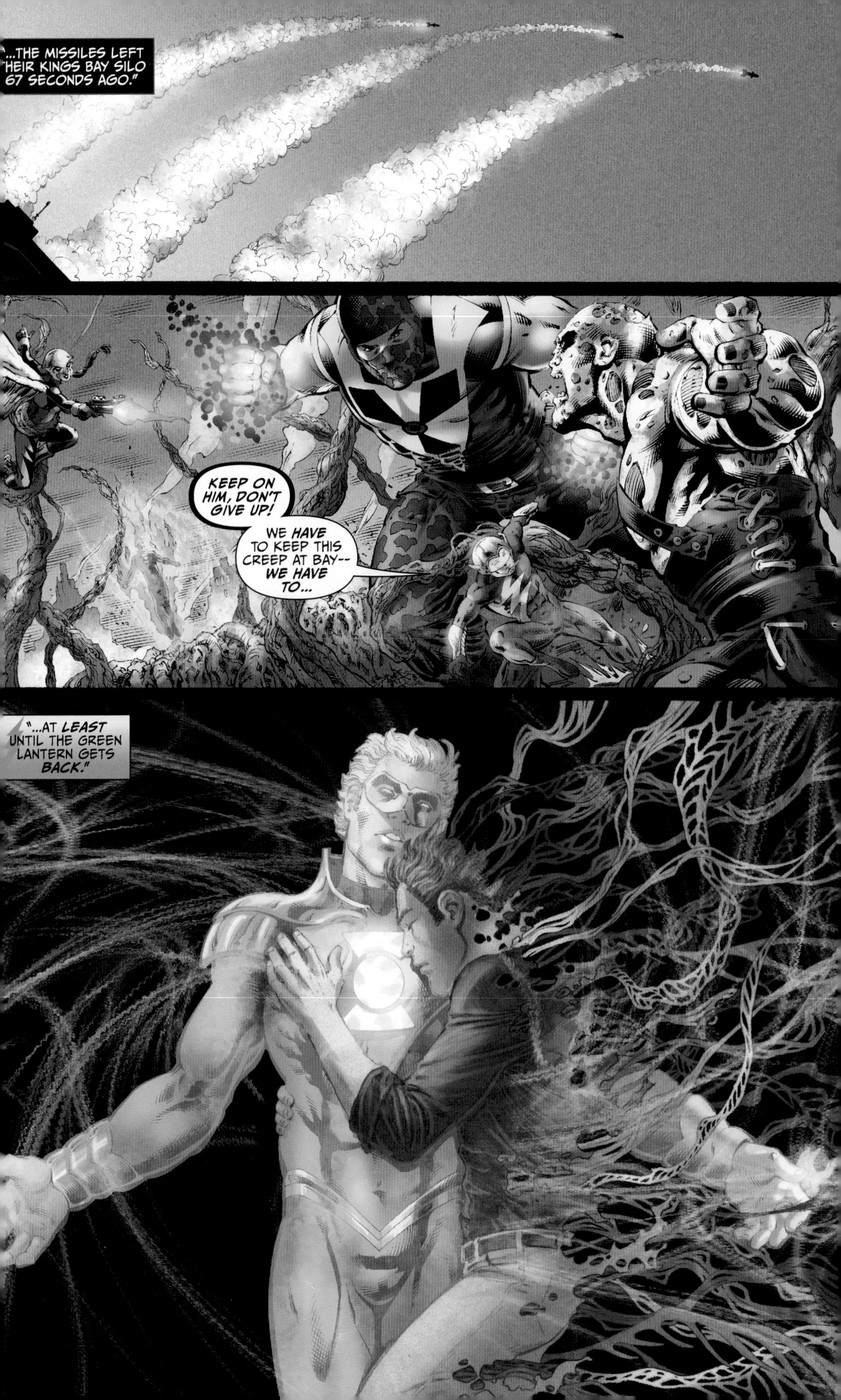
"...THE MISSILES LEFT HEIR KINGS BAY SILO 67 SECONDS AGO."
KEEP ON HIM, DON'T GIVE UP!
WE HAVE TO KEEP THIS CREEP AT BAY-- WE HAVE TO...
"...AT LEAST UNTIL THE GREEN LANTERN GETS BACK."

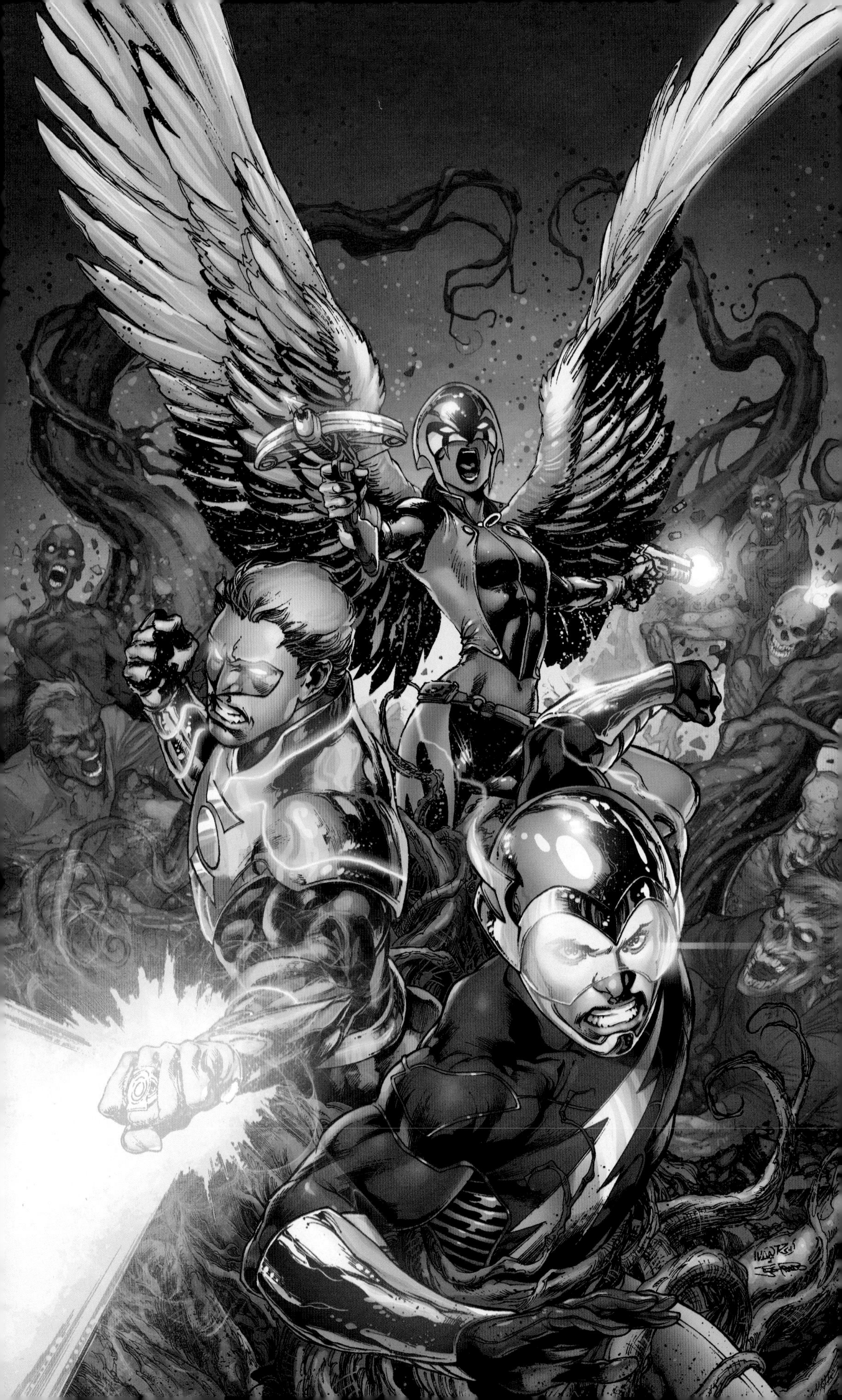

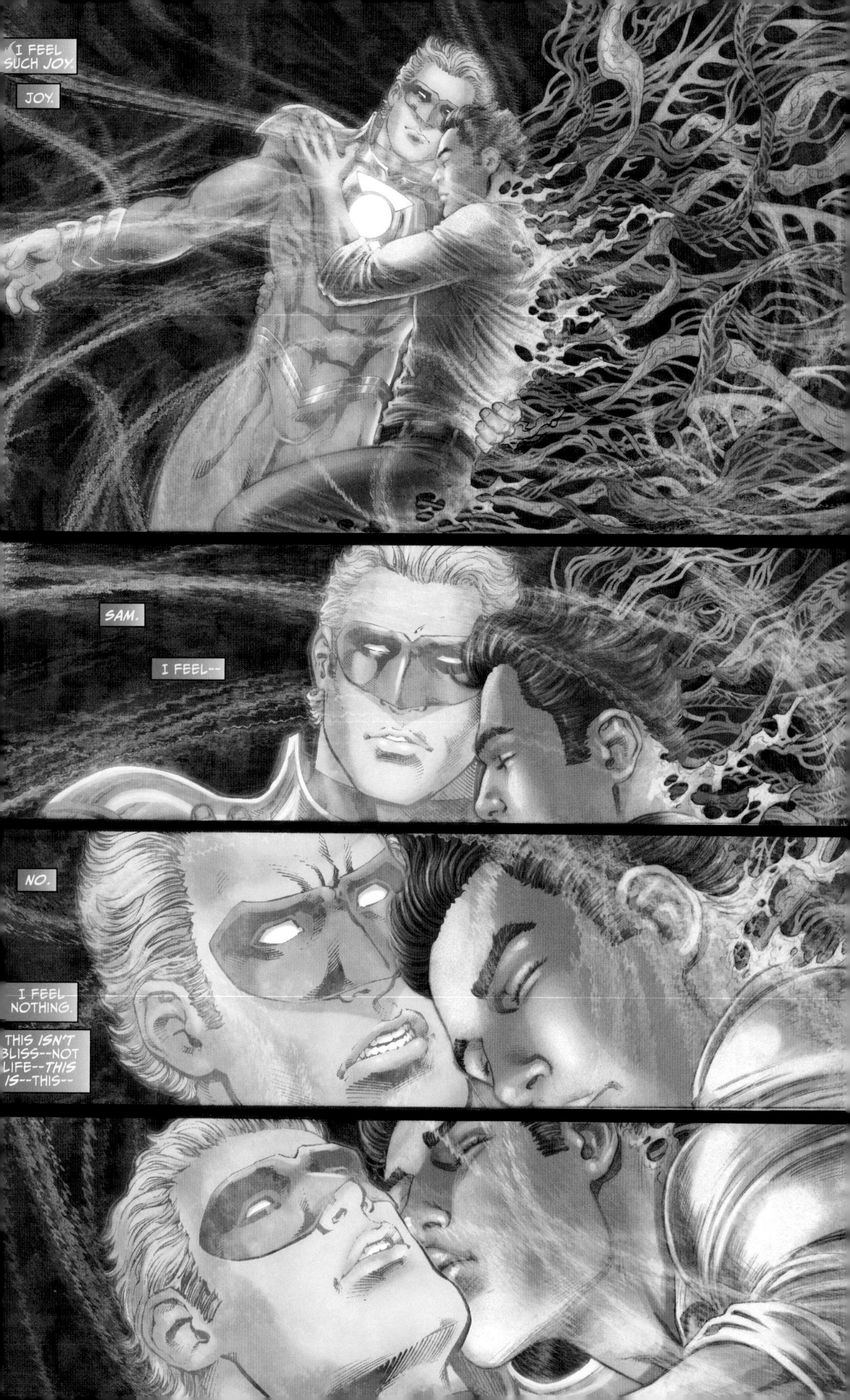
I FEEL SUCH JOY.
JOY.
SAM.
I FEEL--
NO.
I FEEL NOTHING.
THIS ISN'T BLISS--NOT LIFE--THIS IS--THIS--

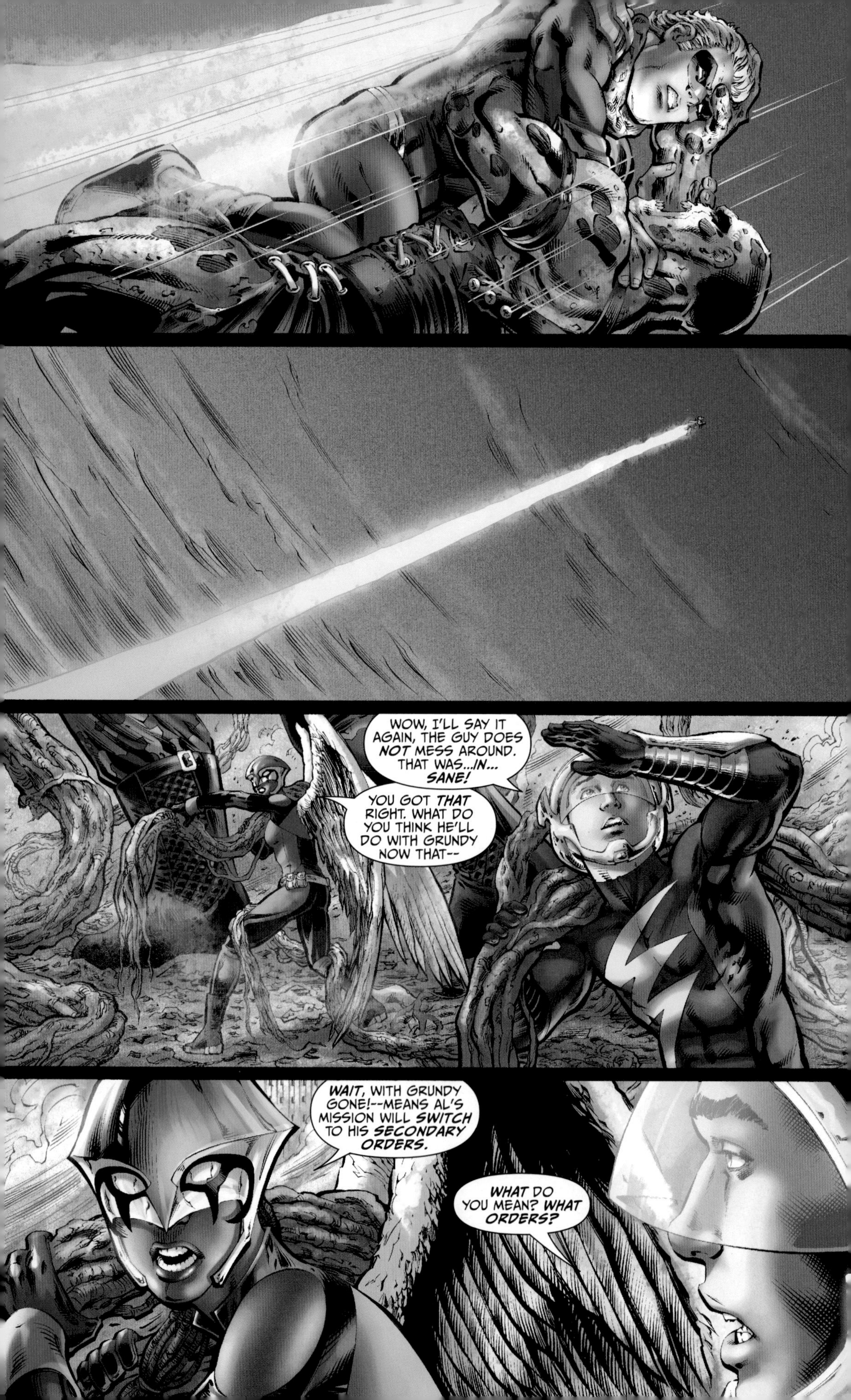
WOW, I'LL SAY IT AGAIN, THE GUY DOES NOT MESS AROUND. THAT WAS...IN... SANE!
YOU GOT THAT RIGHT. WHAT DO YOU THINK HE'LL DO WITH GRUNDY NOW THAT--
WAIT, WITH GRUNDY GONE!--MEANS AL'S MISSION WILL SWITCH TO HIS SECONDARY ORDERS.
WHAT DO YOU MEAN? WHAT ORDERS?

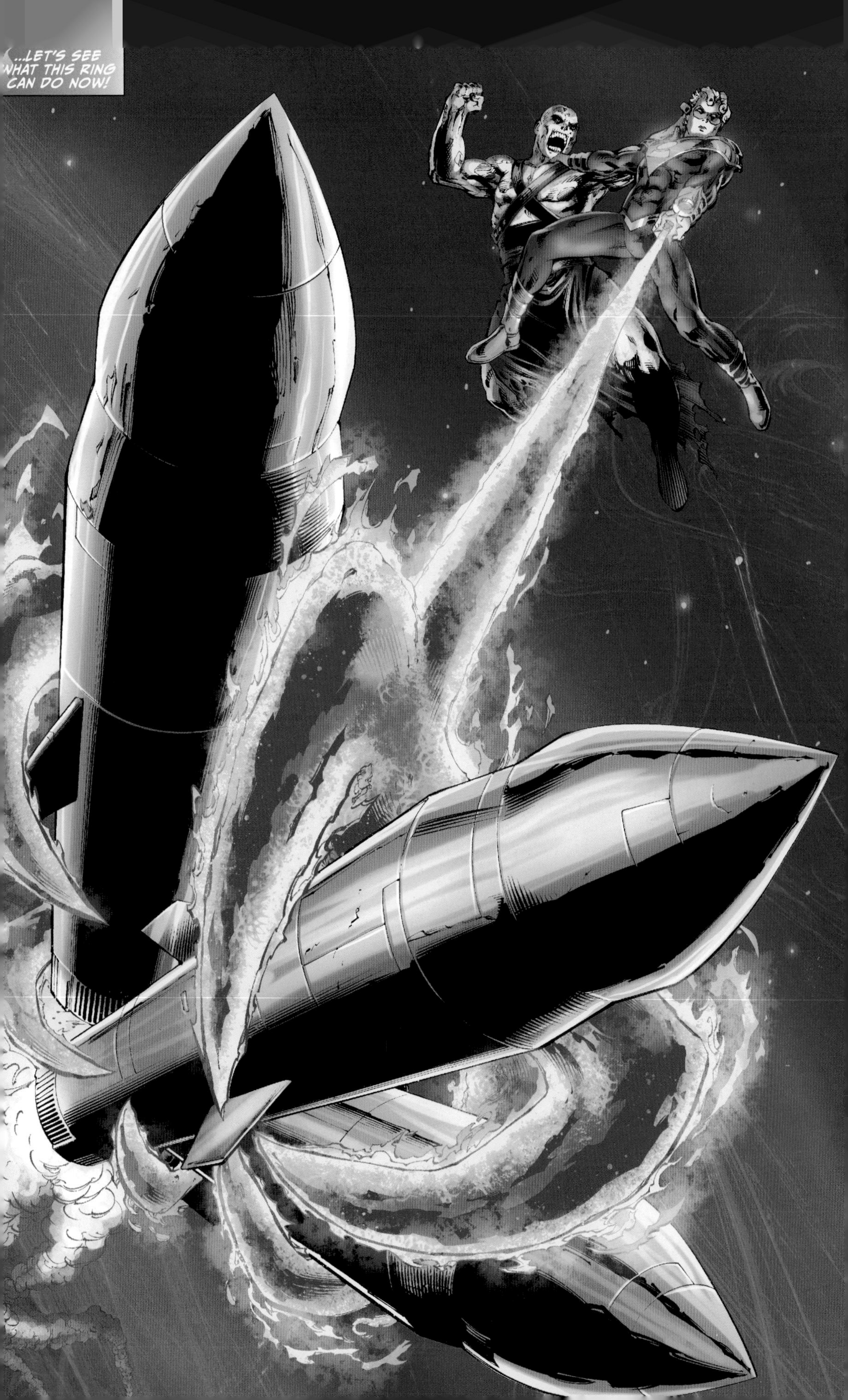
...LET'S SEE WHAT THIS RING CAN DO NOW!

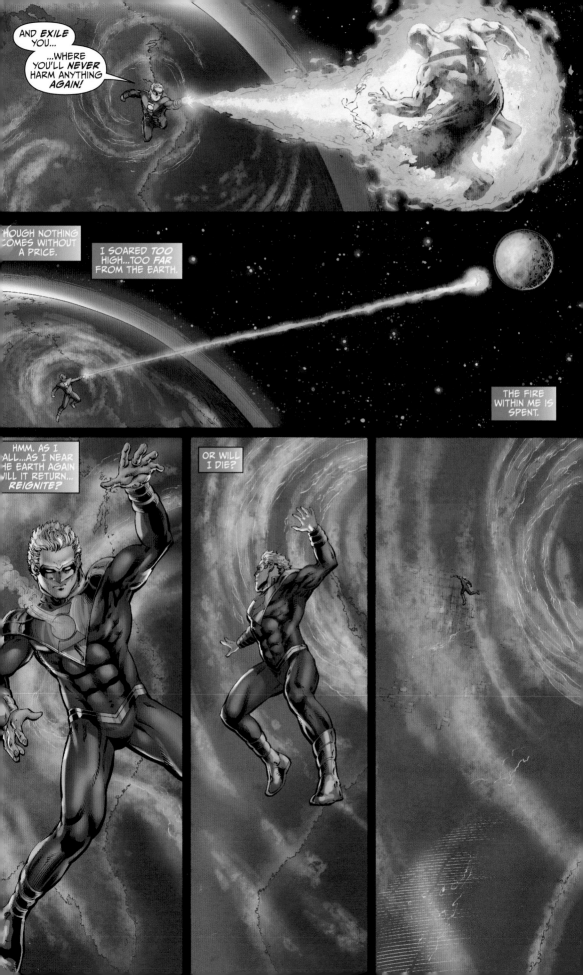

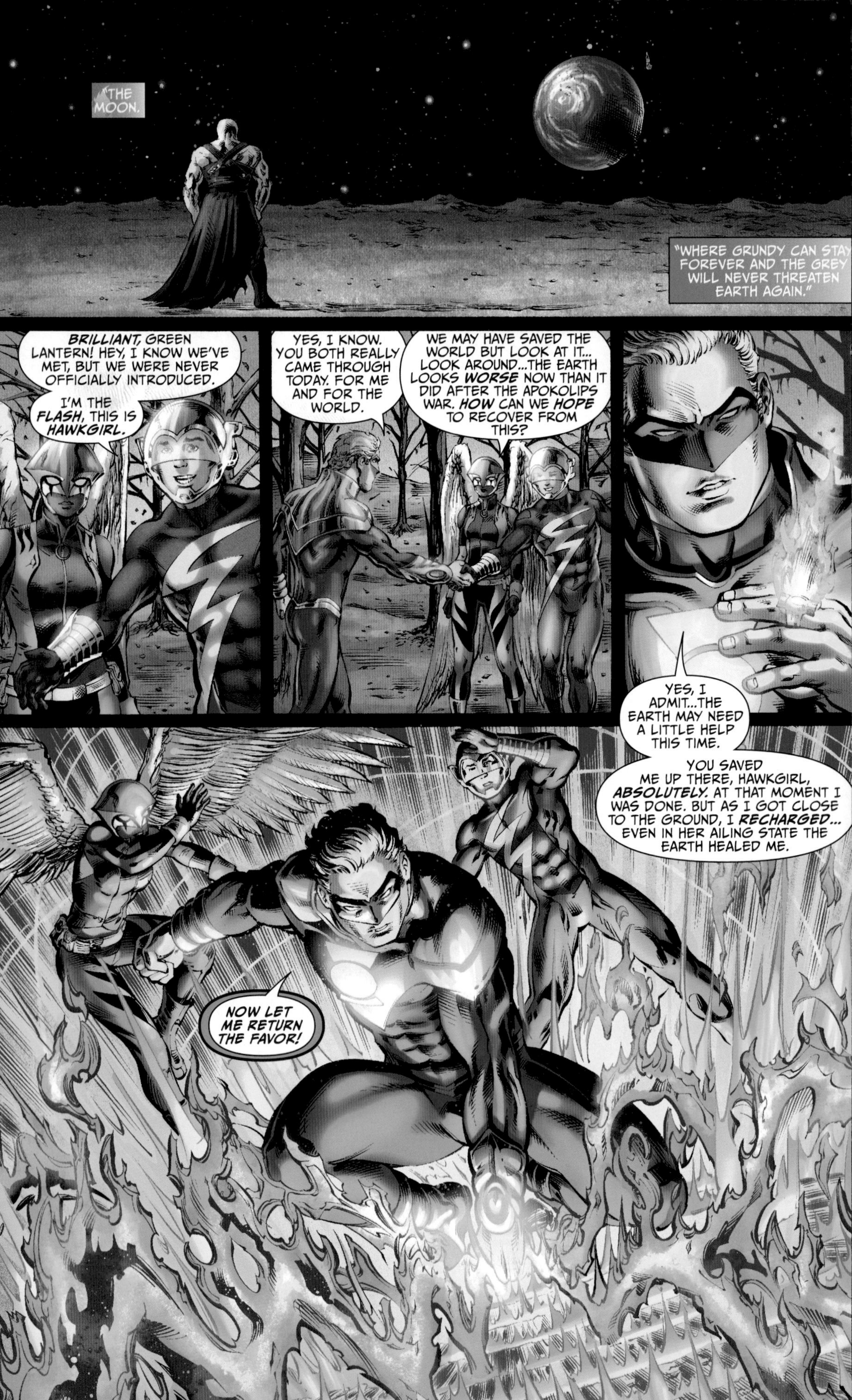
THE MOON.
"WHERE GRUNDY CAN STAY FOREVER AND THE GREY WILL NEVER THREATEN EARTH AGAIN."
BRILLIANT, GREEN LANTERN! HEY, I KNOW WE'VE MET, BUT WE WERE NEVER OFFICIALLY INTRODUCED.
I'M THE FLASH, THIS IS HAWKGIRL.
YES, I KNOW. YOU BOTH REALLY CAME THROUGH TODAY. FOR ME AND FOR THE WORLD.
WE MAY HAVE SAVED THE WORLD BUT LOOK AT IT... LOOK AROUND...THE EARTH LOOKS WORSE NOW THAN IT DID AFTER THE APOKOLIPS WAR. HOW CAN WE HOPE TO RECOVER FROM THIS?
YES, I ADMIT...THE EARTH MAY NEED A LITTLE HELP THIS TIME.
YOU SAVED ME UP THERE, HAWKGIRL, ABSOLUTELY. AT THAT MOMENT I WAS DONE. BUT AS I GOT CLOSE TO THE GROUND, I RECHARGED... EVEN IN HER AILING STATE THE EARTH HEALED ME.
NOW LET ME RETURN THE FAVOR!

EARTH 2 #1 variant cover art by Bryan Hitch & Paul Mounts

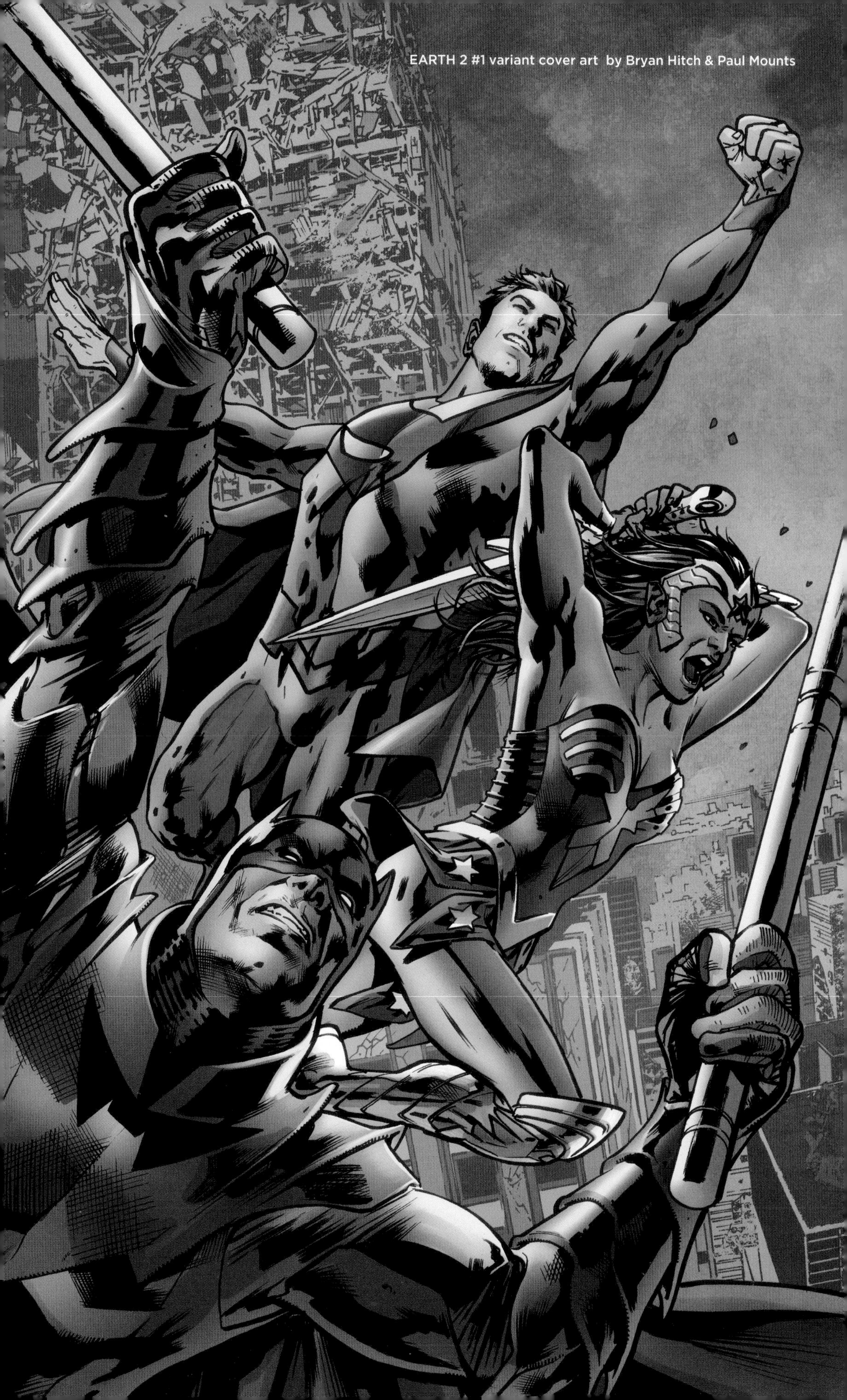

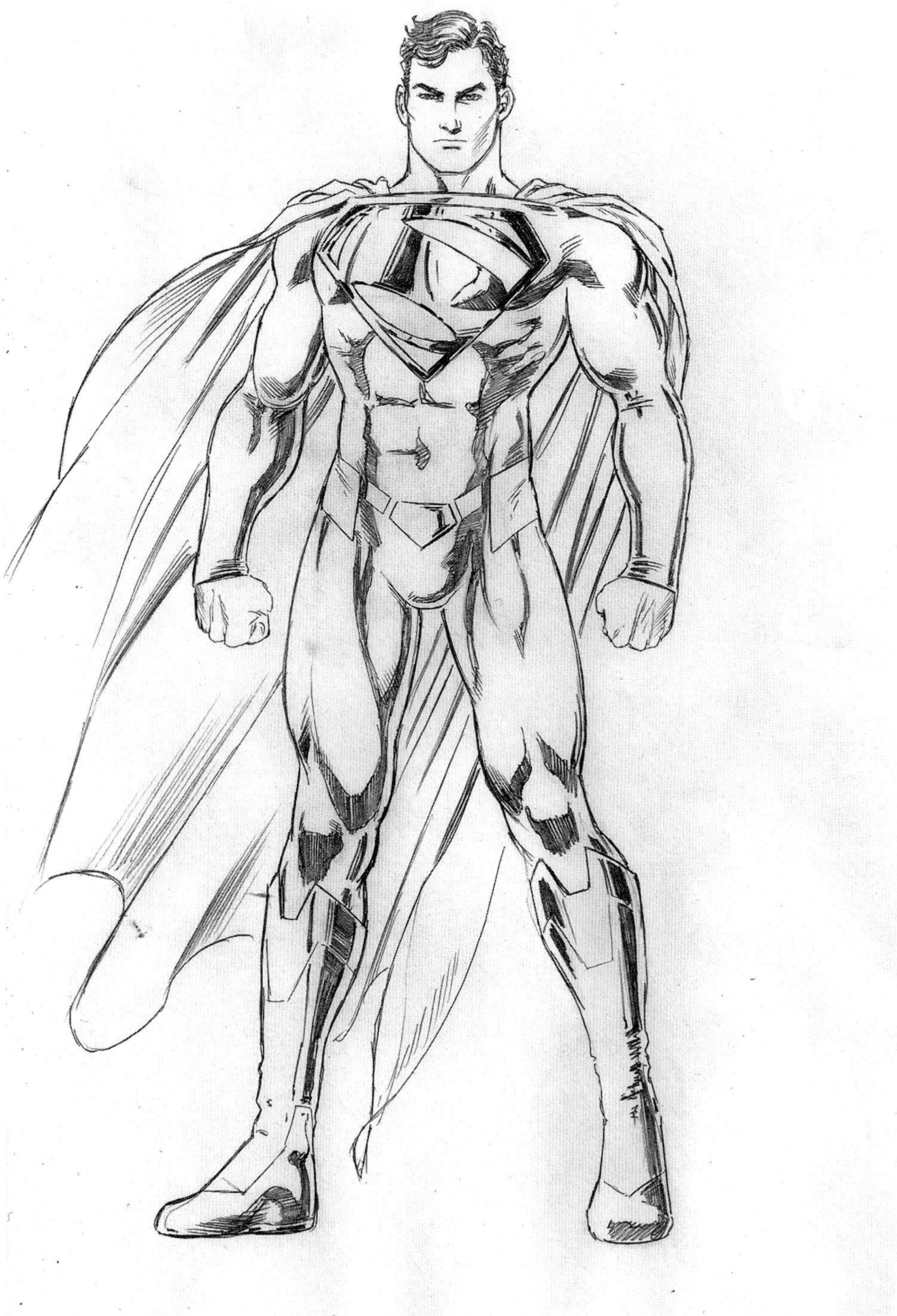

Superman by Nicola Scott

Wonder Woman by Nicola Scott

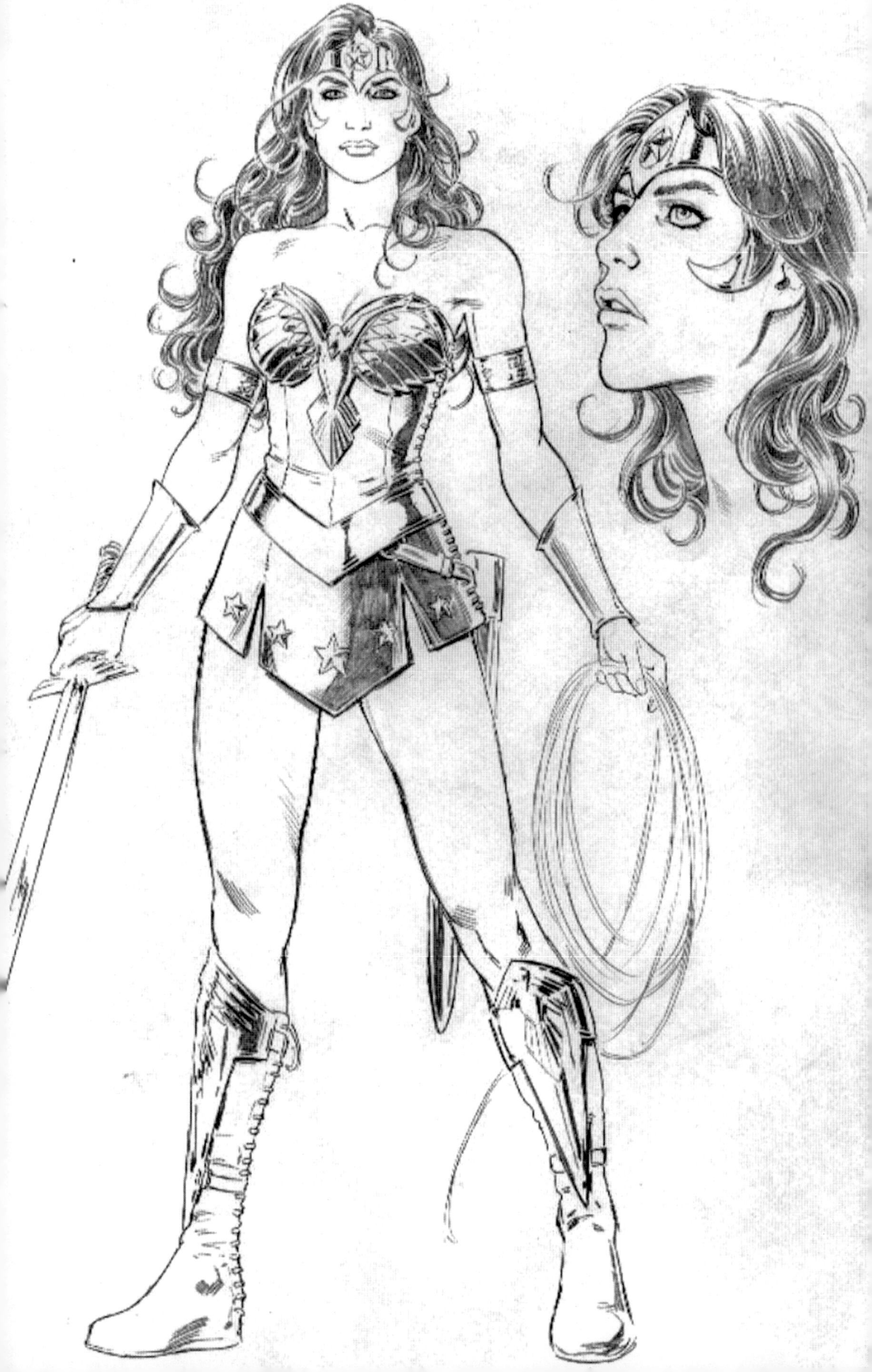

Character head shots
(Hawkgirl, Atom, The Flash and
Green Lantern) by Nicola Scott.

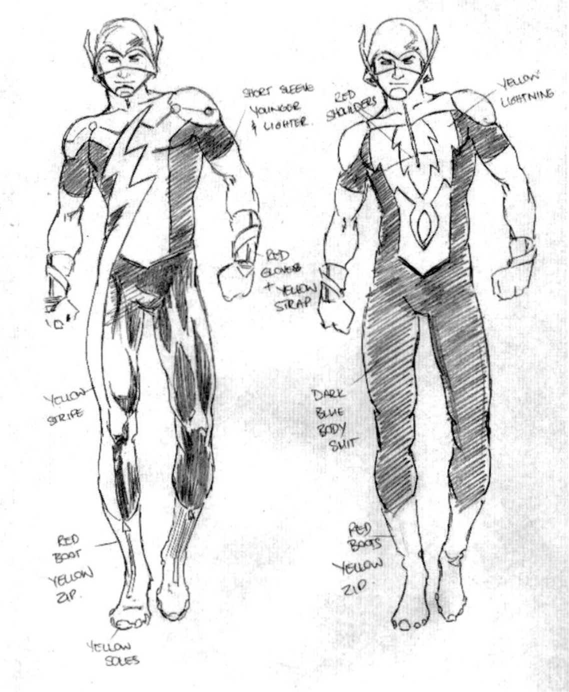

The Flash by Nicola Scott

The Sandmen by Nicola Scott

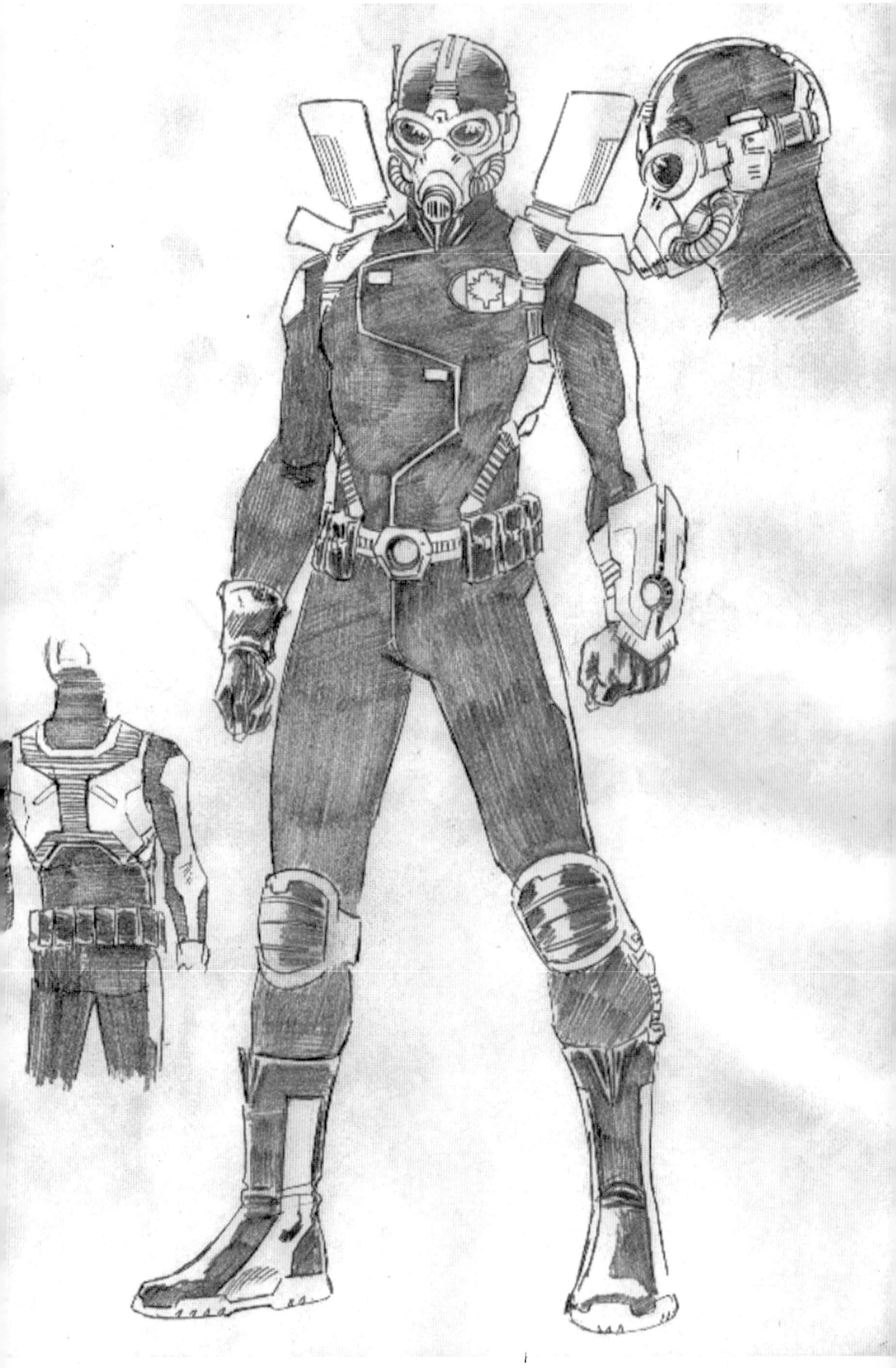

Batman sketch by Jim Lee

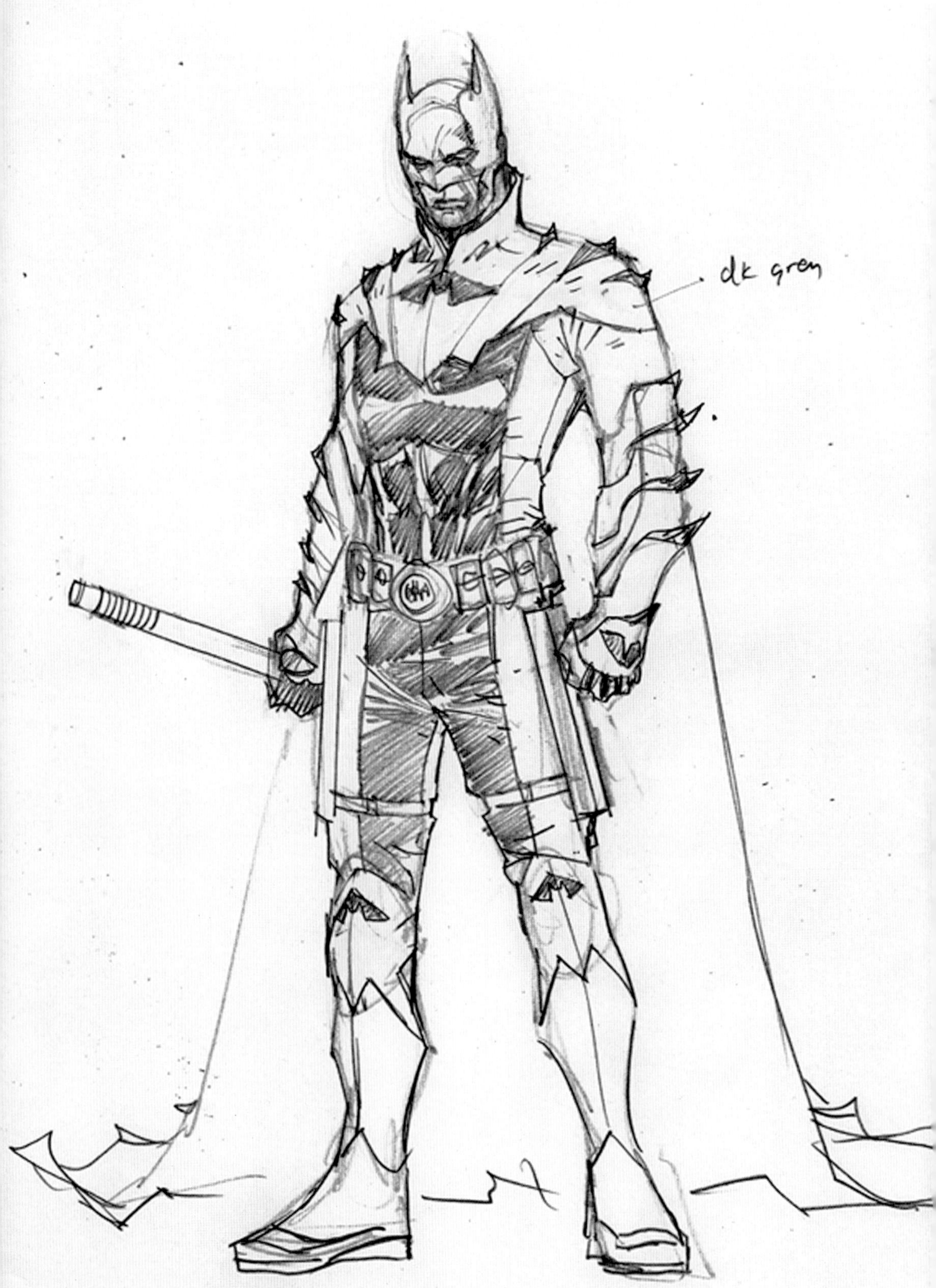
dk grey

Green Lantern by Joe Prado

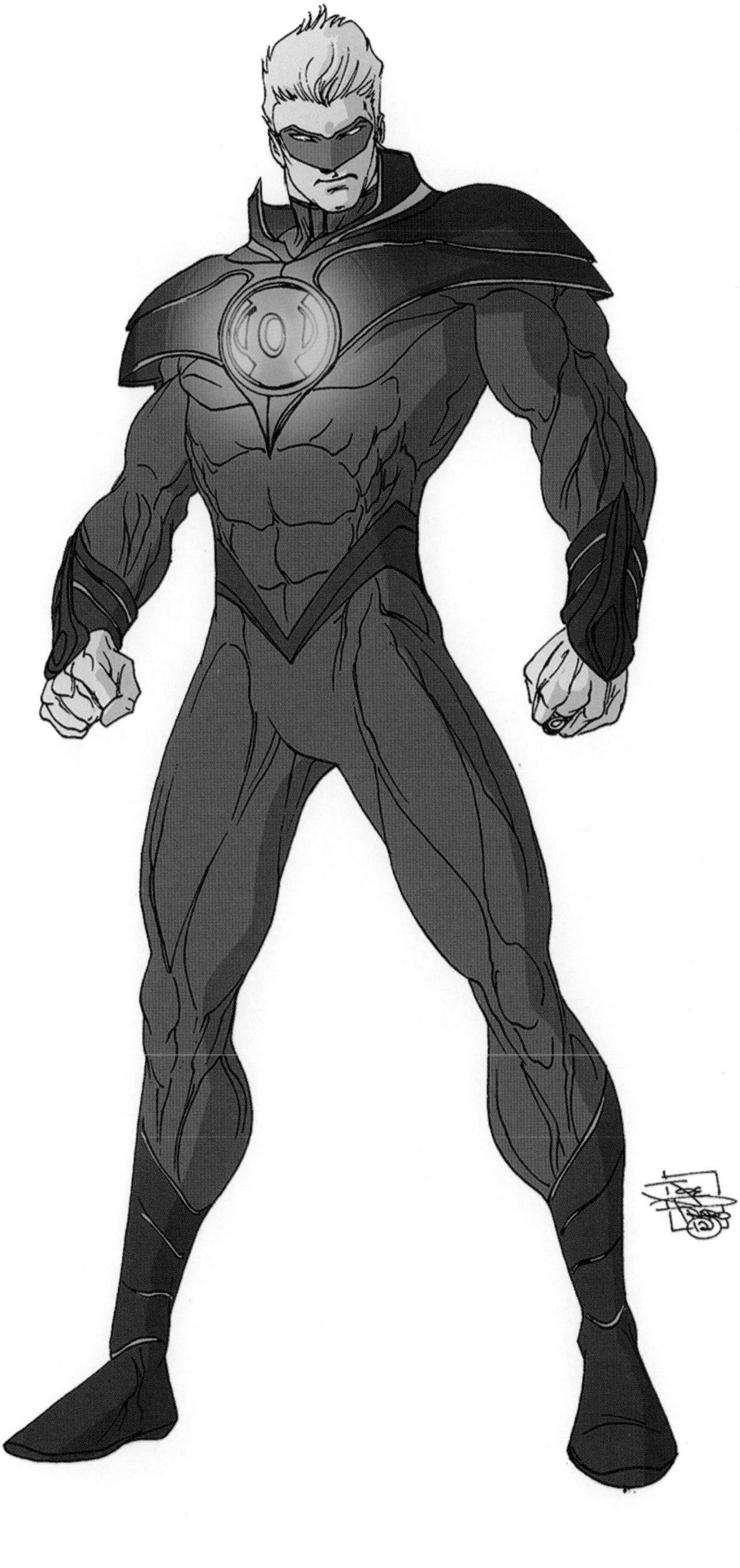

Steppenwolf by Jim Lee

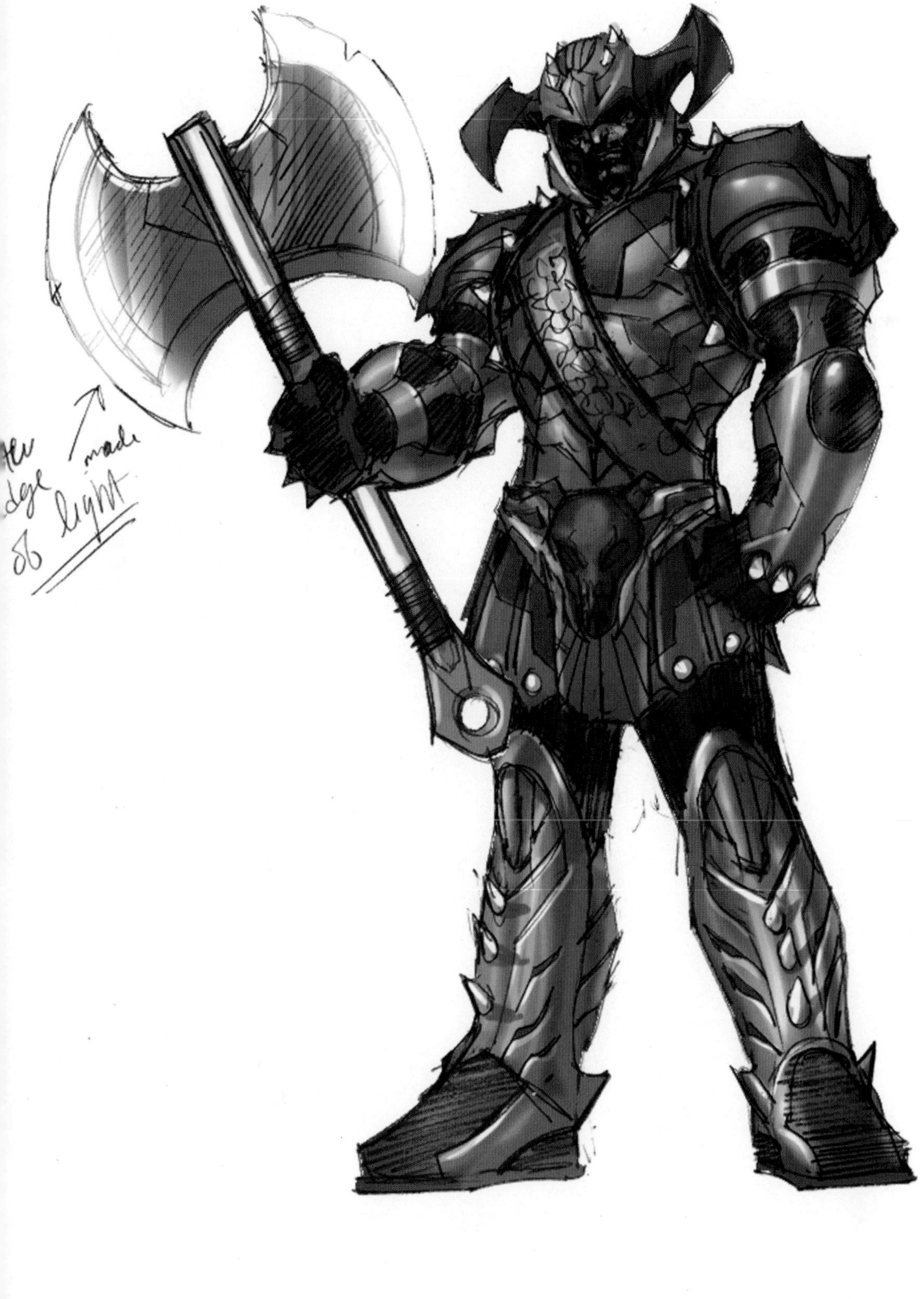
made
light

Solomon Grundy by Jim Lee

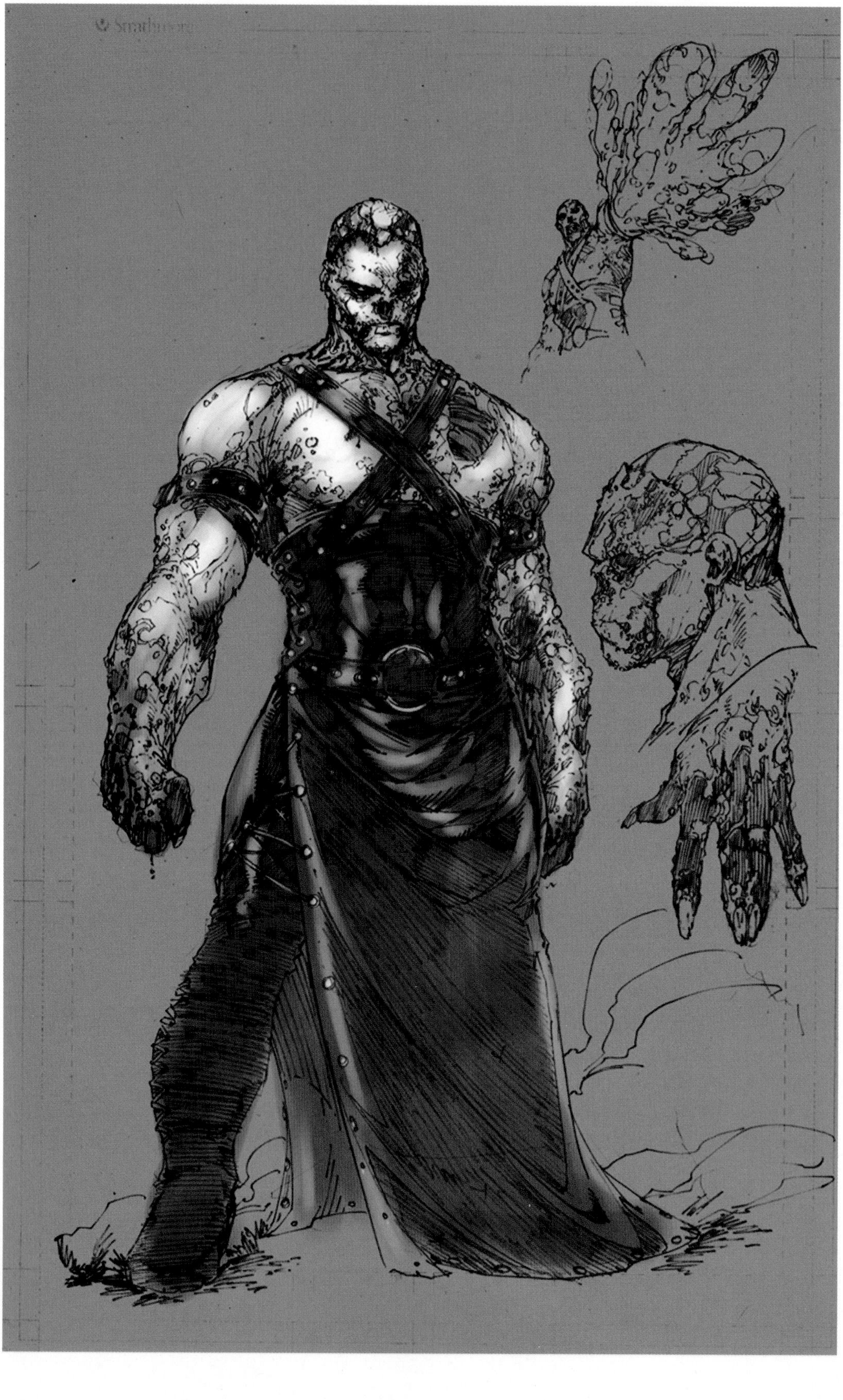

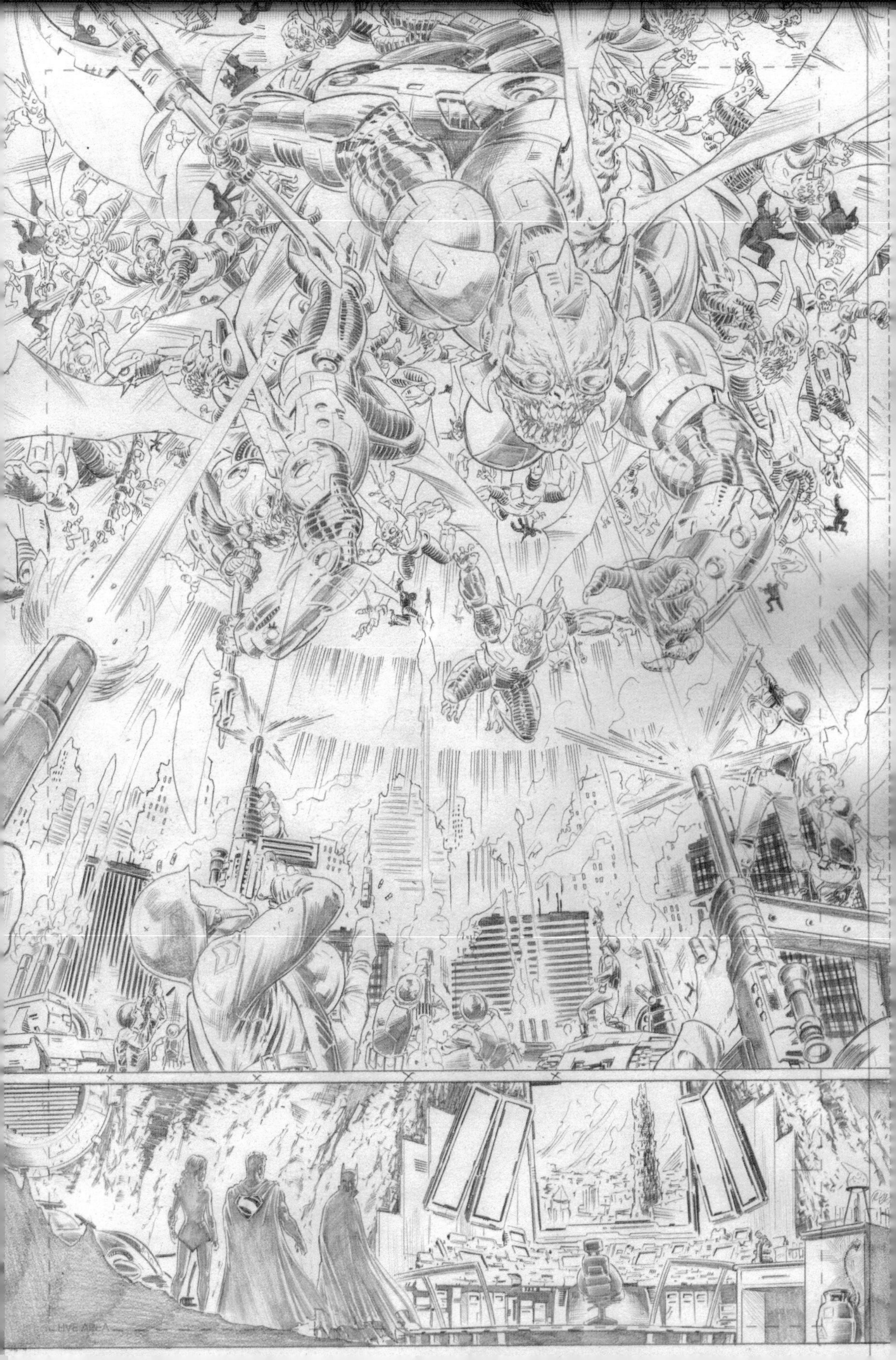

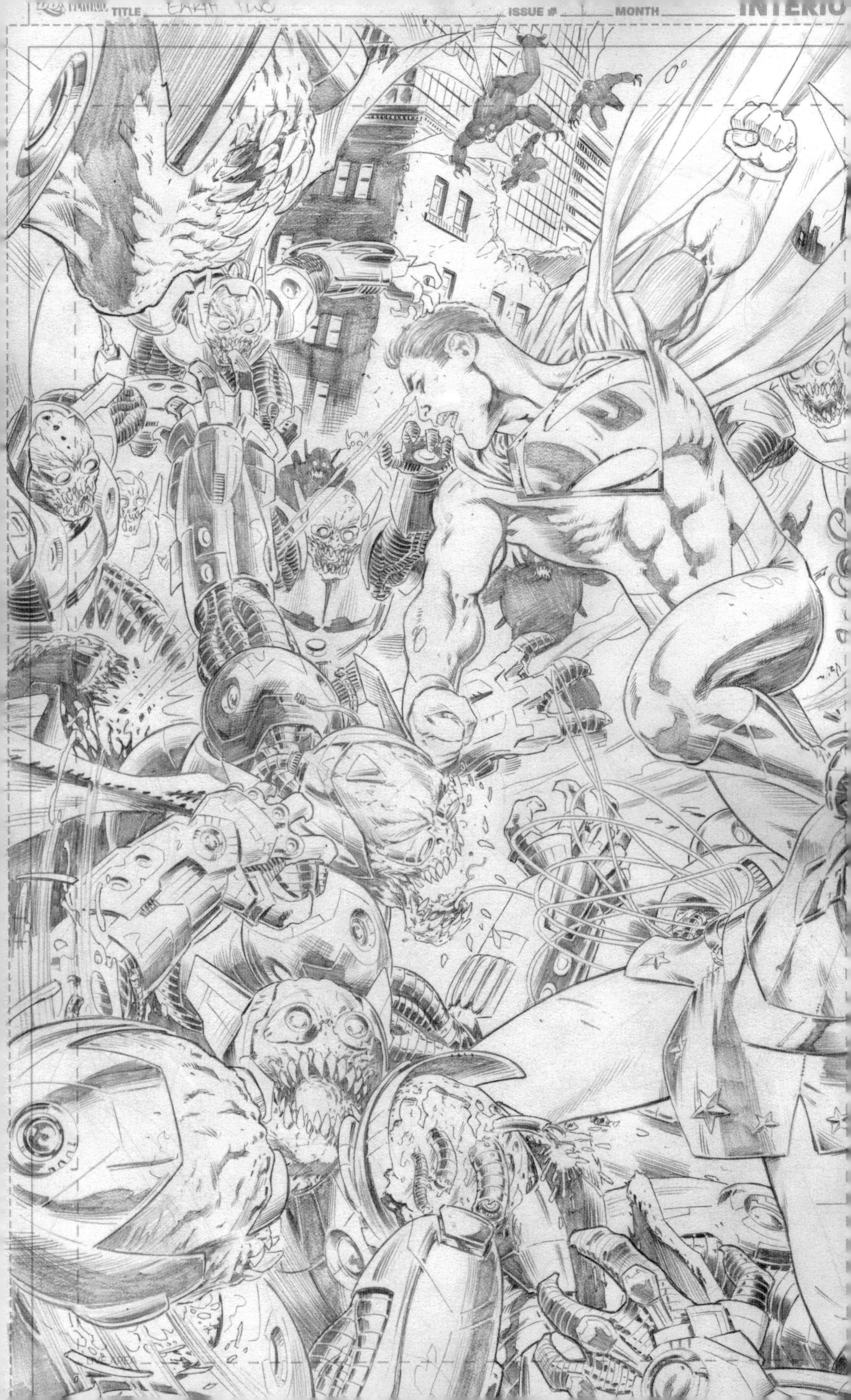
TITLE EARTH TWO
ISSUE # 1
MONTH
INTERIO

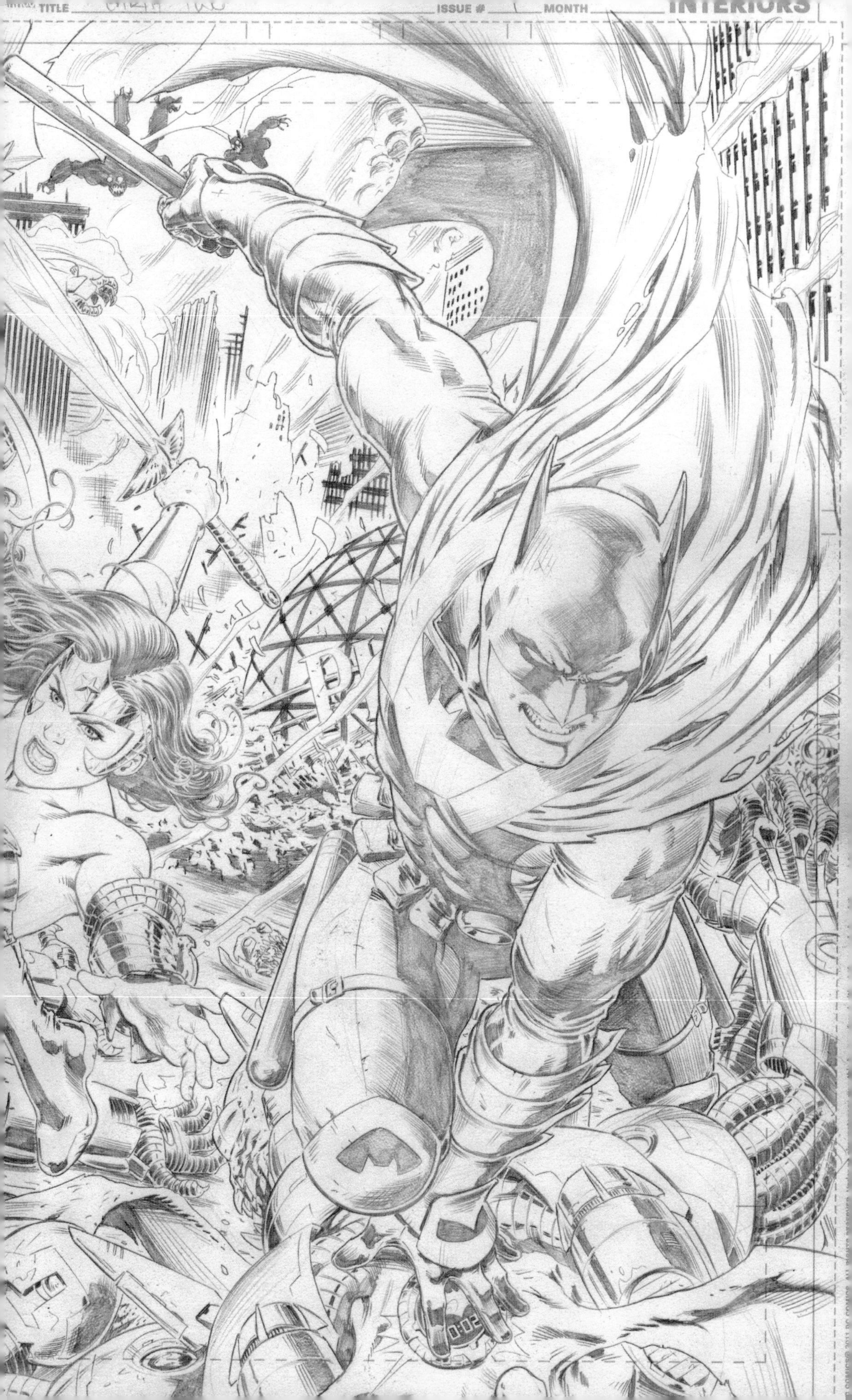
TITLE
ISSUE #
MONTH
INTERIORS
0:02

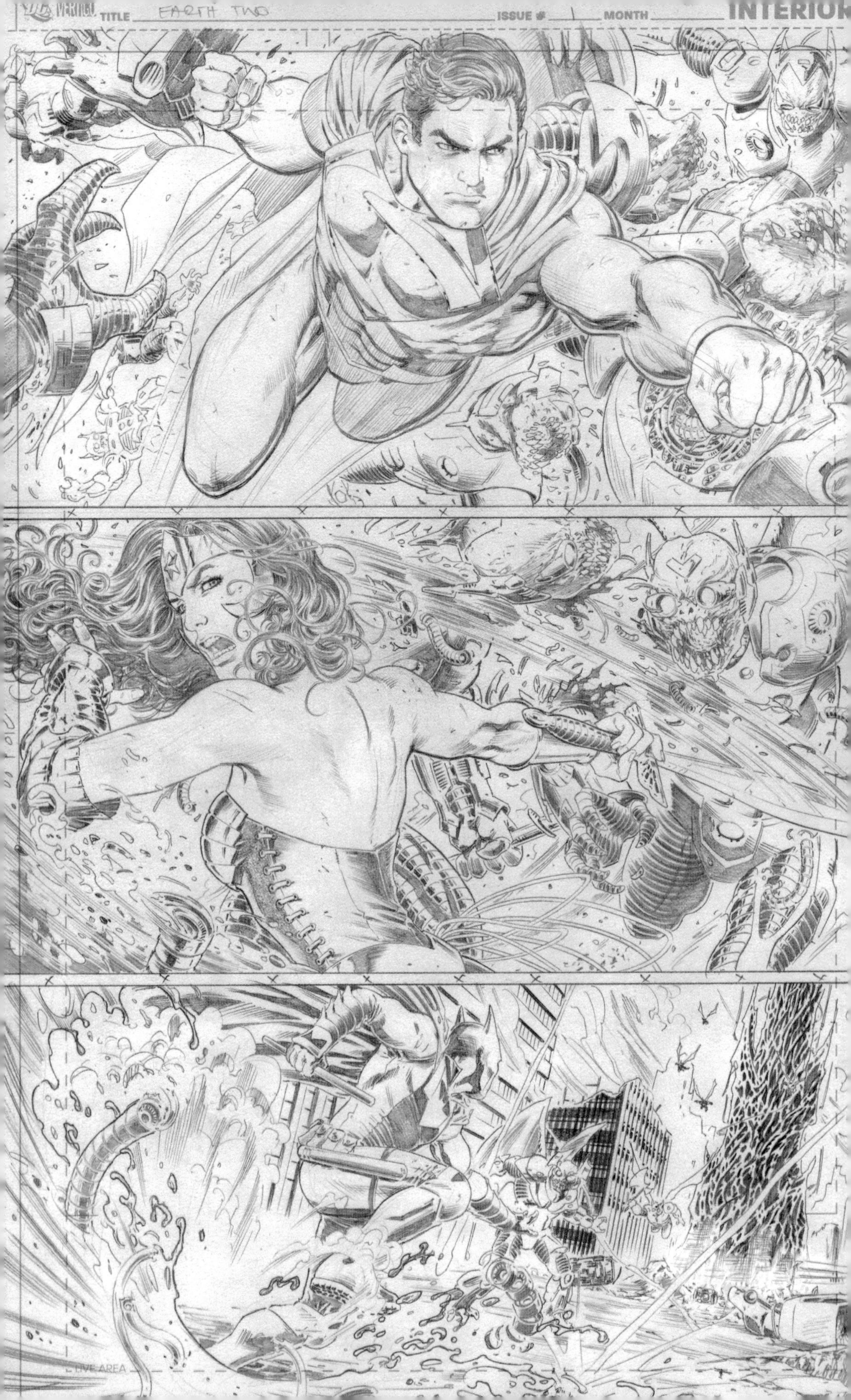
TITLE EARTH TWO
ISSUE # 1
MONTH
INTERIOR
LIVE AREA

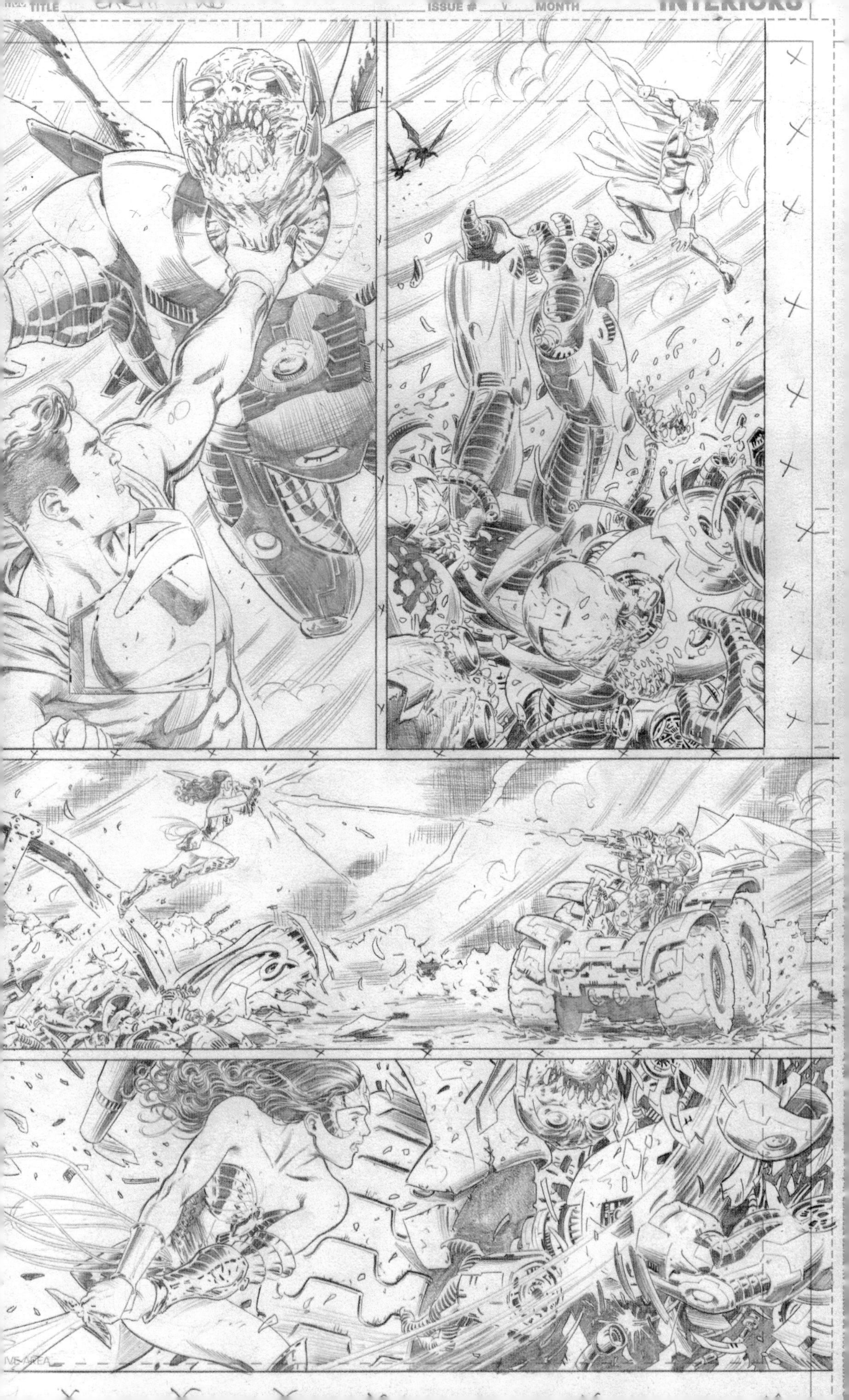
TITLE
ISSUE #
MONTH
INTERIORS

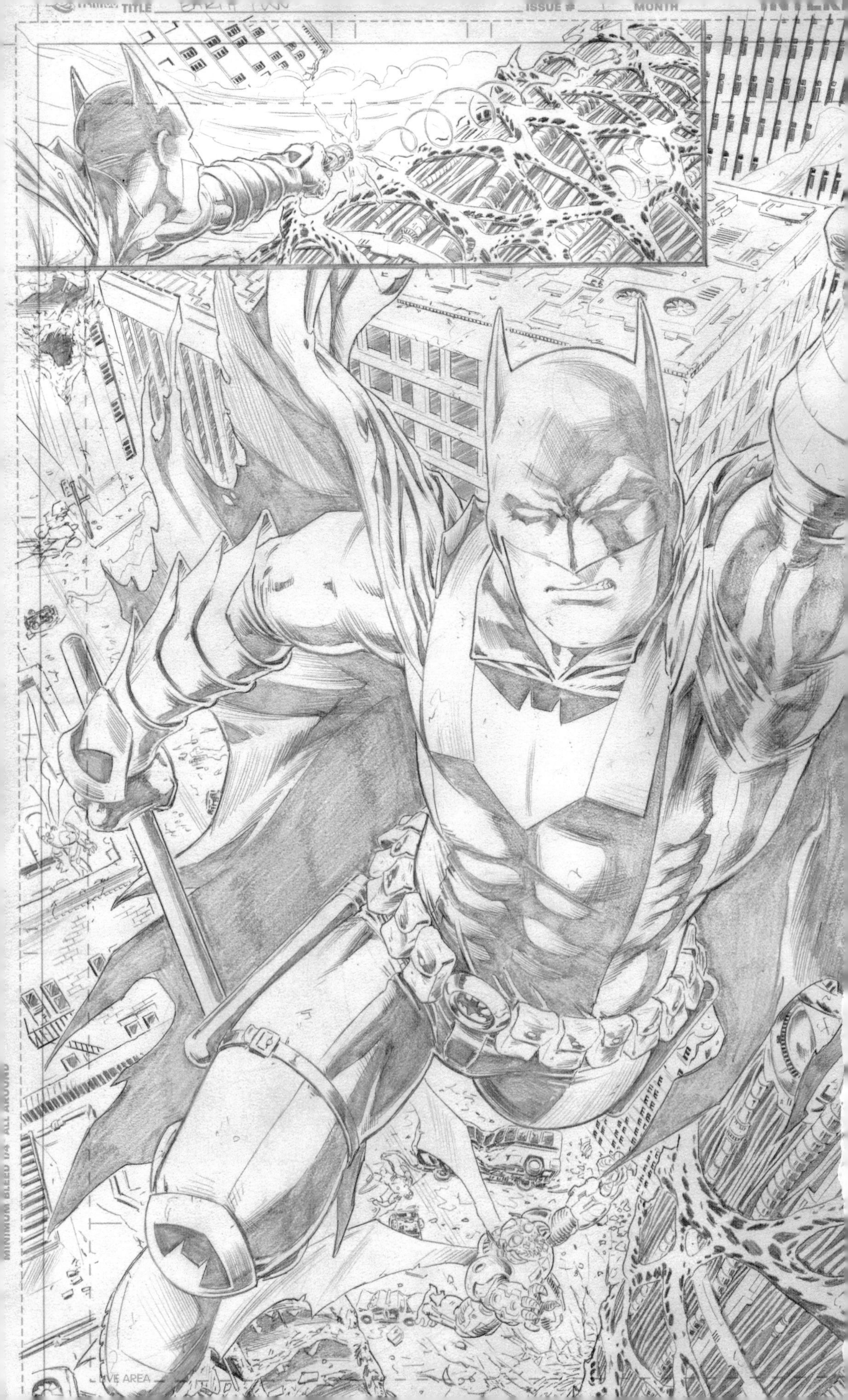
TITLE
ISSUE #
MONTH
LIVE AREA